STRESS TOLERANCE AND PLANT PRODUCTIVITY

ENV BOOKS SERIES

STRESS TOLERANCE AND PLANT PRODUCTIVITY

Editors

Dr. Prasann Kumar
Assistant Professor
Department of Agronomy, School of Agriculture
Lovely Professional University, Jalandhar - 144 411
(Punjab) (India)
&
Dr. Pawan Kumar 'Bharti'
Society for Environment, Health Awareness of
Nutrition & Toxicology (SEHAT)
B-225/5D, Top Floor, Subhash Gali
Road No. 7, Block B, Ashok Nagar
Shahdara, Delhi -110 093
(India)

Associate Editors

Dr. Alka Chauhan
Society for Environment Health Awareness of
Nutrition & Toxicology (SEHAT)
B-225/5D, Top Floor, Subhash Gali
Road No. 7, Block B, Ashok Nagar
Shahdara, Delhi -110 093
(India)
&
Mr. Jaswant Ray
F/119, Pandav Nagar, Meerut - 250 003 (U.P.)

DPH

DISCOVERY PUBLISHING HOUSE PVT. LTD.
INDIA

Published by:
Namit Wasan
DISCOVERY PUBLISHING HOUSE PVT. LTD.
4383/4B, Ansari Road, Darya Ganj
New Delhi-110 002 (India)
Phone : +91-11-23279245, 43596064-65
Fax : +91-11-23253475
E-mail : discoverypublishinghouse@gmail.com
namitwasan9@gmail.com
sales@discoverypublishinggroup.com
web : www.discoverypublishinggroup.com

***First Edition:* 2018**

ISBN: 978-93-86841-56-8

Stress Tolerance and Plant Productivity

Printed at:
Infinity Imaging Systems
Delhi

ENV Books Series, India

Calls descriptive and error free chapters for upcoming volumes of books on various environmental issues. Send your manuscripts to envbooks@gmail.com

Founding Editor (Editor-in-Chief)

Dr. Pawan Kumar 'Bharti'

Society for Environment, Health, Awareness of Nutrition & Toxicology (SEHAT-India)
1775, Sohanganj, Near Clock Tower, Delhi-7, (India)
E-mail:*gurupawanbharti@rediffmail.com*

Other Important Titles by Editor-in-Chief:

1. **Advances in Biotechnology and Ecological Sciences**
   Bharti, P.K., Chauhan, A. and Ray, J. (eds.)
   (ISBN: 978-93-5056-358-8).
2. **Advances in Agriculture and Ecology**
   Bharti, P.K.; Chauhan, A. and Ezeaku Peter Ikemefuna (eds.)
   (ISBN: 978-93-5056-362-5).
3. **Agriculture and Environmental Biotechnology**
   Bharti, P.K. and Chauhan, A. (eds.)
   (ISBN: 978-93-5056-479-0).
4. **Agriculture Crops and Food Security**
   Bharti, P.K., and Chauhan, A. (eds.)
   (ISBN: 978-93-5056-881-1)
5. **Agriculture Development and Sustainable Environment**
   Ray, J. and Bharti, P.K. (eds.)
   (ISBN: 978-93-5056-759-3).
6. **Agriculture Ecology and Environment**
   Bharti, P.K. and Olubukola O. Babalola (eds.)
   (ISBN: 978-93-5056-480-6).
7. **Agriculture Ecology, Sustainable Development and Agribusiness Management**
   Mehta Piyush; Sharma Pankaj; and 'Bharti' P.K. (eds.)
   (ISBN: 978-93-5056-851-4).
8. **Agriculture, Environment and Nano-science**
   Bharti, Pawan K. (ed.)
   (ISBN: 978-93-5056-760-5).
9. **Agriculture Production and Climate Change**
   Khalid, Monowar Alam; Bharti, P.K. and Chauhan, Alka (eds.)
   (ISBN: 978-93-86841-54-4).

10. **Agricultural Practices and Crop Disease Control**
Chauhan Alka and Sharma Anubhuti (eds.)
(ISBN: 978-93-5056-859-0).

11. **Agro-biodiversity:** ***Conservation and Sustainable Development***
Sharma, Pankaj; Singh, Narayan; and Bharti, P.K. (eds.)
(ISBN: 978-93-505-782-1).

12. **Agro-forestry and Climate Change**
Bharti, Pawan K. and Singh, Narayan (eds.)
(ISBN: 978-93-5056-514-8).

13. **Agro-forestry and Sustainable Agriculture**
Sharma, Pankaj; Bharti, P.K. (eds.)
(ISBN: 978-93-5056-786-9).

14. **Air Pollution and Ecosystem Health**
Swami Abhishek and Bharti, P.K. (eds.)
(ISBN: 978-93-5056-877-4).

15. **Analytical Techniques in Chemical and Biological Sciences**
Mala, Deep & 'Bharti', P.K. (eds.)
(ISBN: 978-93-86841-59-9).

16. **Aquaculture and Fisheries Environment**
Gupta, S.K. and Pawan K. Bharti (eds.)
(ISBN: 978-93-5056-408-0).

17. **Aquatic Biodiversity and Pollution**
Bharti, P.K.; Chauhan, A. and Kaoud, H.A.H. (eds.)
(ISBN: 978-93-5056-359-5).

18. **Aquatic Ecology and Biotechnology**
Bharti, P.K. and Zaki, M.S.A. (eds.)
(ISBN: 978-93-5056-451-6).

19. **Aquatic Environment and Toxicology**
Bharti, Pawan K. (ed.)
(ISBN: 978-93-5056-236-9).

20. **Biodiversity, Biotechnology and Environmental Conservation**
Bharti, P.K. and Bhandari, G. (eds.)
(ISBN: 978-93-5056-750-0).

21. **Biodiversity, Biotechnology & Pollution Control**
Bharti, P.K., and Chauhan, A. (eds.)
(ISBN: 978-93-5056-887-3)

22. **Biodiversity of Aquatic Ecosystem:** ***Significance, Threat and Conservation***
Bharti, P.K. and Kaoud, H.A.H. (eds.)
(ISBN: 978-93-5056-297-0).

23. **Biological Diversity and Ecology**
Arya, M.K.; Bharti, P.K. and Ritesh Joshi (eds.)
(ISBN: 978-93-5056-785-2).

24. **Bioremediation and Microbial Biotechnology**
Gupta, Sandeep; and Bharti, P.K. (eds.)
(ISBN: 978-93-5056-783-8).

25. **Biotechnological Approaches and Water Ecosystem**
Zaki, M.S.A.; and Bharti, P.K. (eds.)
(ISBN: 978-93-5056-779-1).

26. **Biotechnology, Agro-ecology and Environment**
Chauhan, Avnish and Bharti, P.K. (eds.)
(ISBN: 978-93-5056-757-9).

27. **Biotechnology and Environmental Management**
Arya Arun; Maheswari Raaz K., & Bharti, P.K (eds.)
(ISBN: 978-93-5056-862-0).

28. **Clean Technologies and Environmental Protection**
Chauhan, A.; Sharma, S. and Bharti, P.K. (eds.)
(ISBN: 978-93-5056-731-9).

29. **Climate Change and Agriculture**
Bharti, P.K. and Chauhan, Avnish (eds.)
(ISBN: 978-93-5056-148-5).

30. **Climate Change and Biodiversity**
Bharti, P.K. and Chauhan, Avnish (eds.)
(ISBN: 978-93-5056-360-1).

31. **Climate Change, Disaster Management and Environment**
Chauhan, Alka; Bharti, P.K. (eds.)
(ISBN: 978-93-5056-784-5).

32. **Conservation and Cultivation of Medicinal Plants**
Bharti, P.K. and Singh Narayan (eds.)
(ISBN: 978-93-5056-740-1).

33. **Crop Irrigation and Farming System**
Chauhan, Alka and P.K. Bharti (eds.)
(ISBN: 978-93-86841-40-7).

34. **Crop Productivity and Plant Disease Management**
Chauhan, Alka; Bharti, P.K. and Sadana, Deepti (eds.)
(ISBN: 978-93-5056-791-3).

35. **Ecotourism, Environmental Problems & Sustainable Development**
Singh, Soubam Premchandra; Rathoure, Ashok Kr., and
Bharti, P.K. (eds.)
(ISBN: 978-93-86841-57-5).

36. **Eco-toxicology and Eco-technology**
Bharti, P.K. and Zaki, M. (eds.)
(ISBN: 978-93-5056-313-7).

37. **Energy Technologies for Clean Environment**
Bharti, Chhavi Kumar and Bharti, P.K. (Eds.)
(ISBN: 978-93-86841-22-3).

38. **Environmental Biotechnology and Application**
Bharti, P.K. and Chauhan, Avnish (eds.)
(ISBN: 978-93-5056-262-8).

39. **Environmental Conservation and Biotechnology**
Chauhan, A. and P.K. Bharti (eds.)
(ISBN: 978-93-5056-512-4).

40. **Environmental Economics and Sustainability**
José G. Vargas-Hernández; Khalid Alam Monowar and Bharti, P.K. (eds.)
(ISBN: 978-93-86841-37-7).

41. **Environmental Health and Problems**
Bharti, P.K. and Gajananda, Kh. (eds.)
(ISBN: 978-93-5056-263-5).

42. **Environmental Pollution and Biodiversity**
Bharti, P.K.; Chauhan, Avnish and Kumar, P. (eds.)
(ISBN: 978-93-5056-149-2).

43. **E-waste and Environmental Issues**
Bhalla, R., and Bharti, P.K. (eds.)
(ISBN: 978-93-5056-886-6)

44. **Experiments on Enhancement of Agricultural Yield**
Chauhan, Alka and P.K. Bharti (eds.)
(ISBN: 978-93-86841-50-6).

45. **Farming Techniques and Crop Production**
Chauhan Alka; Sharma Anubhuti; Ray Jaswant and 'Bharti' P.K. (eds.)
(ISBN: 978-93-5056-855-2).

46. **Faunal Biodiversity and Biotechnology**
Sethi, V. Kumar; Bharti, P.K. (eds.)
(ISBN: 978-93-86841-44-5).

47. **Fisheries and Toxicology**
Zaki, M.S.A.; Bharti, P.K. and Chauhan, A. (eds.)
(ISBN: 978-93-5056-452-3).

48. **Fish Habitat and Aquaculture**
Bharti, P.K.; Gupta Kr. Sanjay (eds.)
(ISBN: 978-93-5056-744-9).

49. **Forest and Biodiversity Conservation**
Chauhan Alka; Bharti, P.K. (eds.)
(ISBN: 978-93-5056-873-6).

50. **Food Processing, Management and Nanotechnology**
Chauhan, Avnish; Bharti, P.K. (eds.)
(ISBN: 978-93-5056-796-8).

51. **Food Technology and Research Advancement**
Chauhan, Avnish; Bharti, P.K. (eds.)
(ISBN: 978-93-86841-49-0).

52. **Freshwater Ecosystem and Xenobiotics**
Bharti, P.K.; Zaki, M. and Chauhan, A. (eds.)
(ISBN: 978-93-5056-299-4).

53. **Geospatial Technology and Ecosystem Assessment**
'Bharti' Chhavi Kumar; Chauhan, Alka & Bharti, P.K. (eds.)
(ISBN: 978-93-86841-36-0).

54. **Geospatial Technology and Water Management**
Chauhan, Alka; Bharti, P.K. (eds.)
(ISBN: 978-93-5056-885-9).

55. **Heavy Metals and Metalloids in Biosphere:** ***Impacts & Assessment***
Chauhan, Avnish, Gupta, Sandeep; and Bharti, P.K. (eds.)
(ISBN: 978-93-5056-860-6).

56. **Heavy Metals and Pesticides in Environment**
'Bharti', P.K.; Bhalla, Resham; Chauhan, Abhishek & Mala, Deep (eds.)
(ISBN: 978-93-86841-60-5).

57. **Land Reclamation, Soil Quality and Agriculture**
Bharti, P.K., and Chauhan, A. (ed.)
(ISBN: 978-93-5056-882-8).

58. **Limnology and Aquatic Science**
Sharma, S., and Bharti, P.K. (eds.)
(ISBN: 978-93-5056-735-7).

59. **Medicinal and Nutritional Values of Plants**
Chauhan, Alka; Bharti, P.K. (eds.)
(ISBN: 978-93-5056-883-5).

60. **Medicinal Plants:** ***Distribution, Utilization and Significance***
Sharma, P.; Bharti, P.K. and Narayan Singh (eds.)
(ISBN: 978-93-5056-734-0).

61. **Microbial Applications and Environment**
Bharti, Pawan K. (ed.)
(ISBN: 978-93-5056-515-5).

62. **Microbial Ecology and Habitat**
Bharti, Pawan K. (ed.)
(ISBN: 978-93-5056-514-8).

63. **Microbial Environment and Bioremediation**
Chauhan Alka; K. Rathoure Ashok; and K Maheshwari Raaz (eds.)
(ISBN: 978-93-5056-856-9).

64. **Microbiological and Pharmacological Aspects of Biodiversity**
Sharma, P., Sharma, N.G.; Sharma, P., and Bharti, P.K. (ed.)
(ISBN: 978-93-5056-878-1).

65. **Natural Ecosystem and Climate Change**
Bharti, P.K., and Kh. Gajananda (ed.)
(ISBN: 978-93-5056-745-6).

66. **Nutraceuticals and Pharmaceuticals from Medicinal Plants**
Bharti, P.K., Khan, M.M. Abid Ali and Rathoure, Ashok Kumar (ed.)
(ISBN: 978-93-86841-55-1).

67. **Organic Farming and Bio-fertilizers**
Sethi, Vinaya Kumar; and Bharti, P.K. (eds.)
(ISBN: 978-93-86841-23-0).

68. **Pest Management and Agro-Techniques**
Biswas, Asim; Bharti, P.K., Chauhan, Avnish (eds.)
(ISBN: 978-93-5056-794-4).

69. **Physical and Chemical Analysis of Environment**
Mala, Deep; Bharti', P.K. & Bhalla, Resham (eds.)
(ISBN: 978-93-86841-61-2).

70. **Plant Biotechnology and Industrial Applications**
Chauhan, A., and Bharti, P.K. (ed.)
(ISBN: 978-93-5056-884-2).

71. **Plant Disease Management:** ***Control & Elimination Strategies***
Chauhan, A., and Bharti, P.K. (ed.)
(ISBN: 978-93-86841-41-4).

72. **Plant Response to Environmental Stress**
Chauhan, Alka; 'Bharti', P.K. and Chauhan, Avnish (eds.)
(ISBN: 978-93-86841-58-2).

73. **Prakriti me Aushadhi (*in Hindi*)**
Singh, J.R.; Bharti, P.K. and Bharti, B.
(ISBN: 978-93-5056-200-0).

74. **Production of Fruits and Vegetables:** *Technologies and Challenges*
Chauhan, Avnish; Bharti, P.K. and Chauhan, Alka (ed.)
(ISBN: 978-93-86841-25-4).

75. **Seed Technology, Plant Growth and Cropping System**
Tyagi, P.K. and Bharti, P.K. (eds.)
(ISBN: 978-93-5056-738-8).

76. **Seed Treatment, Plant Health and Agro-technology**
Chauhan, A. and Bharti, P.K. (eds.)
(ISBN: 978-93-5056-810-1).

77. **Soil Characteristics and Agro-ecology**
Avnish Chauhan and Bharti, P.K. (eds.)
(ISBN: 978-93-5056-758-6).

78. **Soil Contamination and Conservation**
Ezeaku, P.I. and Bharti, P.K. (eds.)
(ISBN: 978-93-5056-737-1).

79. **Soil Quality and Contamination**
Bharti, P.K. and Chauhan, Avnish (eds.)
(ISBN: 978-93-5056-361-8).

80. **Sustainable Aquaculture Management**
Gupta, S.K.; Bharti, P.K (eds.)
(ISBN: 978-93-5056-797-5).

81. **Waste Disposal and Management**
Bharti, P.K.; Tabassum, B. and Bajaj, P. (eds.)
(ISBN: 978-93-5056-729-6).

82. **Waste Generation and Utilization**
Bajaj Priya; Tabassum, B., and Bharti, P.K. (eds.)
(ISBN: 978-93-5056-792-0).

83. **Waste Management and Environmental Health**
Tabassum, B., Bajaj Priya, and Bharti, P.K. (eds.)
(ISBN: 978-93-5056-777-7).

84. **Water Resources:** *Mapping Monitoring and Management*
Tyagi, P.K., Chauhan, Avnish and Bharti, P.K. (eds.)
(ISBN: 978-93-5056-861-3).

85. **Water Resources and Agriculture**
Bharti, P.K. and Ezeaku Peter Ikemefuna (eds.)
(ISBN: 978-93-5056-481-3).

86. **Waste Resources Management:** *Monitoring and Assessment*
Gupta, Sandeep and Bharti, P.K. (eds.)
(ISBN: 978-93-5056-799-9).

Preface

Factors affecting the distribution of plants on earth are Temperature; season; Altitude; Rainfall; Wind; Soil; Slope; Land Tenure; Market; Transport; Capital; Technology; and Government. Most plants cannot grow if the temperature falls below 6 C or the soil is frozen for five consecutive months. As a consequence, many areas are unsuitable for crop production.

Shorter the required growing seasons the capability for that crop for growing in a cold environment increase. This affects temperature so it also affects farming. When the temperature is constantly high with sufficient precipitation high yield crops such as rise can be grown. The higher the altitude, lower the temperature and pressure. Water is obviously a key factor in plant growth. The greater the average temperature the greater the amount of water required for plant growth. Seasonal variation is important in as different crops require water at different times. Ex: Coffee must have a period of drought before and during the harvesting. Maize needs heavy rain in the same period. Rice is the principal crop in the tropics because it requires substantial quantities of water. (a high yield crop). In summers temperatures are very high, encouraging high rates of evapo-transpiration and consequently very dry soil and a low water table. There is a soil water deficit. These conditions are not conducive to plant growth. Wind can have a destructive effect on crops. At its most severe a hurricane can physically destroy thousands of acres of farmland. Less severe but also but also harmful are the winds that dry soils so reducing moisture and increasing the potential for soil erosion. Soil type will influence crop cultivation because different crops prefer different soils. Clay soil with their high water retention are well suited to rice while sandy soils with good drainage are best for root vegetables. Soil type can be influenced by the input of lime, clay or fertilizer, but this can only make limited differences. The angle of slope will affect the type, depth and moisture content of soil. It will also affect the rate of soil erosion. These terraces are cut into steep slopes to retain the soil that otherwise would be easily removed by heavy rains. The degree to which the farm can be mechanized is influenced by the slope. In the developed world large percentage of farmers are owner-occupiers. In the developing world farmers are less likely to be owner-occupiers. Instead, they will probably be tenants or landless labourers. For any commercial farm to succeed there must be a demand. If the demand for a crop drops, then profits will fall. That crop will then be replaced by a more profitable one. It is an important factor in determining the location of farm types. If the product is bulky such as potatoes, then it should be grown close to the market place to cut down on transport costs. If the food is perishable, then again, it should be grown close to the market place. The effect of transport has been greatly reduced in the developed world because of innovations such as refrigerated lorries. It is still an important factor in many parts of the developing world. The transportation available and the transport network will have a large influence on the distribution of agricultural system. Many subsistence farms could not cell surpluses even if they had them because of the costs involved in transporting the surpluses to the market place. In the developed world, there is a well established system of supportive banks, private investors and government subsides. This means that the agriculture is likely to be capital intensive and highly mechanized. New technology is always increasing efficiency and yields, but technology costs money.

The present book updates the subject matter and recent findings on stress tolerance in plants against abiotic and biotic stresses, heavy metals, Pathogens, water availability, along with the management strategies.

Thanks are due to publisher and contributors from various institutions and universities.

The book will be helpful for the researchers, academia working in the field of stress tolerance in plants against abiotic and biotic stresses, heavy metals, Pathogens, water availability, along with the management strategies.

–Editors

(envbooks@gmail.com)

Contents

Pages: 1-14

Stress Tolerance and Plant Productivity
Edited by: Mr. Prasann Kumar and Dr. Pawan Kumar 'Bharti'
ISBN: 978-93-86841-56-8
Edition: 2018
Published by: Discovery Publishing House Pvt. Ltd., New Delhi (India)

1 Role of Paclobutrazol for the Mitigation of Water Logged Stress in Cicer Arietinum L.

Prasann Kumar

ABSTRACT

The chickpea is a cool season pulse crop and is grown in several countries worldwide as a food source. Chickpea is the third most important food legume crop and India is the largest producer contributing to 65% of world's chickpea production. Chickpea seeds contain on an average 23% protein, 64% total carbohydrates (47% starch, 6% soluble sugar), 5% fat, 6% crude fiber and 3% ash. High mineral content has been reported for phosphorus (340 mg/100 g), calcium (190 mg/100 g), magnesium (140 mg/100 g), iron (7 mg/100 g) and zinc (3 mg/100 g).

Key words: Agriculture, Biotic, Cicer, Diffuse, Efficient, Gap.

INTRODUCTION

Recent studies have also shown that they can assist in lowering cholesterol in the bloodstream (Pittaway *et al.* 2008). Besides this, it also improves the soil fertility due to its nitrogen fixing ability (Maiti 2001). The major chickpea growing countries are India, Pakistan and Turkey in Asia, Ethiopia in Africa, California and Washington State in the U.S.A. Mexico and Australia. The total cultivated area of chickpea in the world is about 8.57 m.ha. And annual world production is 7.35 mtonns. The average productivity is estimated to be around 858 kg/ha (FAO 2001). Chickpea (*Cicer arietinum* L.) is widely cultivated and an important food grain legume in Indian sub-continent. In India during 2013-14 chickpea was cultivated in an area of about 8.32 million hectares with a production of about 9.8 million tones and 925 - kg/ha productivity (AICRP-chickpea). In Madhya Pradesh during 2013-14 chickpea was cultivated in an area about 3.4 million hectares with production of 2.5 million tones and 1220 kg/ha productivity

Assistant Professor, Department of Agronomy, School of Agriculture, Lovely Professional University, Jalandhar - 144 411, Punjab (India)

(www.mpkrishi.org). In Jabalpur, during 2013-14 chickpea was cultivated in an area of about 66000 hectares with a production of 49000 tones and 745kg/ha productivity.Chickpea is an essential crop for arid and semi-arid regions and is mostly cultivated in dry and rainfed areas (Varshney *et al.* 2009). It is a resistant, deep-rooted plant and successfully grown under conditions which limit growth of other plants. Fertilizers and pesticides are occasionally used on chickpeas. Urea is one of the most widely used foliar N-fertilizers, characterized by a high leaf penetration rate and low cost and most plants can absorb rapidly and hydrolyze in the cytosol (Witte *et al.* 2002). Urea can also increase the level of storage N compounds, such as amino acids and proteins, thus, foliar spray of urea could directly affect N metabolism under stressful conditions and therefore amino acidsynthesis. Two varieties of chickpea: the larger light tan *Kabuli* and variously coloured desi chickpea. They are green when picked early and vary through tan or beige, speckled, dark brown to black. Its different types are variously known as gram. The chickpea is considered the third most important pulse in the world, being widely grown in many subtropical and warm-temperate regions. Chickpea is the common name for an annual plant, of the Fabaceae (or Leguminosae) family that is widely cultivated for its typically yellow-brown, pea like seeds.It is the only cultivated crop within the Cicer. This light brown colored pulse is considered to be a good source of protein. It is a legume crop mostly sown. The plant grows to 20-50 cm (8-20 in) high and has small, feathery leaves on either side of the stem.Chickpeas are a type of pulse, with one seedpod containing two or three peas. It has white flowers with blue, violet, or pink veins. The chickpea or garbanzo bean (kabuli chana) is a cool-season annual that requires about 100 days to reach harvest. The chickpea is a tender annual legume, a bushy plant that grows to about 18 inches tall and has pairs of dark green, compound leaflets that look like vetch. Chickpeas are frost tolerant, but grow best where daytime temperatures range between 70 and 80° and where night time temperatures do not dip below 65°F. Sow chickpeas in the garden as early as 2 or 3 weeks before the average last frost in spring. Chickpea (*Cicerarietinum*) has become an accepted legume crop in the wheat producing areas of eastern Australia, where legumes are now an integral component of the cropping system. Chickpeas are grown on the alkaline gray clays and black earths (vertisols), where they are shown in late autumn/early winter and harvested in early summer.

Planting and spacing: Chickpeas should be sown 1½ to 2 inches deep, spaced 3 to 6 inches apart. Thin successful plants to 6 inches apart; cut way thinned plants at soil level with scissors so as not to disturb roots. Space rows 18 to 24 inches apart. Do not soak seed before sowing and avoid heavy watering after sowing to keep seeds from cracking. Chickpeas allowed to grow a bit crowded will offer each other support. Chickpeas will be ready for harvest about 100 days after planting. Chickpeas for fresh eating can be picked when pods are still immature and green; they can be eaten like snap beans. For dried chickpeas, harvest the entire plant when the leaves have withered and turned brown; place the plant on a flat, warm surface and allow the pods to dry. Collect the seed as the pods split. Seeds that will barely dent when bitten are sufficiently dry (Figure 1.1).

Fig. 1.1: Seeds of Chickpea
Source: Based on Review of Literature

Chickpea seed has 38-59% carbohydrate, 3% fiber, 4.8-5.5% oil, 3% ash, 0.2% calcium, and 0.3% phosphorus. Digestibility of protein varies from 76-78% and its carbohydrate from 57-60%. Raw whole seeds contain per 100 g: 357 calories, 4.5-15.69% moisture, 14.9-24.6 g protein, 0.8-6.4% fat, 2.1-11.7 g fiber, 2-4.8 g ash, 140-440 mg Ca, 190-382 mg P, 5.0-23, 9 mg Fe, 0-225 mg b-carotene equivalent, 0.21-1.1 mg thiamin, 0.12-0.33 mg riboflavin, and 1.3-2.9 mg niacin. Sprouting is said to increase the proportionate amounts of ascorbic acid, niacin, available iron, choline, tocopherol, pantothenic acid, biotin, pyridoxine, inositol, and vitamin K. Malic and oxalic acid exudation from the leaves of the plant may soil and damage trousers and shoes.Wild species often have similar glandular secretions" (Duke, 1981). The limiting amino acid concentrations are 0.52 for methionine, 1.45 for lysine and cystine, 0.71 for threonine and 0.16 for tryptophan.The amino acid composition of seeds with 19.5% protein, 5.5% oil is (per 16 g N): 7.2 g lysine, 1.4 g methionine, 8.8 g arginine, 4.0 g glycine, 2.3 g histidine, 4.4 g isoleucine, 7.6 g leucine, 6.6 g phenylalanine, 3.3 g tyrosine, 3.5 g threonine, 4.6 g valine, 4.1 g alanine, 11.7 g aspartic acid, 16.0 g glutamic acid, 0.01 g hydroxyproline, 4.3 g proline, and 5.2 g serine. "Percent fatty acid composition is: 'Desi': oleic 52.1, linoleic 38.0, myristic 2.74, pactic 5.11, and steatic 2.05; 'Kabuli': oleic 50.3, linoleic 40.0, myristic 2.28, palmitic 5.74, stearic 1.61, and arachidic 0.07%. The leaves contain 4-8% protein".

Days to flower initiation: The salicylic acid treatment is not significant in respect to phenology of the crop. The days to first flowering in chickpea genotypes ranged minimum from 45 days (IC 4958) to maximum 53 days (Tyson) (Patel and Hemantranjan 2012). The earliness in flower initiation is due to use of plant growth retardants (Figure 1.2).

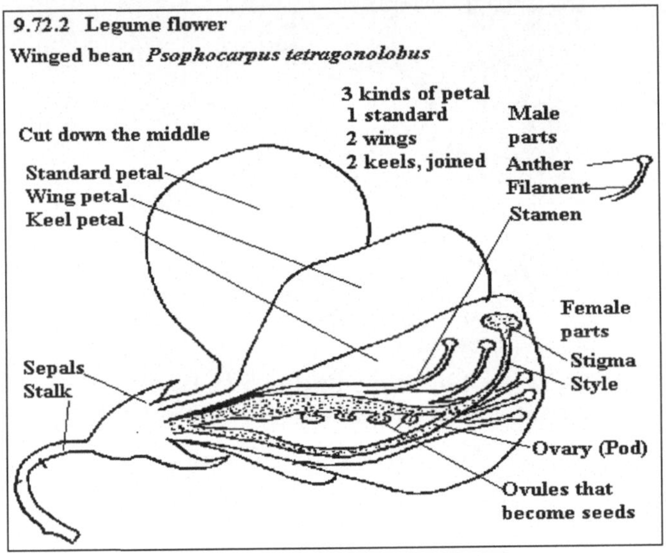

Fig. 1.2: Schematic diagram of legume flower

Source: Based on Review of Literature

Effects of Waterlogging

Chickpeas are particularly sensitive to waterlogging during flowering and podding. The effect of timing of waterlogging on chickpeas was examined in two pot trials. In the first experiment pants were waterlogged for ten days from 21 days after sowing (DAS), at flowering or at mid-pod fill, plus combinations of these times. Waterlogging at any stage reduced seed yield; waterlogging at 21 DAS had the least effect, reducing yield relative to the non-waterlogged control by 35%. The ability of the plant to survive and regrow following waterlogging decreased with increasing physiological age: mortality rate averaged 0, 30 and 100% after waterlogging at 21 DAS, flowering and pod fill, respectively. Tolerance to waterlogging was not enhanced by previous exposure to waterlogging.In the second experiment, waterlogging was imposed at six different times shortly before or after flowering begins. Ability to survive waterlogging declined sharply as flowering commenced: mortality rate increased from 13% when waterlogging was imposed six days before flowering to 65% one day after flowering, and 100% when waterlogging began 7.5 days after flowering. Scientist suggests that survival and recovery after waterlogging may have been inhibited in flowering plants by an inadequate supply of nitrogen or carbohydrates.The experiments were conducted in a glasshouse with daily maximum/minimum temperatures limited to 28/15° C. Tyson was sown into 20 cm diameter pots containing 4.2 kg air-dry, cracking gray clay (TypicPellustert) which had been pasteurized in a steam steriliser for 16 hours. Phosphate fertilizer (50 kg ha -1 P as triple superphosphate) was incorporated before sowing inoculated seed. After emergence, plants were thinned to four per pot in Experiment 1 and five per pot in Experiments 2 and 3. Waterlogging was imposed by immersing pots in water-filled buckets and maintaining the water level at the soil surface for ten days, after which pots were allowed to drain:

Experiment 1

Five treatments were included in a randomized complete block design with five replicates:

(1) Control; (2) BA + GA: Benzyladenine + gibberellic acid (each 25 mg L-1, with 3 mL L^{-1} "Agra160"ionic surfactant, active ingredient nonyl phenol ethylene oxide, 600 g L-l), when the buds were just visible, at waterlogging, and on the fifth day of waterlogging; (3) Leaf: leaflets removed immediately before and during, but not after waterlogging; (4) Bud: buds removed when pedicels began to elongate, prior to and during, but not after waterlogging. All treatments were waterlogged. Waterlogging was imposed individually to each pots when the pedicel had begun to elongate at the most advanced apex of at least two plants in the pot. One additional pot of four plants was maintained as a non-waterlogged reference for measurements of leaf diffusive resistance, which was undertaken daily during waterlogging, between 1100 and 1400 hours, using a Delta-T diffusion porometer. The abaxial surface of the terminal leaflet of the youngest fully expanded leaf on the tallest branch was measured on each plant, and the result expressed relative to the average of the four non-waterlogged plants. Measurements were discontinued when the resistance of a leaf was eight times greater than the non-waterlogged plants. Height from soil surface to uppermost leaf node was measured before waterlogging and at harvest,30 days after the end of waterlogging. The number of green leaves on "new shoot" and mortality rate per pot were recorded before harvest. Plants were divided into root, nodules, "new shoots" and "old shoots" (see Cowie *et al.*, 1996 for definitions of "green leaf', "dead", "new shoots" and "old shoots"). Plant material was dried at 80° for 48 hours and weighed.

Experiment 2

The experiment comprised two sowing times, ten days apart, two bud treatments (retained and removed), and two waterlogging treatments (waterlogged and nonwaterlogged control), arranged in a complete factorial design, giving eight treatments. Treatments were replicated three times, and the whole experiment was duplicated to allow two complete harvests. Buds were removed when pedicels began to elongate. The waterlogging treatment was imposed on the two sowing times simultaneously, at a stage when older plants (Sowing 1) had been flowering, on average, for seven days and the most advanced younger plants.

ROLE OF PACLOBUTRAZOL IN AMELIORATION OF WATER DEFICIT STRESS IN CHICKPEA

Chickpea (*Cicerarietinum* L.) as a third major cool season grain legume in the world has an important role in the poor people's diet. India is the largest producer of chickpea. Traditionally, this crop is cultivated under marginal and rainfed areas. Therefore, drought is one of the major constraints in chickpea production.At present, the application of bioregulators attracts more attention to protect plants from abiotic stresses. Paclobutrazol (PBZ) interferes with gibberellins biosynthesis and provides plant protection against water deficit stress. Thus, the present study was undertaken using two contrasting chickpea varieties viz. desi (Pusa 362) and kabuli (Pusa 1108) for identifying optimum dose of paclobutrazol for foliar and drenching applications under water deficit condition and to analyze the physiological and biochemical alterations to gain insight into the mechanism of paclobutrazol induced water deficit stress tolerance. Initially, a preliminary experiment was conducted with varying dose of paclobutrazol for both foliar and drenching applications and Water deficit stress was imposed by restricting water supply until severe symptoms of wilting were visible.Before the imposition of water stress, plants were treated exogenously with an identified optimum dose of paclobutrazol. Based on relative water content, membrane stability index, photosynthetic pigments and photosynthesis rate, optimum dose of PBZ for foliar spray (60 ppm) and drenching (120 ppm) were identified and used for main experiment. Main experiment was comprised two main treatments (i.e. Sufficient watered and water deficit condition) and four sub-treatments (PBZ foliar spray (60 ppm), PBZ drenching (120 ppm), water spray and water drenching). The main result of the experiment showed decrease in RWC, MSI, rate of photosynthesis, stomatal conductance, transpiration rate, Fv/Fm ratio, water use efficiency, chlorophylls, carotenoids, growth parameters, harvest index, drought tolerance efficiency, yield and its attributes and disrupted chloroplast grana under imposed water deficit stress condition. Applications of paclobutrazol maintained higher values of all these parameters and maintained the integrity of chloroplast structure under imposed water stress and also stimulated faster recovery after water deficit stress termination in both chickpea varieties. Biochemical analysis revealed that total soluble sugars, total free amino acids and proline content increased under imposed water deficit stress and paclobutrazol maintained these at a higher level and hence has a role in osmo-protection. Paclobutrazol reduced the rate of lipid peroxidation and hence provided reduced membrane leakage. It also enhanced the activity of antioxidant enzymes and provided stress tolerance ability to both chickpea varieties. Paclobutrazol increased the level of abscisic acid and thus contributed in stress tolerance. In general PBZ drenching in terms of physio-biochemical responses were found better over the foliar application of PBZ. From the present study it can be concluded that paclobutrazol maintained RWC, MSI, photosynthetic activity, photosynthetic pigments and protected the photosynthetic machinery by enhancing the level of osmolytes, antioxidant activities and level of endogenous hormones and thereby induced water deficit stress tolerance and enhanced the yield (Figure 1.3) (Table 1.1)

Fig. 1.3: Chickpea plant growth and development

Source: Based on Review of Literature

Table 1.1: Properties of paclobutrazol

Chemical Formula	Properties
Melting point	164
Boiling point	384
Bulk density (g ml^{-1}/specific gravity)	1.23
Solubility in water	26 mg/L (20)

Source: http://sitem.herts.ac.uk/aeru/ppdb/en/Reports/504.htm

Paclobutrazolis a plant growth retardant and triazole fungicides (Table 1.1). It is a known antagonist of the plant hormone gibberellin. It acts by inhibiting gibberellin biosynth reducing internodal growth to give stouter stems, increasing root growth, causing early fruitset and increasing seedset. Paclobutrazol (PBZ) has also been shown to reduce frost sensitivity in plants. Paclobutrazol is used by arborists to reduce shoot growth and has been shown to have additional positive effects on trees and shrubs. Among those are improved resistance to drought stress, darker green leaves, higher resistance against fungi and bacteria, and enhanced development of roots. Cambial growth, as well as shoot growth, has been shown to be reduced in some tree species. Paclobutrazol is absorbed by roots and stems, and to a lesser extent, with leaves. Therefore, it can be applied as a spray, sprench, drench, or bulb or young-plant dip. Plants absorb paclobutrazol with 30 minutes, and so crops can be watered relatively soon after PGR application without losing efficacy. Once absorbed, the products have a fairly long residual effect, so they are often used on aggressive bedding plants and herbaceous perennials, as well as potted flowering plants such as poinsettia. In addition, paclobutrazol is used as a spray on some vigorous plug and liner crops, especially during periods of warm weather. Paclobutrazol is a compound which contains nitrogen heterocycle.

ROLE OF PACLOBUTRAZOL IN AMELIORATION OF WATER DEFICIT STRESS IN CHICKPEA

Chickpea (*Cicer arietinum* L.) is cultivated under marginal and rainfed areas. Therefore, drought is one of the major constraints in chickpea production. At present, the application of bioregulators attracts more attention to protect plants from biotic stresses. Paclobutrazol (PBZ) interferes with gibberellins biosynthesis and provides plant protection against water deficit stress.Thus, the present study was undertaken using two contrasting chickpea varieties viz. Desi (Pusan 362) and Kabuli (Pusa 1108) for identifying optimum dose of paclobutrazol for foliar and drenching applications under water deficit condition and to analyze the physiological and biochemical alterations to gain insight into the mechanism of paclobutrazol induced water deficit stress tolerance. Initially, a preliminary experiment was conducted with varying dose of paclobutrazol for both floor and drenching applications and Water deficit stress was imposed by restricting water supply until severe symptoms of wilting were visible. Before the imposition of water stress, plants were treated exogenously with an identified optimum dose of paclobutrazol. Based on relative water content, membrane stability index, photosynthetic pigments and photosynthesis rate, optimum dose of PBZ for foliar spray (60 ppm) and drenching (120 ppm) were identified and used for main experiment. Main experiment was comprised two main treatments (i.e. Sufficient watered and water deficit condition) and four sub-treatments (PBZ foliar spray (60 ppm), PBZ drenching (120 ppm), water spray and water drenching). Main results of the experiment showed decrease in RWC, MSI, rate of photosynthesis, stomatal conductance, transpiration rate, Fv/Fm ratio, water use efficiency, chlorophylls, carotenoids, growth parameters, harvest index, drought tolerance efficiency, yield and its attributes and disrupted chloroplast grana under imposed water deficit stress condition. Applications of paclobutrazol maintained higher values of all these parameters and maintained the integrity of chloroplast structureunder imposed water stress and also stimulated faster recovery after water deficit stress termination in both chickpea varieties. Biochemical analysis revealed that total soluble sugars, total free amino acids and proline content increased under imposed water deficit stress and paclobutrazol maintained these at a higher level and hence has a role in osmo-protection. Paclobutrazol reduced the rate of lipid peroxidation and hence provided reduced membrane leakage. It also enhanced the activity of antioxidant enzymes and provided stress tolerance ability to both chickpea varieties. Paclobutrazol increased the level of abscisic acid and thus contributed in stress tolerance. In general PBZ drenching in terms of physio-biochemical responses were found better over the foliar application of PBZ. From the present study it can be concluded that paclobutrazol maintained RWC, MSI, photosynthetic activity, photosynthetic pigments and protected the photosynthetic machinery by enhancing the level of osmolytes, antioxidant activities and level of endogenous hormones and thereby induced water deficit stress tolerance and enhanced the yield.Paclobutrazol reduce the rate of lipid peroxidation and hence provided reduced membrane leakage. It also enhanced the activity of antioxidant enzymes and provided stress tolerance ability to both chickpea varieties. Paclobutrazol increased the level of abscisic acid and thus contributed in stress tolerance. In general PBZ drenching in terms of physio-biochemical responses were found better over the foliar application of PBZ. From the present study it can be concluded that paclobutrazol maintained RWC, MSI, photosynthetic activity, photosynthetic pigments and protected the photosynthetic machinery by enhancing the level of osmolytes, antioxidant activities and level of endogenous hormones and thereby induced water deficit stress tolerance and enhanced the yield.

How does paclobutrazol act?

Available evidence strongly suggests that flower initiation depends on the presence of an unknown flowerpromoting factor or factors synthesized in the leaves. At the same time, there are other factors in the shoots which work against the flowering factor or factors. It is believed that a group of plant hormones called gibberellins act as inhibitors to flowering. When paclobutrazol is applied to the soil, it moves up through the roots into the shoots and, due to its anti-gibberellin properties, blocks the synthesis of flowering inhibitors, thereby allowing the flower-promoting factor(s) to work (Figure 1.4).

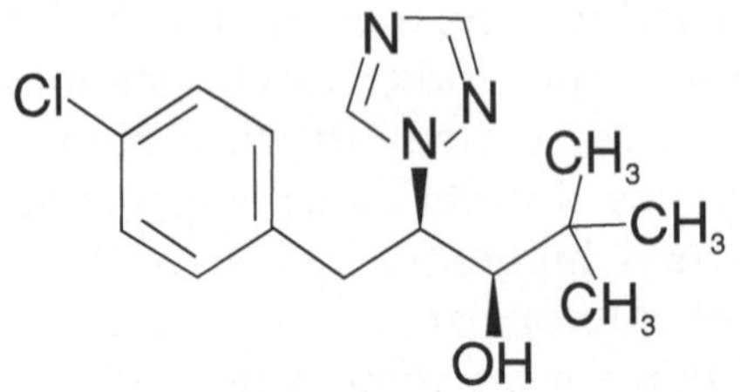

Fig. 1.4: Chemical structure of Paclobutrazol
Source: Based on Review of Literataure

Plant Growth Retardants: Their Mode of Action

The growth behavior and yield formation of crop plants are governed by their genetic potential, climatic conditions, and the supply of nutrients. Specific control of these processes by the application of plant bioregulators of natural or synthetic origin is increasingly emerging in recent years. Because of their specific properties in regulating shoot growth, the plant growth retardants have become the most widely used groups of bioregulators in agricultural and horticultural practice.For detailed summaries of commercially realized and possible future applications of growth retardants the reader is referred to reviews by Davies *et al.* (1988), Rademacher (1991), and Hoffmann (this volume). When applied in appropriate concentrations, growth retardants modify plant architecture in a typical fashion. Number of internodes and leaves. Concomitantly, the green colour of the foliage is intensified and leaf thickness and epicuticular wax may increase. In contrast to the shoot, the growth retardants maintain or slightly enhance root formation. Therefore, the root-shoot ratio is clearly changed in favour of the root. The morphological effects of growth retardants are accompanied by alterations in the development and physiological behavior of treated plants. The most striking changes include reduction of water consumption, retardation of senescence, and improved resistance to environmental stresses. As a result of this bio-regulation, the economically most important use of growth retardants is in improving lodging resistance and yield formation, particularly in cereals (Bruinsma, 1982; Jung, 1984). Extremely effective compounds have been discovered and developed in recent years. These include substances with a nitrogen containing heterocycle, such as pyrimidine (e.g. in ancyrnidol), 4-pyridine (in inabenfide), triazole (e.g. in uniconazole, "paclobutrazol", triapenthenol, BAS 111, and norbomanodiazetine (in tetcyclacis), and compounds with a cyclohexanetrione (acylcyclohexanedione) structure as the chemical feature. (E)-1-(4-Chlorophenyl)-4,4-dimethyl-2-(1,2,4-triazol-1-yl)-1-penten-3-ol

(S-3307), a new plant growth retardant, was investigated to determine the inhibitory sites in gibberellin biosynthesis and the comparative effects of its stereoisomers in a cell-free system from *Cucurbita maxima*. After treatment with S-3307, the incorporation of [^{14}C] mevalonic acid into GA_{12}-aldehyde and GA_{12} clearly was inhibited, and kaurene accumulated. Feeding experiments showed that S-3307 inhibited the oxidation of kaurene, kaurenol and kaurenal, but did not affect the oxidation of kaurenoic acid. Thus the reaction sites of S-3307 in gibberellin biosynthesis were shown to be the three oxidation steps from kaurene to kaurenoic acid. Because S-3307 has an asymmetric center and a tri-substituted double bond, there are four stereoisomers; two optical isomers and two geometrical isomers. The activities of these isomers as a growth retardant and gibberellin biosynthesis inhibitor were examined with a rice seedling assay and the cell-free system. The relative activity of these isomers was basically the same in the two assay methods. The (S)-(E) form was the most active, being 7-fold more active in the cell-free system and 70-fold more active in the bioassay than the (R)-(E) form. The (RS)-(Z) form showed no activity in the cell-free system, but weak dwarfing effects in the rice seedling assay.

Paclobutrazol (Pbz) Induces Morphological Adaptations that Enhance Tolerance to Deficit Irrigation

Water deficit or drought stress is diligently regulated *via* active participation of ABA, jasmonic acid, salicylic acid, auxins and brassinosteroids. Pbz application has shown a positive impact on drought tolerance potential of crop plants. Paclobutrazol application resulted in a reduction in plant height irrespective of growth conditions. Reduced size in Paclobutrazol-treated plants may be linked with its inhibitory action on the GAs, which are involved in cell division. Paclobutrazol application also increased stem width and leaf number in all the conditions tested. Paclobutrazol (at 1.6 ppm) significantly reduced leaf area (LA) (28% and 24%) in both irrigated and deficits irrigated conditions. Integrating leaf and root observations, Paclobutrazol application led to decreased LA/RA ratio in irrigated plants. The Pbz-induced change in LA under deficit irrigation may be linked to improved water use efficiency. Water use efficiency (WUE) increased in 0.8 I and 1.6 I plants as compared to irrigated control. However, in case of deficit irrigation, the WUE increased only in 0.8 DI plants. The 0.8 DI plants have WUE close to irrigated control plants, which suggest that the Pbz induced higher WUE in deficit irrigated plants affording them improved WUE as irrigated control plants (Figure 1.5).

Effects of PBZ application (0, 0.8 and 1.6 ppm) in irrigated (I) and deficit-irrigated (DI) tomato plants on the endogenous content of (A) abscisic acid (ABA) and expression of ABA biosynthesis genes (B, C) *SlZEP, SlNCED and SlAAO1*, and relative content of (D) spermidine (Spd) and expression of (E) spermidine synthase gene (*SlSPDS*) in the leaf tissue of 105-days old tomato plants. Letters (A, B and a, b, c) indicate significant differences (one way ANOVA, $p < 0.05$) from the control in irrigated and deficit-irrigated conditions, respectively.

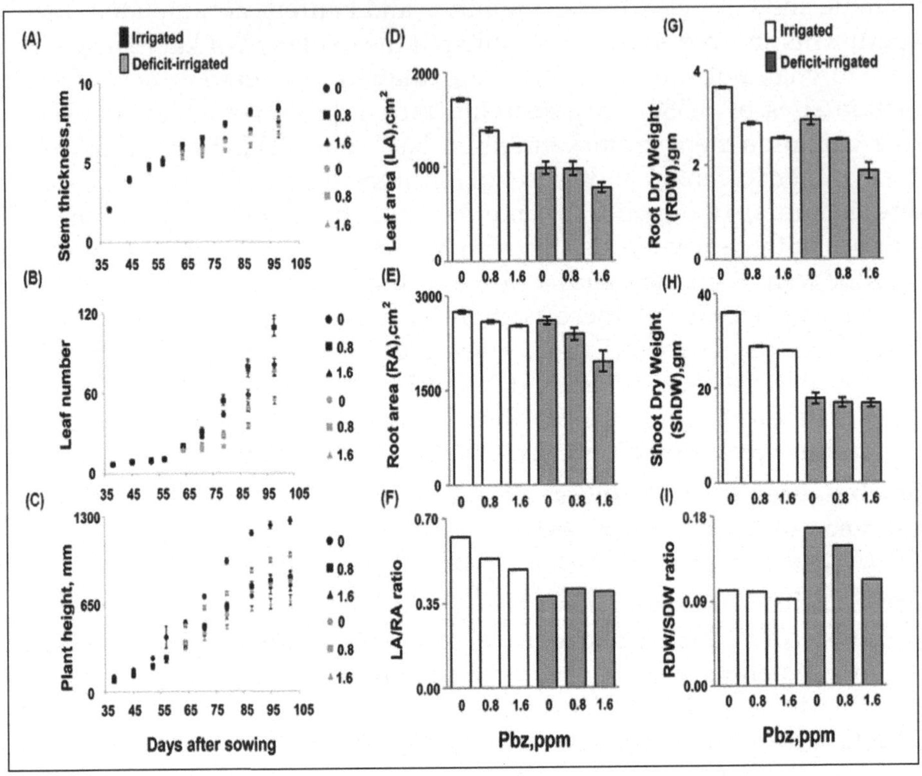

Fig. 1.5: Paclobutrazol induced morphological adaptations under deficit irrigation

Biosynthesis

Paclobutrazol and flurprimidol both significantly reduced growth compared to controls when applied at 0.5 mg/plant, but XE-1019 was more effective. All three gibberellin (GA) biosynthesis inhibitors effective retarded growth at a dosage of I mg/plant.A number of commercially important plant growth regulators are retards or inhibitors (Nickell 1982, Steffens 1980). Several are classed as giberellin (GA) biosynthesis inhibitors and have uses or potential uses in commercial agriculture.Examples include triazole compounds represented by palclobutrazol. Other new triazole compounds also have plant growth-regulating activity. A pyrimidine, has been shown to be a potent inhibitor of plant growth via the GA biosynthesis inhibition route. Other potent GA biosynthesis inhibitors include ancymidol. Several triazoles including triadimefon, inhibit ergosterol biosynthesis in fungi and have become commercially important fungicides. Triadimefon applied at 10 mg/plant had essentially no effect on growth, but at 50 and

100 mg/plant it caused significant but less dramatic growth retardation when compared with the GA inhibitors. Major differences in effectiveness among the triazole GA biosynthesis inhibitors may be due to longevity of effect as well as to the extent of inhibition. The plant growth retardants PBZ should be applied to the crops only once at the vegetative growth stage.One method to manipulate flowering is to use the plant growth regulator, paclobutrazol. The post-harvest application of a small amount of paclobutrazol to the soil significantly promotes flowering and fruiting in the following year. Trials over the last two years have shown the following benefits from the treatment: A significant increase in flowering leading to increased yields. The early flowering considerably enhanced fruit maturity. Treated trees flowered three to four weeks early, which reduced the time to fruit maturity by at least two weeks. Visually, the fruit developed a better external colour. The application of paclobutrazol to soil as a drench around the tree trunk (collar drench) is the most effective method, as it ensures proper uptake by the tree. The required quantity is mixed in approximately one litre of water and poured onto the soil around the trunk in a circular band. In the Top End, the ideal time to apply paclobutrazol is from soon after harvest to early January. In dry conditions, a light irrigation is recommended after application. Foliar sprays have been ineffective.

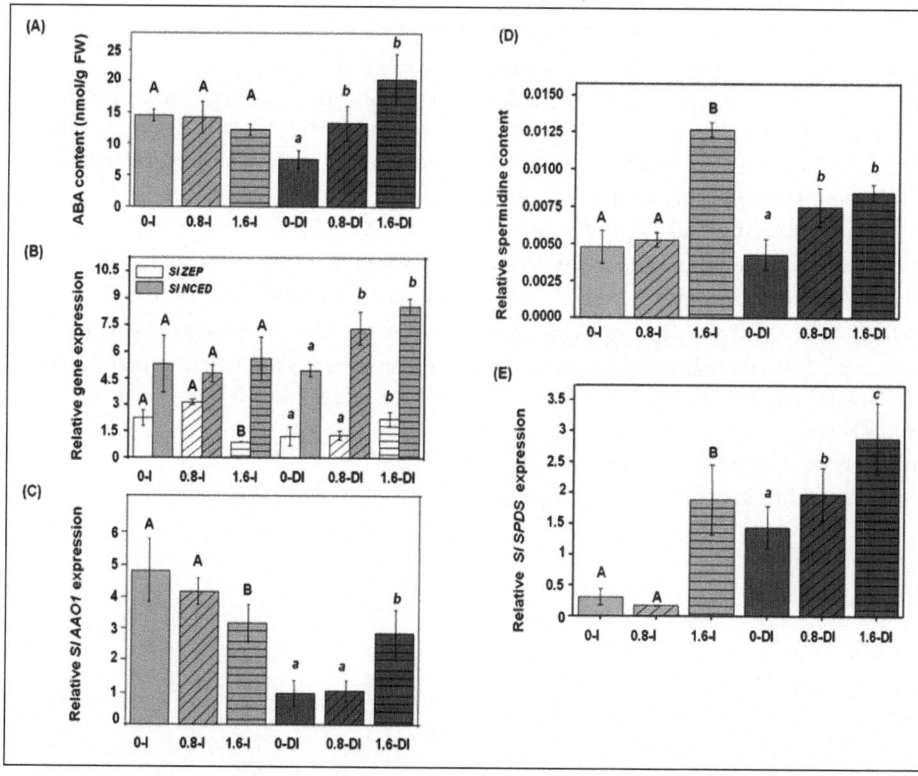

Fig.1.6: ABA content, Relative Spermidine, Relative gene expression

CONCLUSION

The present research investigation entitled effect of foliar application of plant growth retardants on growth, partitioning, productivity and quality of Chickpea as influenced by plant growth retardants. It can be concluded from the present investigation that foliar application of plant growth retardants significantly improved the physiological mechanism to enhance the yield potential in chickpea especially paclobutrazol. Plant height significantly reduces due to application of plant growthretardants. Paclobutrazol (PBZ) has also been shown to reduce frost sensitivity in plants. Paclobutrazol increased the level of abscisic acid and thus contributed in stress tolerance. Paclobutrazol reduced the rate of lipid peroxidation and hence provided reduced membrane leakage. Paclobutrazol maintained RWC, MSI, photosynthetic activity, photosynthetic pigments and protected the photosynthetic machinery by enhancing the level of osmolytes, antioxidant activities and level of endogenous hormones and thereby induced water deficit stress tolerance and enhanced the yield.

REFERENCES

The Plant List: A Working List of All Plant Species". Retrieved 22 October 2014.

http://www.icrisat.org/chickpea/taxonomy/frachc.htm.

https://www.harvesttotable.com/how_to_grow_chickpeas_garbanzo/

http://krishikosh.egranth.ac.in/bitstream/1/68048/1/T-83710.pdf.

Cubero, J.I. 1987. Morphology of Chickpea. p. 35-66. In: M.C. Saxena and K.B. Singh (eds.), The Chickpea. CAB. International, Wallingford, Oxon, OX10 8DE, UK.

A.L. Cowie, R.S. Jessop and D.A. 1996. MacLeod Plant and Soil. 183(1): 97-103.

Grossi; *et al.* (2005). "Effects of Paclobutrazol on Growth and Fruiting Characteristics of Pitanga Ornamental Pepper". ActaHorticulturae. 683: 333-336.

http://krishikosh.egranth.ac.in/handle/1/5810018882.

Role of Paclobutrazol, http://krishikosh.egranth.ac.in/handle/1/5810018882.

Mode of Action, https://link.springer.com/chapter/10.1007/978-94-011-2458-4-97.

Pal, S. *et al.* 2016. Paclobutrazol Induces Tolerance in Tomato to Deficit Irrigation through Diversified Effects on Plant Morphology, Physiology and Metabolism. Sci. Rep. 6, 39321.

https://www.nature.com/articles/srep39321#f1.

Biosynthesis, https://link.springer.com/article/10.1007/BF02054159.

Pages: 15-30

Stress Tolerance and Plant Productivity
Edited by: **Mr. Prasann Kumar and Dr. Pawan Kumar 'Bharti'**
ISBN: 978-93-86841-56-8
Edition: **2018**
Published by: **Discovery Publishing House Pvt. Ltd., New Delhi (India)**

2 Crop Adaptation and their Distribution

Prasann Kumar

ABSTRACT

Distribution of commercial crop production throughout the world is governed by many factors, with the main ones being climate, soils, topography, insect pressure, plant disease and economic conditions. Crop adaptation is determined primarily by genotype-environment interaction, the suitability of a crop to a particular region depending largely on the climatic features of the region in relation to the requirements for normal growth and development of the crop.

Key words: Agriculture, Biotic, Crop, Drought, Effect, Forage, Grass.

INTRODUCTION

Adaptation of crop plants depends on many factors, and is best considered in relation to a set of conditions (environmental, edaphic (soil) and biotic) rather than to a single factor alone. In many situations, one factor (e.g. water availability) may dominate the prevailing conditions, and the nature of the plant's response then largely reflects its adaptation to the existing level of that factor. More typically, adaptation is expressed as a response to a combination of factors (e.g. temperature and daylength) and the nature of the response then reflects the plant's adaptation to the factors in combination. The success of a plant in a particular environment rarely depends on possession of a single adaptive character. Development is the progression of a plant through the successive stages of its normal life cycle. The life cycle is best considered in two main phases, *Vegetative* and *Reproductive*, each of which includes one or more stages:

Assistant Professor, Department of Agronomy, School of Agriculture, Lovely Professional University, Jalandhar - 144 411, Punjab (India)

Vegetative

- Establishment – seed germination, emergence and, ultimately, independence of seed reserves.
- Vegetative growth – initiation, development and expansion of leaves, stems and roots.

Reproductive

- Floral initiation – the transition of stem apices (growing points) from vegetative (producing leaf and stem primordia [buds]) to reproductive (producing inflorescence structures and floral primordia).
- Flowering and pollination (anthesis), resulting in fertilized ovules which will develop into seeds (grains).
- Seed growth (grain filling) to a maximum wet weight at physiological maturity.
- Seed (grain) maturation – grain dries naturally to a moisture content suitable for harvesting and storage.
- Harvest ripeness – dry (12-14% moisture) grain ready for harvest.

Reproductive development in plants is controlled more by regulatory than by assimilatory processes. The consequences of this are that reproductive development can proceed relatively independently of growth, and can be modified by selecting more readily than growth. In many cases, the adaptation of crops to harsher environments has depended more on changes in the length and timing of their life cycles - allowing them to escape the most adverse conditions - than on changes in their ability to tolerate such environments. In contrast to those for growth, the external governing factors for development are principally environmental, with daylength and temperature the most important. As the most regular and predictable component of climate, daylength is the most potent and universal controlling element in the timing of life cycles of both wild and cultivated plants, and the modification of their responses to daylength has been a major factor in the spread and adaptation of many crop plants (Evans, 1996).

Growth

Growth is the increase in plant biomass (dry matter) over time. About 95% of biomass are the net result of photosynthetic gains and respiratory losses, with the remaining 5% derived from nutrient uptake. Growth is affected by the supply and the level of availability of all factors that are essential to normal plant metabolism and function. The major factors are:

- Water
- Nutrient elements
- Light (the visible component of incoming solar radiation – it includes the red and blue wavelengths which provide energy for photosynthesis)

- Gases, particularly carbon dioxide (CO_2) for photosynthesis and oxygen (O_2) for respiration.

All of these are usually infinite supply and are frequently the subject of competition between plants or species in a community.

Factors for which plants compete

The main factors are:

- Water
- Nutrients
- Light (solar radiation)
- Gases (carbon dioxide [CO_2] and oxygen [O_2])

Early Cultivation Crops

- Derived from local wild strains.
- First species were grasses(cereals).
- Wheat, barley first, Persian Gulf area around 10,000 years ago.
- About 7000 years ago
  - Rise in Asia
  - Corn in Central America
- About 5500 years ago, sorghums and millets in Africa.
- 5000 years ago rye in SW Asia.
- 3000 years ago oats in Europe.
- Cotton first cultivated in India, Egypt, Africa and the America about 5500 years ago.

Origins of agriculture, the active production of useful plants or animals in ecosystems that have been created by people. Agriculture has often been conceptualized narrowly, in terms of specific combinations of activities and organisms-wet-rice production in Asia, wheat farming in Europe, cattle ranching in the Americas etc. Over time, some plants and animals have become domesticated, of dependence on these and other human interventions for their long-term propagation and survival.

FACTORS AFFECTING CROP DISTRIBUTION AND ADAPTATIONS

Climatic factors include:

1. Temperature

Most plants cannot grow if the temperature falls below 6° C or the soil is frozen for five consecutive months. As a consequence, many areas are unsuitable for crop cultivation.

2. The growing season

The number of days between the last frost of the spring and the first of the autumn. Different crops require different lengths of growing seasons. Cotton needs 200 days, so could not survive in a British climate. Cereal crops are grown in the South-east of Britain as this is the area most likely to meet the necessary growing season. The shorter the required growing season the further north that crop can be grown. Oats can be found in Northern parts of the UK because they have a very short growing season (Figure 2.1).

Fig. 2.1: Crops along with their growing season

Source: Based on Review of Literature

3. Altitude

This affects temperature so it also affects farming. In the Alps for example, you will find dairy farming in valley bottoms and coniferous forestry further up.When temperatures are consistently high with sufficient precipitation high yield crops such as rise can be grown. These have the added advantage of producing up to three crops a year.

4. Rainfall

Water is obviously a key factor in plant growth. The greater the average temperature the greater the amount of water required for plant growth. Seasonal variation is important as different crops require water at different times. Coffee, for example, must have a period of drought before and during harvest whilst maize would benefit from heavy rain in the same period. A farmer is therefore looking for rainfall reliability so that he can select the most appropriate crop for the area. Rice is the principal crop in the tropics because it requires substantial quantities of water, is a very high yield crop and has good nutritional value. With the addition of consistent high temperatures, it can also produce two or three crops a year. In the Mediterranean crop growth is affected by the summer drought despite high annual rainfall. The rainfall is very high in the winter months, but infiltration rates are comparatively low. In summer temperatures are very high, encouraging high rates of evapo-transpiration and consequently very dry soil and a low water table. There is a soil moisture deficit. These conditions are not conducive to plant growth (Figure 2.2).

Fig. 2.2: Rain is an important ingredient in crop growth
Source: Based on the review and literature

5. Wind

Wind can have a destructive effect on crops. At its most severe a hurricane can physically destroy thousands of acres of farmland. Less severe but also harmful are the winds that dry soils so reducing moisture and increasing the potential for soil erosion.

6. Soil

Soil type will influence crop cultivation because different crops prefer different soils. Clay soils with their high water retention are well suited to rice whilst sandy soils with good drainage are best for root vegetables. Soil type can be influenced through the input of lime, clay or fertilizer, but this can only make limited differences.

7. Slope

The angle of slope will affect the type, depth and moisture content of soil. It will also affect the rate of soil erosion. Some of the most unique farming landscapes of Bali are a consequence of having to cultivate steep slopes that are prone to soil erosion. Here terraces are cut into steep slopes to retain the soil that otherwise would be easily removed due by the heavy rains. The need to cultivate such steep slopes is a consequence of population pressure and very small farms due to generations of sub-dividing amongst the sons (Figure 2.3).

Fig. 2.3: Bali farming

Source: Based on the Review of Literature

The degree to which a farm can be mechanized is influenced by slope. Many vineyards in Germany are still harvested by hand at great cost because of the steep slopes. This is despite the fact that Germany is one of the richest countries in the world with capital to take advantage of the latest technology. The principles behind the changing environments are like:

- Adaptation of a crop species is reflected in its responses to the combined environmental, edaphic and biotic features of its growing environment.
- Adaptation reflects the heritable features of a plant that enable it to survive, reproduce, or both, in a given environment.
- Acclimation reflects the non-heritable modifications to the plant phenotype caused by exposure to environmental stresses that enable it to tolerate further and more severe stress.
- Growth is an increase in plant biomass over time, and is determined by the level of availability of all factors necessary for normal plant metabolism and function.
- Development is the progression of a plant through the successive stages of its normal life cycle.

- Economic performance in grain crops is dependent on the successful completion of all development phases from establishment to harvest maturity.
- Development in most modern crop cultivars is dependent more on temperature than daylength and is accelerated by high temperatures, resulting in a shortened life cycle.
- The outcomes of competition reflect the relative adaptation of competing plants in optimising their capture or use of essential factors for growth that are in limited supply.
- Competitive ability in modern crop cultivars is a function of area, activity and distribution in space and time of absorptive surfaces (roots for water and nutrients; leaves for light and CO2) in crowded, productive situations.
- Water supply and temperature, sometimes aided by the buildup of pests and diseases, determine the maximum length of the growing season, the range of crops that can be grown, their optimum duration and likely yield.
- Adaptation to temperature is a major factor governing the natural distribution of plants, and is a principal determinant in the selection of crop species for any location.
- The adaptation of crop species to harsh environments has depended more on changes in the length and timing of their life cycles that allow avoidance of harsh conditions, than to changes in their tolerance to those conditions.
- Reducing daylength dependence in crop cultivars increases the flexibility of their life cycles, allowing greater manipulation of their planting dates, flowering times and growing periods.
- Underwater limited rainfed conditions, earlier flowering and maturity can be critical to yield performance, as they enable flowering and grain fill before available water is exhausted.
- Production principles for rainfed temperate crops reflect strategies to capitalise on available water during the growing period, while minimizing frost risk at flowering and high temperatures and water stress during grain filling.
- Production principles for rainfed summer crops focus on frost escape, water availability throughout the growing period, and minimization of water and high-temperature stresses during flowering and grain filling.
- The principal production strategies to minimize the impact of climatic constraints are cultivar selection, planting time and, to a lesser extent, planting rate.

- Late planting of most crops results in accelerated development, a short vegetative phase, low biomass at anthesis and reduced yield potential.
- The optimum planting time for any crop is determined by the combination of cultivar adaptation, soil temperature and available soil water.

NEW RESEARCHES RELATED TO ADAPTATION AND CHANGING CLIMATE

Crops and Food

Researches investigate the use of genetics and processing interventions to avoid intolerance to gluten protein; reduction of anti-nutritional factors in faba bean; targeting increased levels of beneficial compounds associated with improved cardiovascular and brain function.

Crops and Soil

CP is currently investigating how we can improve the use of phosphate through manipulation of plant nutrient uptake and utilization traits as well as oil mychorriza; reduction of pesticide residues through robotic precision application; more effective use of biological nitrogen fixation in cropping systems.

Crops and Climate

Scientists undertake modeling work to determine the impact of climate change on crop production; genetics of tolerance to drought; impact of heat on grain quality, an apple and cocoa productivity; root traits for drought resistance. An adaptation of a crop is very much important in case of the changes in the normal condition of the crop.In case of any deviation in the required conditions, the crop can get adapted and make sure the usual mechanism of the plant is carried out. The plant makes several changes for the sake of survival. Crop distribution is one of the major reasons which affects the biodiversity of the world. The distribution occurs according to many factors.It is the ability of a crop to respond positively to changes in agricultural conditions. The plant gets the ability to exploit environmental attributes,both natural and agronomic. It may be due to the genetically controlled trait."Any feature of an organism which has survival value under the existing conditions of its habitats.Such a feature of features may allow the plant to make fuller use of the nutrients, water, temperature or light. It gives protection against the adverse factors such as temperature extremes, water stress, disease or insect pressures." (Figure 2.4)

ADAPTIVE CHARACTERISTICS

1. Shading of leaves during the dry long seasons-helps to reduce water loss (Figure 2.5).
2. More rapid and extensive development of leaf canopy-reduce water evaporation, catches sun light more,increasing shading and suppression of the inferior plant (Figure 2.6).

Fig. 2.4: Crops and climate

Source: Based on the Review of Literature

Fig. 2.5: Shading of leaves

Source: Based on the Review of Literature

Fig. 2.6: Rapid and extensive development of leaf canopy

Source: Based on Review of Literature

3. Rough leaf surface-shield stomata by limiting the direct stomatal exposure to the sun,prevents the water removal by transpiration (Figure 2.7).

Fig. 2.7: Rough leaf surface
Source: Based on the Review of Literature

4. Leaf rolling-reduce the removal of water, limits direct stomatal exposure to solar radiation and wind (so the transpiration is reduced) (Figure 2.8).

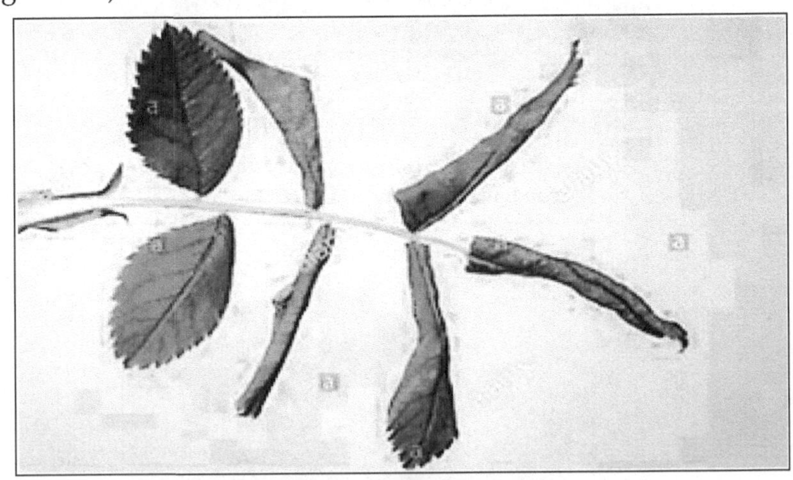

Fig. 2.8: Leaf rolls in plants
Source: Based on the Review of Literature

5. Indehiscent fruits with numerous seeds to promote-effective dispersal, the possibility is more in case of reproduction (Figure 9).

Fig. 2.9: Indehiscent fruits

Source: Based on Review of Literature

6. Many of the local grain crops in the region such as sorghum and millet follow the C4-photosynthetic pathway (capable of converting very high light intensities) which is more efficient than C3 (Figure 2.10).

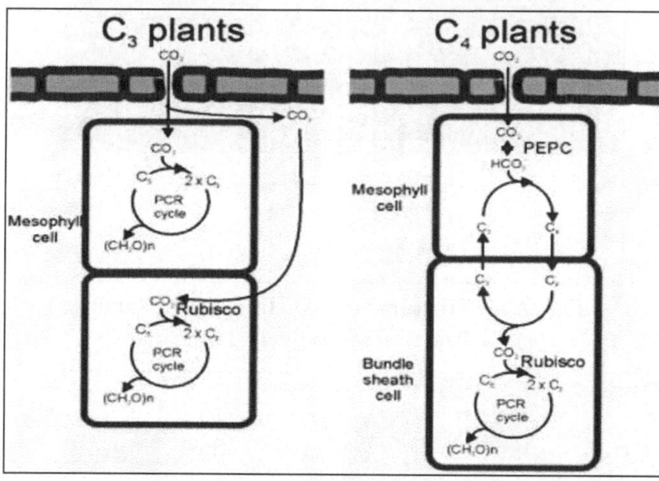

Fig. 2.10: C3 and C4 plants cycle

Source: Based on review of Literature

7. Glossy outermost surface on the leaves-reduces water removal by transpiration and evaporation (Figure 2.11).
8. Strong root system-can absorb water from a large area (Figure 2.12).
9. Leaves are converted to fine tips-cactus (Figure 2.13).

Fig. 2.11: Glossy surface of the leaves of the plants
Source: Based on the Review of Literature

Fig. 2.12: Fibrous root system of the plant
Source: Based on the Review of Literature

Fig. 2.13: Cactus of the plant
Source: Based on Review of Literature

TEMPERATURE

It influences the growth and the development of all the crops.The adequate temperature has to be there for the proper metabolism, including all the enzymatic actions. Ex:photosynthesis. The effect of temperature on plants varies widely, and it is influenced by the factors such as exposure to sunlight, moisture drainage, elevation, difference between day an night temperature and approximity to surrounding rock structure(thermal heat mass). When the temperature alters the yield of the plants get affected. Pollination is one of the most sensitive phenological stages of temperature extremes across all species and during this developmental stage temperature extremes would greatly affect production. Ex:tomatoes get effected very much when it is exposed to about >90 degrees F. Different plant has their different favourable conditions. Ex:lettuce and broccoli around 55-70 F. Warm season plants such as squash, marigolds best when the temperatures are between 70-85 p F. The growth of a plant which shows the maximum level will differ from one plant to another.

AMOUNT OF WATER AVAILABLE

Water is one of the most important factors affecting the growth and development of a plant. It provides a medium for the water soluble nutrients to dissolve and enzymes for their functioning. Plants get water from the soil. The amount of available water may get affected by different reasons like, Cutting down of trees in bulk-deforestration. The constructions which affect the fountains. When the amount of free water is reduced by the conversion of free water to bound water etc. Recovery from water stress is slower and the yield penalty is greater is usually greater than in sorghum or millet. The plants become wilt and close its stomata up to an extend to prevent further water loss. While sunken stomates and rough leaf surfaces in arid zone plants. Plants such as sorghum, millets and maize exhibit leaf rolling under water stress.

CARBON DIOXIDE

It is fundamental to the crop carbohydrate production (important for crop productivity and yield) and overall plant metabolism. Atmospheric carbondioxide concentrations have risen dramatically over the past 200 years and may reach 450-1000 micrio mol by the end of this century, according to the Ingovermental Panel on Climate Change(IPCC2007). Rising carbondioxide levels will likely boost the overall productivity of many crops, although important tropical grasses likemaize, sugarcane and sorghum and some cellulosic biofuel crops do not respond as well to elevated carbondioxide levels. Increase in productivity could be offset though, by pressure such as insect and fungal pests, ozone, and more variable precipitation, although the degree to which this occurs will depend on the physiology and biochemistry of each crop. Crop adaptation will be critical to ensure that crops can maintain or even increase productivity amidst a carbondioxide enriched environment. Spotlight on carbondioxide and C3 and C4 crops. Crops with C3 photosynthesis (soybeen, rice and wheat) respond more positively in increasing carbondioxide than C4 crops (maize, sugarcane, biofuel grasses such as switchgrass, miscanthus). C3 crops are more susceptible to increases in temperature. Given that environmental factors, carbondioxide concentration, temperature and water availability will likely change simultaneously (as well as impact biotic factors). It is therefore difficult to make accurate predictions about crop production under elevated concentrations of carbondioxide.

BIOLOGICAL STRESSES

Biological stress on cropping system includes weed, insects, viruses, bacteria and fungi. Temperature is considered as the most important factor in determining how insects affect crop production and yield. For example, some populations of insect species, such as, flea beetles are showing signs of overwintering because of warmer winter temperatures. Viral, bacterial and fungal pathogens also respond greatly to temperatures,as season lengthens and winters, moderate due to climate change,pressure from plant, microbial and insect pests are expected to rise due to an increased capacity for over-wintering, greater movement of organisms and expanded adaptation zones.

CONCLUSION

Factors affecting the distribution of crops. Physical (1) Temperature; (2) The growing season; (3) Altitude; (4) Rainfall; (5) Wind; (6) Soil; (7) Slope; (8) Land Tenure; (9) Market; (10) Transport; (11) Capital; (12) Technology; (13) Government. Most plants cannot grow if the temperature falls below 6 C or the soil is frozen for five consecutive months. As a consequence, many areas are unsuitable for crop production. The number of days between the last frost of the spring and the first of the autumn. Different crops require different lengths of growing seasons.Cotton needs 200 days, so can not survive in a British climate. Shorter the required growing seasons the capability for that crop for growing in a cold environment increase. This affects temperature so it also affects farming. When the temperature is constantly high with sufficient precipitation high yield crops such as rise can be grown. The higher the altitude, lower the temperature and pressure. Water is obviously a key factor in plant growth. The greater the average temperature the greater the amount of water required for plant growth. Seasonal variation is important in as different crops require water at different times. Ex:Coffee must have a period of drought before and during the harvesting. Maize needs heavy rain in the same period. Rice is the principal crop in the tropics because it requires substantial quantities of water. (a high yield crop). In summers temperatures are very high, encouraging high rates of evapo-transpiration and consequently very dry soil and a low water table. There is a soil water deficit. These conditions are not conducive to plant growth. Wind can have a destructive effect on crops. At its most severe a hurricane can physically destroy thousands of acres of farmland. Less severe but also but also harmful are the winds that dry soils so reducing moisture and increasing the potential for soil erosion. Soil type will influence crop cultivation because different crops prefer different soils. Clay soil with their high water retention are well suited to rice while sandy soils with good drainage are best for root vegetables. Soil type can be influenced by the input of lime, clay or fertilizer, but this can only make limited differences. The angle of slope will affect the type, depth and moisture content of soil. It will also affect the rate of soil erosion. These terraces are cut into steep slopes to retain the soil that otherwise would be easily removed by heavy rains. The degree to which the farm can be mechanized is influenced by the slope. In the developed world large percentage of farmers are owner-occupiers. In the developing world farmers are less likely to be owner-occupiers. Instead, they will probably be tenants or landless labourers. For any commercial farm to succeed there must be a demand. If the demand for a crop drops,then profits will fall. That crop will then be replaced by a more profitable one. It is an important factor in determining the location of farm types. If the product is bulky such as potatoes, then it should be grown close to the market place to cut down on transport costs. If the food is perishable, then again, it should be grown close to the market place. The effect of transport has been greatly reduced in the developed world because of innovations such as refrigerated lorries. It is still an important factor in many parts of the developing world. The transportation available and the transport network will have a large influence on the distribution of agricultural system. Many subsistence farms could not cell surpluses even if they had them because of the costs involved in transporting the surpluses to the market place. In the developed world, there is a well established system of supportive banks, private investors and government subsides. This means that the agriculture is likely to be capital intensive and highly mechanized. New technology is always increasing efficiency and yields, but technology costs money. Therefore the gap between the developed and developing world is growing. Government policies will have a direct or indirect effect on the prevailing agricultural system. The communist governments encouraged collectives as already seen while farming is indirectly manipulated by the agricultural policies.

REFERENCES

http://as.wiley.com/WileyCDA/WileyTitle/productCd-0813820162.html

http://iari.bestbookbuddies.com/cgi-bin/koha/opac-detail.pl?biblionumber=45675

http://www.powershow.com/view4/479946NTI3Y/Crop_Adaptation_and_Distribution_powerpointo ppt presentation

http://www.reading.ac.uk/apd/research/apd-rescp.aspx

http://www.sciencedirect.com/science/article/pii/S1002007109002810

https://rjoas.com/issue-2012-11/i011_article_2012_02.pdf

https://www.csu.edu.au/__data/assets/pdf_file/0006/.../Chapter3_Kelleher.pdf

https://www.csu.edu.au/__data/assets/pdf_file/0006/2805558/Chapter3_Kelleher.pdf

https://www.researchgate.net/publication/ 285145048_Adaptive_characteristics_of_the_symbiotic_association_and_nitrogen_symbiotic_fixation_in_young_plants_of_Lonchocarpus_muehlbergianus_Haasl_a_leguminous_tree_native_from_%27Cerrado%27

https://www.theguardian.com/environment/2012/feb/27/climate-change-adaptation

https://www.usda.gov/topics/farming/crop-production

Pages: 31-57

Stress Tolerance and Plant Productivity
Edited by: **Mr. Prasann Kumar and Dr. Pawan Kumar 'Bharti'**
ISBN: 978-93-86841-56-8
Edition: **2018**
Published by: **Discovery Publishing House Pvt. Ltd., New Delhi (India)**

3 Impact of Climate Change on Plant - Pollinator Interaction

Pushpavathi Y*; Thomson T and Ashoka Reddy Y

ABSTRACT

Pollinators are a key component of global biodiversity, providing vital ecosystem services to crops and wild plants. Approximately 80% of all flowering plant species are specialized for pollination by animals, mostly insects. There is clear evidence of recent declines in both wild and domesticated pollinators, and parallel declines in the plants that rely upon them. Pollinator declines can result in loss of pollination services which have important negative ecological and economic impacts that could significantly affect the maintenance of wild plant diversity, wider ecosystem stability, crop production, food security and human welfare. Insects and plants react differently to changed temperature, creating temporal (phenological) and spatial (distributional) mismatches with severe demographic consequences for the species involved. Mismatches may affect plant by reduced insect visitation and pollen deposition, while pollinators experience reduced food availability. The effect of climate change on pollinators depends upon their thermal tolerance and plasticity to temperature changes. Data on the impacts of climate change on crop pollination is still limited, and investigations in this direction are very limited. This chapter deals with the potential effects of climate change on pollinators, including direct effects and indirect effects through their floral resources. Measures to enhance and conserve pollinators are also suggested.

INTRODUCTION

Pollinators play an important functional role in most terrestrial ecosystems and represent a key ecosystem service that is vital to the maintenance of both wild plant communities and agricultural productivity.

Department of Fruit Science, Dr. Y.S.R. Horticultural University, Venkataramanna gudem, West Godavari District - 534101 (Andhra Pradesh) (India)

Pollination is a keystone process in both human managed and natural terrestrial ecosystems. It is critical for food production and human livelihoods, and directly links wild ecosystems with agricultural production systems. To achieve successful pollination, many angiosperms depend on external agents like animals, wind and water. However, many food crops, barring cereals, are entomophilous in nature and rely on insects for pollination. The pollinators in turn benefit by obtaining floral resources such as nectar or pollen or both. In agroecosystems, pollinators are essential for orchard, horticultural and forage production, as well as the production of seed for many root and fibre crops.

Worldwide, the number of flower-visiting species is estimated to be around 150,0005. Bees account for 25,000 to 30,000 species and together with flies, butterflies, moths, wasps, beetles and some other insect orders encompass the majority of pollinating species. Vertebrate pollinators include bats, non-flying mammals (several species of monkey, lemur, rodents, tree squirrel, coati, olingo and kinkajou) and birds (hummingbirds, sunbirds, honeycreepers and some parrot species).

Major groups of pollinators include bees (*Apis* spp. and non- *Apis* sp.), wasps, butterflies, flies and beetles. However, pollinators such as bees, birds and bats affect 35% of the world's crop production, increasing outputs of 87 of the leading food crops worldwide, plus many plant-derived medicines in our pharmacies (FAO 2009). The total economic value of crop pollination worldwide has been estimated at €156 billion annually (Gallai *et al.* 2009). The dependence of ecosystems on animal pollinators is stronger in the tropics than the global average: less than 3% of all tropical lowland plants rely on wind for pollination (Kjohl *et al.* 2011). The area covered by pollinator dependent crops has increased by more than 300% during the past 50 years (Aizen and Harder 2009). European bee, *Apis mellifera,* and Indian honeybee, *Apis cerana,* are the most widely used and managed pollinators followed by bumblebees. Approximately 73% of the world's cultivated crops are pollinated by bees, 19% by fl ies, 6.5% by bats, 5% by wasps, 5% by beetles, 4% by birds and 4% by butter flies and moths (Abrol 2009). In the recent years, there has been a concern about declines in both wild and domesticated pollinators and parallel declines in the plants that rely upon them. A large proportion of horticultural crops are potentially vulnerable to declines in honeybees and other pollinator insects. Complete pollinator loss would translate into a production deficit over current consumption levels of –12% for fruits and –6% for vegetables. Among different factors responsible for pollinator decline are habitat loss and fragmentation, chemical intensive agriculture, invasive species and climate change (Potts *et al.* 2010), Climate change is thought to be one of the serious threats to pollination services and it is a major issue now a days which is negatively harming the insect pollinators (Hegland *et al.* 2009).

Different scientists notice that we may be in the middle of global pollination crisis (Biesmeijer *et al.*, 2006). But the knowledge of the effects of climate change on plant – pollinators interactions is still limited (Visser and Both, 2005) and it is found that systematic studies on this aspect are very few elsewhere and almost none in India, except for the very recent initiation of research projects under the umbrella of National Initiative on Climate Resilient Agriculture (NICRA) being implemented by the Indian Council of Agricultural Research (ICAR), Government of India. Hence regarding such context this chapter reviews about the impact of climate change on pollinators.

DEPENDENCE OF WORLD CROPS ON POLLINATORS

Out of the 115 crops whose pollen vectors were determined in a recent global study, over 75% depend to some degree upon animal pollination. Among the leading crops that benefit from animal pollination, 13 are entirely reliant upon animal pollinators, 30 are greatly dependent and 27 are moderately dependent. A few crops rely entirely on pollinators for reproduction; without pollinators, a crop could only be produced with human help via hand pollination. These include cocoa, one of the most important cash crops in tropical countries, the vitamin-rich and tasty kiwifruit, passion fruit, annona and sapodilla fruits, as well as vanilla, squashes and pumpkins, cantaloupes and watermelons, and Brazil- and macadamia nuts. Most crops showed a production increase between 5 and 50% as a result of pollination by animals (mainly bees). However, that there are multiple gaps in the knowledge of pollination requirements, which may vary between varieties and geographic locations. The understanding of the pollination needs of many crops has recently been revised, as they are grown under increasingly intensive practices where the underappreciated wild pollination service may be impacted. In addition to gaps in knowledge about pollination requirements, there is also a dynamic aspect about knowledge development in this area, as production systems evolve and change. In particular, as production systems intensify, there has been an increase in awareness of the importance (and value) of previously supplied wild pollination services (Klein *et al.* 2007).

CURRENT STATUS OF POLLINATOR DECLINE

Thomas *et al.* (2004) have found that 71% of butterfly species have decreased and 3.4% became extinct over the past 20 years, illustrating the greatest net loss compared to native vascular plants (28% decrease in 40 years) and birds (54% decrease in 20 years) of the same area in the UK.

Most species of non migratory butter flies that reach the northern margins of their geographic ranges in Britain have declined over the last 30 years. The "pollination crisis" that is evident in declines of honeybees and native bees worldwide is due to disruption of critical balance between the two mutually interacting organisms. Anthropogenic climate change is widely expected to drive species extinct by hampering individual survival and reproduction, by reducing the amount and accessibility of suitable habitat, or by eliminating other organisms that are essential to the species in question. Changes in habitats and climates have resulted in substantial reductions in biodiversity, and evidence has been accumulating that insect biodiversity is at risk as well. Of particular concern, the pollinators and the plants that are linked to one another within communities show coincident declines. Many agricultural crops and natural plant populations are dependent on pollination and often on the services provided by wild, unmanaged, pollinator communities. Despite widespread concern about declines in pollination services, little is known about the patterns of change in most pollinator assemblages. Depending on the assemblage and location, pollinator declines were most frequent in habitat and flower specialists, in univoltine species and/or in nonmigrants. In conjunction with this evidence, outcrossing plant species that are reliant on the declining pollinators have themselves declined relative to other plant species. Gallai *et al.* (2009) had estimated the extent of honeybee decline in last 15-25 years in different countries (Tables 3.1 and 3.2).

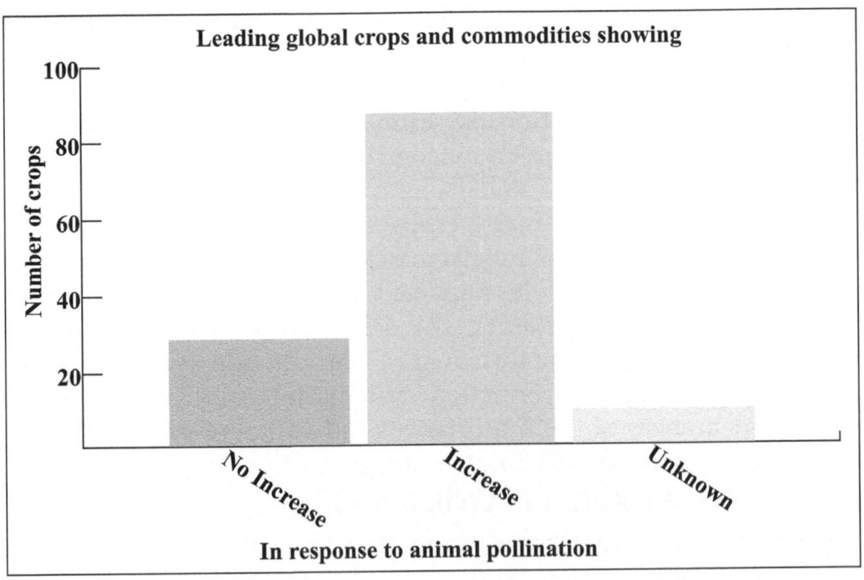

Economic impacts of insect pollination of the world agricultural production used directly for human food and listed by the main categories ranked by their rate of vulnerability to pollinator loss

Crop Category	Average Value of a Production Unit	Total Production Economic Value (EV)	Insect Pollination Economic Value (IPEV)	Rate of Vulnerability (IPEV/EV)
	€ per metric tonne	10^9€	10^9 €	%
Stimulant crops	1225	19	7.0	39.0
Nuts	1269	13	4.2	31.0
Fruits	452	219	50.6	23.1
Edible oil crops	385	240	39.0	16.3
Vegetables	468	418	50.9	12.2
Pulse	515	24	1.0	4.3
Spices	1003	7	0.2	2.7
Cereals	139	312	0.0	0.0
Sugar crops	177	268	0.0	0.0
Roots and tubers	137	98	0.0	0.0
All categories		1618	152.9	9.5

Impact of honeybee (*Apis cerana*) pollination on fruit productivity

Crop	Increase in Fruit Set (%)	Increase in Fruit Weight (%)	Increase in Fruit Size (Length, Diametre) (%)	References
Apple	10	33	15, 10	Verma and Dulta, 1998
Peach	22	44	29, 23	Partap *et al.*, 2000
Plum	13	39	11, 14	Partap *et al.*, 2000
Citrus	24	35	9, 35	Partap, 2000
Strawberry	112	48	Misshapen fruits decreased by 50 percent	Partap, 2000

Source: Partap *et al.*, 2000

The role of honeybees in the pollination pome and stone fruit

Fruit	Variety	Fruit set (per cent)		Yield/tree (kg)
Apples	Yates	Open* Enclosed**	2408	1259
Pears	Winter Nelis	Open Enclosed	535	8812
Apricot	Trevatt	Open* Enclosed**	1911	9967
Cherry	Moss Early	Open Enclosed	362	352
Peach	Golden Queen	Open Enclosed	2622	216155++
Peach	Crawford	Open Enclosed	2810	4718
Plum	Satsuma	Open Enclosed	62	3815

Russel lGoodman Knoxfield September, 1994

Percentage Increase in Yield of Orchard Crops due to Bee Pollination

Crops	% Increase in yield
Apple	180-6950
Pear	240-6014
Plum	6.7-2739
Cherry	56.1-1000
Strawberry	17.4-91.9
Raspberry	291.3-462.5
Litchi	4538-10246
Citrus	7-233.3
Grapes	756.4-6700
Squash	771.4-800
Guava	70-140
Papaya	22.4-88.9
Mosambi	36-750
Orange	471-900

Table 3.1: Population decline of honeybees in world scenario

Country	Decline (%) Duration	Duration
Germany	57	Last 15 years
UK	61	Last 10 years
USA	>50	Last 20 years
Poland	>35	Last 15 years
India	>40	Last 25 years
Brazil	>53	Last 15 years
Netherland	58-65	Last 25 years
China	>50	Last 20 years

Source: Gallai *et al.* 2009

CLIMATE CHANGE AND POLLINATORS

The Intergovernmental Panel on Climate Change (IPCC) reports an approximate temperature increase ranging from 1.1°C to 6.4°C by the end of this century and that the increases in temperature will be greatest at higher latitudes (IPCC 2007). The biological impacts of rising temperatures depend upon the physiological sensitivity of organisms to temperature change. Deutsch *et al.* (2008) found that an expected future temperature increase in the tropics, although relatively small in magnitude, is likely to have more deleterious consequences than changes at higher latitudes. The reason for this is that tropical insects are relatively sensitive to temperature changes (with a narrow span of suitable temperature) and that they are currently living in an environment very close to their optimal temperature. Deutsch *et al.* (2008) point out that in contrast, insect species at higher latitudes – where the temperature increase is expected to be higher – have broader thermal tolerance and are living in cooler climates than their physiological optima. Warming may actually enhance the performance of insects living at these latitudes. It is therefore likely that tropical agroecosystems will suffer from greater population decrease and extinction of native pollinators than agroecosystems at higher latitudes. Coope (1995) gives three possible responses of species to climate change, viz., adaptation to the new environment, migration to another suitable area and extinction. The first response is unlikely since expected climate change occurs too rapidly for populations to adapt by genetic change. With increase in temperatures, many species move towards poles and higher altitudes. Tropical pollinators may respond to different temperature cues than pollinator species at higher latitudes. Temperature-induced activity patterns may also differ, depending on pollinator size, age and sex. Winter temperature might also be of importance for pollinators.

The effects of climate change on pollinators depend upon their thermal tolerance and plasticity to temperature changes. There is an urgent need to investigate the thermal tolerance of important crop pollinators and differences in thermal tolerance among *Apis* species and subspecies. Environmental cues controlling the phenology of important pollinators might include maximum daily temperature, lack of frost, number of degree days (number of days with a mean temperature above a certain threshold), day length and snow cover. Bees are the most important group of pollinators, and like other insects, they are ectothermic, requiring elevated body temperature for flying. The temperature of their surroundings determines their activity (Willmer and Stone 1997). The high surface-to-volume ratio of small bees leads to rapid absorption of heat at high ambient temperatures. All bees with body weight above 35 mg (*Apis, Bombus, Xylocopa* and *Megachile)* are capable of endothermic heating (Bishop and Ambruster 1999).

Behavioural responses of pollinator insects to avoid extreme temperatures have the potential to significantly reduce pollination services (Corbet *et al.* 1991). Shifts in climate are bound to cause changes in behaviour of pollinators. The time taken for thermoregulation at higher temperatures comes at the cost of foraging. With increase in temperatures, the efficiency of pollen removal and deposition will change, and pollinators are at risk of overheating, especially in regions where ambient temperatures are high and climatic conditions are stable. It is important to investigate the taxonomic differences in pollinator's ability to regulate body temperature and avoid overheating (Hegland *et al.* 2009)

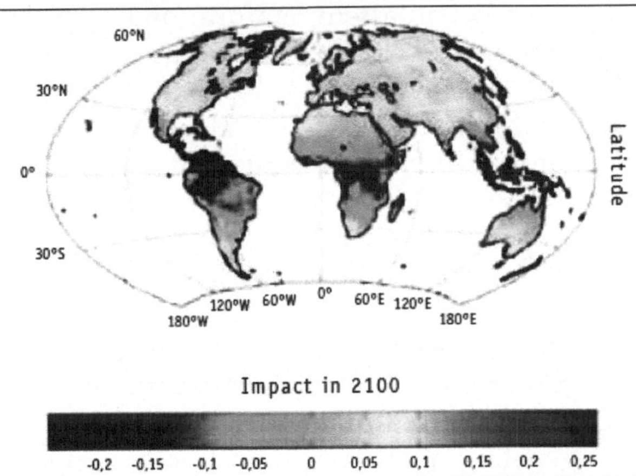

On the basis of patterns in warming tolerance, climate change is predicted to be most deleterious for insects in tropical zones.

Source: Deutsch *et al.* 2008

Coope (1995) gives three possible scenarios for species' responses to large-scale climatic changes:

- Adaptation to the new environment
- Emigration to another suitable area
- Extinction

The first response is unlikely, since the expected climate change will occur too rapidly for populations to adapt by genetic change (evolution). As temperatures increase and exceed species' thermal tolerance levels, the species' distributions are expected to shift towards the poles and higher altitudes. Many studies have already found poleward expansions of plants (Lenoir *et al.* 2008), birds (Zuckerberg *et al.* 2009) and butterflies (Konvicka *et al.* 2003) as a result of climate change. Crop species and managed pollinators may easily be transported and grown in more suitable areas. However, moving food production to new areas may have serious socio-economic consequences. In addition, wild pollinators might not be able to follow the movement of crops.

Insect pollinators are valuable and limited resources (Delaplane and Mayer 2000). Currently, farmers manage only 11 of the 20000 to 30000 bee species worldwide (Parker *et al.* 1987), with the European honey bee (*Apis mellifera)* being by far the most important species. Depending on only a few pollinator species belonging to the *Apis* genus has been shown to be risky. *Apis*-specific parasites and pathogens have lead to massive declines in honey bee numbers. Biotic stress accompanied with climate change may cause further population declines and lead farmers and researchers to look for alternative pollinators. Well-known pollinators to replace honey bees might include the alfalfa leaf-cutter bee (*Megachile rotundata*) and alkali bee (*Nomia melanderi*) in alfalfa pollination (Cane 2002), mason bees (*Osmia* spp.) for pollination of orchards (Maccagnani *et al.* 2003) and bumblebees (*Bombus* spp.) for pollination of crops requiring buzz pollination (Velthuis and van Doorn 2006). Stingless bees are particularly important pollinators of tropical plants, visiting approximately 90 crop species (Heard 1999). Some habits of stingless bees resemble those of honey bees, including their preference for a wide range of crop species, making them attractive for commercial management.

ELEVATED CO_2 AND POLLINATORS

The direct effects of elevated atmospheric carbon dioxide concentrations on pollinators and their mutualistic plant hosts are dif fi cult to predict. Indirectly, elevated atmospheric CO_2 is expected to modify ratios of carbon and nitrogen in plant tissues, possibly leading to changes in patterns of herbivory by organisms such as butter fl y larvae (Rusterholz and Erhardt 1998). How this might affect communities of pollinators is uncertain. Furthermore, increasing concentrations of CO_2 in the atmosphere will probably lead to changes in plant community structure, particularly in the proportions of C_3 and C_4 plants in a given habitat (Bazzaz 1998). It is too early to say whether these effects will influence the conservation status of particular pollinator species. However, stresses to ecosystems that are caused by climate change will act synergistically with other forms of human perturbation (Myers 1992), and the results of such synergisms cannot yet be predicted.

CLIMATE CHANGE AND FLORAL RESOURCES

Plant development is mainly dependent on temperature and photoperiod. As global temperatures increase, crops will be grown in warmer environments that have longer growing seasons (Rosenzweig *et al.* 2008). An increased temperature of 1-2°C may have negative impact on crop at low latitudes and a small positive impact at higher latitudes. Crops facing water stress were found to produce less number of flowers with little attractants for pollinators (Hegland and Totland 2005). Other effects of climate change include changes in nectar and pollen amounts, quality and changes in phenology.

CLIMATE CHANGE AND HABITAT FRAGMENTATION

Pollinators currently at the limits of their climatic range may, under climate change and where suitable habitat is available, colonize new regions, thereby increasing the abundance and diversity of recipient communities. However, compensatory species migration as a result of climate change might be inhibited by habitat loss and fragmentation. In general, low connectivity between habitat remnants is likely to reduce population sizes and increase extinction likelihoods of pollinators that are poor dispersers or habitat specialists (Warren *et al.* 2001). Pollinator communities might therefore become progressively species-poor and dominated by mobile, habitat generalists. Recent evidence suggests that continuing land-use intensification, combined with stochastic events or disease, may eliminate even these generalists. In addition, climate driven changes in pollinator food availability may interact with diminishing nutritional resources (Kleijn and Raemakers 2008) in intensively managed landscapes to further stress pollinators.

EXPECTED ASYNCHRONY OF PLANTS AND THEIR POLLINATORS

Changing climates may cause changes in the time of growth, flowering and maturation of crops, with consequent impacts on crop-associated biodiversity, particularly pollinators. Key biological events such as insect emergence and date of onset of flowering need to occur in synchrony for successful pollination interactions (Abrol 2009). Effective crop pollination is heavily dependent on biological timing, of both the crop and its pollinators. Crops such as mangoes in tropical regions, or almonds or apples in temperate regions, have periods of mass blooming over relatively short periods, requiring a tremendous peak in pollinators. Climate change may have profound impacts on the timing of these events. The extreme weather events that will accompany global warming may have severe impacts on pollinators already stressed from climatic change. Insects and plants react differently to changed temperature, creating temporal (phenological) and spatial (distributional) mismatches with severe demographic consequences for the species involved. Mismatches may affect plant by reduced insect visitation and pollen deposition, while pollinators experience reduced food availability.

Studies have shown that there have been shifts both in the distribution and phenology of many plants and animals in the last few decades indicated by a global advancement of spring events by 2.3 days per decade and a species range shift of 6.1 km per decade towards the poles (Parmesan and Yohe 2003). Memmot *et al.* (2007) simulated the effect of increasing temperatures on a highly resolved plant-pollinator network. They found that shifts in phenology reduced the floral resources available for 17-50% of the pollinator species. A temporal mismatch can be detrimental to both plants and pollinators. Temperature can induce different responses in plants and pollinators. For example, increased spring temperatures may postpone plant flowering time while pollinators might be unaffected. Even if plants and pollinators do respond to the same temperature cues, the strength of the response might differ (Hegland *et al.* 2009). However, Kudo *et al.* (2004) reported that bumblebee queen emergence was unaffected by the advancement of flowering period of spring crops in Japan. Hence, the response of synchrony varies with region and species. Williams *et al.* (2007) found a relationship between climatic niche and declines in British bumblebees, whereas Dormann *et al.* (2008) projected general declines in future bee species richness in Europe. Impacts of climate change occur at all levels starting from the individual level, through population genetics, species level shifts, to the community level. Climate change-induced mismatches in temporal and spatial co-occurrence can potentially disrupt their interactions (Fig. 3.1).

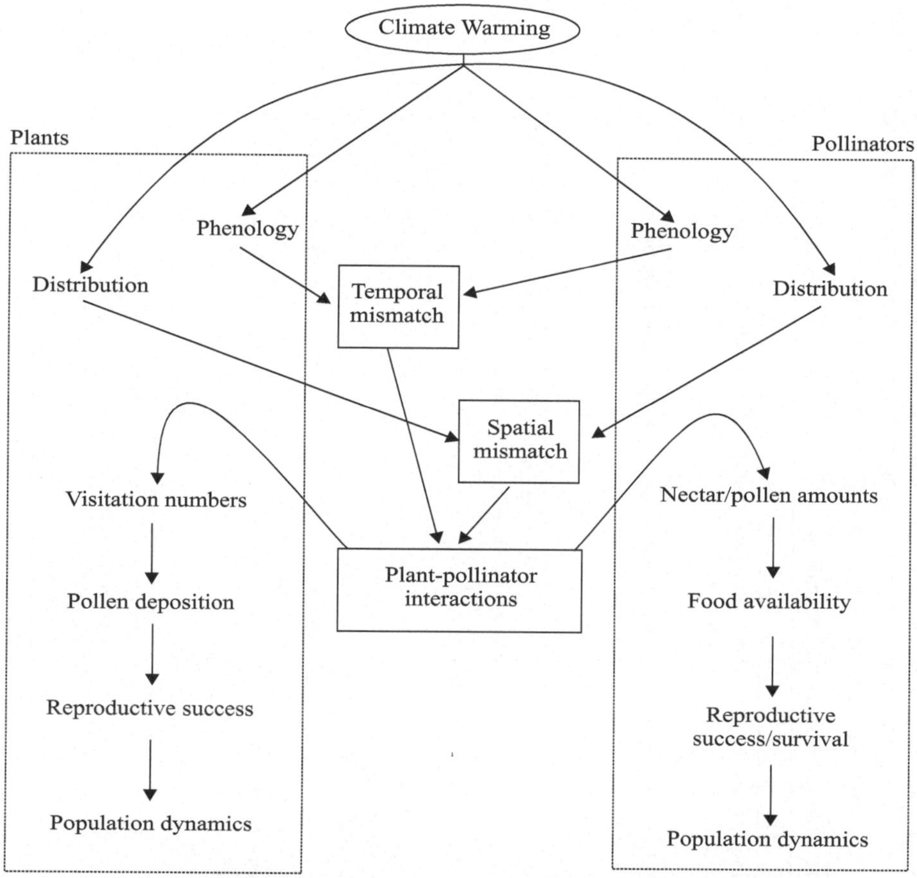

Fig. 3.1: Schematic representation of the climate change-induced effects on plant-pollinator interactions (Hegland *et al.* 2009)

Table 3.2: Climate-change effects on species and communities, potential consequences for plant–pollinator interactions, and derived hypotheses. For potentially contradicting evidence see text. Indication provides evidence from literature given as superscripts

Climate Change Affects	Indication	Consequences	Indication	Hypothesis
(1)	(2)	(3)	(4)	(5)
Phenology of plants and pollinators	Phenological changes reported[1]	Disrupted temporal matching	Phenologies of pollinators advance more than plant phenologies[2]	Partial or full uncoupling of pollinator flight period and flower blooming
Spatial distribution of plants and pollinators Distributional changes reported[1]	Distributional changes reported[1]	Disrupted spatial matching	Potential co occurrence of a butterfly and its larval host plant is projected to be reduced[3]	Increased or full mismatching in pollinator and plant ranges
Pollinator body size distribution	Bergman's rule may apply to insect pollinators[4]	Disrupted morphological matching	Associations between pollinator body size and plant functional type[5,6]	Pollen limitation because of mismatching in (size dependent) pollinator and plant morphology
Nectar quantity and quality Sucrose content changes with temperature[7]	Sucrose content changes with temperature[7]	Disrupted energetic matching	Pollinator behaviour is affected by sucrose content[8]	Pollinator behaviour is affected by sucrose content[8]
Pollinator energy demand	Metabolic rates increase with temperature[9]	Disrupted energetic matching	Sucrose content changes with temperature[7]	Increased energy demands of small pollinators cannot be fully compensated by nectar production in increasingly hotter and dryer regions
	Flight metabolic rate decreases with increasing temperature[1]	Eased energetic matching	Crop loading and foraging behaviour affected by temperature[10]	Large pollinators can spend more time on for aging when cooler regions get warmer

(Table Contd...)

(1)	(2)	(3)	(4)	(5)
Plant community structure	Changes reported[1]	Conditions of competition for pollinators change	Decreased pollinator availability for aparticular plant[11]	Pollen limitation because of decreased plant attractiveness
		Facilitative structure changes	Increased pollinator availability for a particular plant[12,13]	Decreased pollen limitation because of increased pollinator availability
Pollinator community structure	Changes reported[1]	Pollination effectiveness changes	Plant species richness depends on functional diversity and complementarity of pollinators[14,15]	Pollen limitation when functional diversity or complementarity of pollinators

References: 1, Parmesan (2006); 2, Gordo & Sanz (2005); 3, Schweiger *et al.* (2008); 4, Malo & Baonza (2002); 5, Bond (1994); 6, Corbet (2000); 7, Petanidou & Smets (1996); 8, Golubov *et al.* (1999); 9, Gillooly *et al.* (2001); 10, Afik & Shafir (2007); 11, Palmer *et al.* (2003); 12, Moeller (2004); 13, Molina-Montenegro *et al.*(2008); 14, Fontaine *et al.* (2006); 15, Fleming *et al.* (2001).

CONSEQUENCES OF MISMATCHES

Synchronized timing of mutualistic partners may be important for efficient pollination of plants and survival of pollinators. Therefore, one of the major concerns related to global warming and pollination interactions is the demographic consequence of mismatches between plants and pollinators. Assessments of how pollination interactions might respond to climate-driven mismatches must be speculative, because little is known about how warming affects the demography and population dynamics of the involved partners. Furthermore, the effect of climate-driven changes in food (for pollinators) and pollinator availability (for plants) is difficult to predict because our knowledge on the relative importance of bottom-up and top-down forces in population regulation is still poor (Steffan-Dewenter & Schiele 2008). If mismatches are to seriously affect pollinator demography, pollinator population densities and distributions must be controlled by bottom up forces, such as flower abundance. Likewise, whether mismatches will significantly influence plant demography depends on the extent to which plants are top-down controlled through effects of pollinator abundance on pollen availability and mobility.

In plants, a mismatch with important pollinators could reduce pollen deposition through altered visitation (quantity or quality of floral visits), potentially increasing pollen limitation. Among plant species, limitation of reproduction due to insufficient pollination is common (Ashman *et al.* 2004). However, the impact of pollen limitation (i.e. a top-down force) on population dynamics, and its relative importance compared to resource limitation (i.e. bottom-up forces), is still poorly understood, although a few studies have shown that increased seed set or seed mass after supplemental pollination can positively influence recruitment, survival and population growth rates of flowering plants (Price *et al.* 2008).

Another consequence of mismatches is the cascading effects they might have on species interactions occurring later in the season. A crash in early-emerging pollinator populations may affect both early and later flowering species and sequentially flowering species may facilitate each other through maintenance of pollinator populations (Waser & Real 1979). Moreover, in northern regions many plants depend on bumble bees for sufficient pollination. If nest development is restricted by a mismatch between early emerging bumble bee queens and their main food plants, such early season events may influence pollination services later in the season.

In pollinators, we can expect that a mismatch with important forage species primarily will reduce food accessibility through altered availability of carbohydrates (nectar) and proteins (pollen), subsequently affecting pollinator survival and reproduction (Boggs & Ross 1993). The effects of mismatches on pollinator population dynamics may be more severe than with plants, because pollinator dependence on nutrition often is more absolute than flowering plant species_ dependence on pollination. For example, the reproductive success of hummingbirds may be determined by the degree of matching (both timing and peak abundance) with its main flower resources (Waser 1976). In such cases, the potential for bottom-up control on pollinators population dynamics appears evident. The generally shorter life span of pollinators, especially insects, compared to plants makes them more sensitive to climate variability (Morris *et al.* 2008), and this may be one reason why the population dynamics of many pollinators vary profoundly in time and space (Williams *et al.* 2001). Knowledge of the effect floral abundance (i.e. resource availability) has on pollinator population dynamics appears limited, but a recent study by Steffan-Dewenter & Schiele (2008) showed that bottom-up forces, including food availability, were more important than top-down forces (such as rate of parasitism) in regulating the population dynamics of a solitary bee species. An extended flowering period or increased food availability per flower in response to higher temperatures (Petanidou & Smets 1996) may partly compensate for diet reductions due to mismatches in time and space. Importantly, it is not only the presence or absence of an interacting species that determines the output of a mismatch, but also their abundance, because most plants and pollinators are generalists utilizing several mutualistic partners and many mismatches are only partial (Memmott *et al.* 2007). Altered abundance of the interacting species can potentially compensate for or strengthen the consequences of trophic mismatches (Durant *et al.* 2007).

BUFFERS AGAINST MISMATCHES

Despite potential negative effects of mismatches, there are also innate properties found in plant-pollinator interactions that might buffer against their impacts. One prolific study approach the last decade has been to view ecological communities and systems as networks. Pollination ecology has, by studying entire plant-pollinator systems, been able to illustrate some of the robustness that exists in natural systems of mutualistic interactions. Plant-pollinator networks are very heterogeneous with the bulk of species having relatively few interactions, whereas a few species have many more interactions than expected by chance (Jordano *et al.* 2003). Overall, there are more generalist species in pollination networks than previously thought and strict one to one specialist relationships are rare in nature (Waser *et al.* 1996). This generalist tendency in pollination interactions may itself ensure that most species are not severely affected by climate-driven mismatches. Moreover, plant-pollinator networks display a nested structure, where a core of generalist species interact with each other, while most specialists interact only with these generalists (Bascompte *et al.* 2003). Furthermore, most pollination interactions are highly asymmetric, meaning that if a plant is very important to a pollinator (a high percentage of the pollinator_s visits are to this particular plant), the importance of this pollinator to the plant is low (a low percentage of the visits received by the plant comes from this pollinator) (Bascompte *et al.* 2006). The nested structure and predominantly asymmetric nature of the interactions within plant-pollinator networks have been shown to stabilize these systems and make them less sensitive to species extinctions, disturbance and habitat loss (Fortuna & Bascompte 2006). Such perturbations may create mismatches that resemble those expected after climate change. Regardless of these buffering properties, loss of generalist plant species in particular, may put other species of pollinators and plants at higher risk for extinction (Memmott *et al.* 2004).

Studies on variations in plant-pollinator network properties through time have only recently started to appear (Olesen *et al.* 2008). Knowledge of such temporal variation in plant pollinator interactions is crucial for understanding how these systems are affected by altered climatic conditions. The cited studies all show that plant-pollinator interactions are highly dynamic and both the species comprising the networks and the links change dramatically through time. One consequence of this variation is that plant-pollinator systems may be robust against both temporal and spatial mismatches between pairs of species. The dynamic structure of the mutualistic networks might therefore act as a buffer against cascading effects of loss of species and links within the network, although mutualistic networks could also reach a tipping point and collapse under severe disturbance (Memmott *et al.* 2004).

EVOLUTIONARY RESPONSES TO MISMATCHES

The phenology of species has evolved to match environmental conditions. It is, however, reasonable to believe that plants and pollinators may have different mechanisms underlying their phenology and respond to different environmental cues (Visser & Both 2005). Studies suggest that the activity of both plant and pollinating insects show linear relationships with current increases in temperature (Gordo and Sanz 2005). Despite this apparent similarity in responses, the magnitude (i.e. the slopes) of responses may diverge, resulting in a mismatch. A central question is whether the responses of plants and pollinators to increasing temperatures will be parallel or whether the partners will halt or accelerate their future response relative to the other. The answer lies in the potential for adaptation and whether such adaptations will be driven mainly by temperature or whether the interaction itself may shape the organisms_ future responses.

Temporal mismatches among plants and pollinators may alter selection pressures that plants and pollinators exert on each other, and result in rapid evolution in pollination and reproductive traits in plants and foraging and phonological traits in pollinators as indirect responses to climate warming. A pre-requisite for such rapid genetic change is a sufficiently large fitness consequence of the experienced mismatch (Skelly *et al.* 2007). Moreover, to what extent climate warming affects selection pressures depends on whether the species use temperature as cues to track changes in the phenology of their mutualistic partners (see also Future Research). Rapid evolution in response to climate change has been documented for both insects and flowering plants (Franks *et al.* 2007). Species_ generation times may be decisive for their potential to respond to rapid direct or indirect changes of climate warming (Davis *et al.* 2005). Thus, plant species with contrasting life-histories may respond with different speed and pollinators, which generally have shorter generation times, may evolve faster as a response to changing climate conditions than their food plants.

FUTURE RESEARCH

Temperature plays an important role in the life of plants and pollinators, and in the interactions among them. Although temperature is the factor most often studied, many other environmental factors and cues (see also Phenology and Evolutionary responses to mismatches) may also be of great influence and potentially affect species phenology, abundance and distribution. Firm predictions of future impacts of climate warming on ecological interactions may both require knowledge of the importance of different cues to phenology and the covariance between temperature and other cues. Thus, future research focus must include not only direct temperature effects on pollination interactions, but also indirect and correlated effects of climate change. One goal should be to assess separately the direct and indirect effects of climate warming on plant-pollinator interactions. Moreover, different cues or combinations of cues may have a disproportionate influence on phenological events across species, ecosystems and climatic regions. For example, it appears that bumble bee queen emergence in the Rocky Mountains is tied to snowmelt, as is also the case for the plants they pollinate (Inouye 2008). The activity of insects can also be strongly influenced by photoperiodicity and this effect generally increases with altitude and latitude potentially counteracting warming impacts. Mismatches may occur if photoperiodicity is a more important cue for insect emergence than for onset of flowering. Studies should simultaneously assess the importance of different cues in both plants and pollinators. In addition, we know much less about potential biological effects of climate warming on ecological interactions in the tropics than in temperate areas. One central question is whether the relative importance of different environmental cues to species_ phenologies may differ across altitudinal or latitudinal gradients?

The evolutionary response to climate warming and climate-driven mismatches is of great importance for the persistence of ecological interactions. For example, it is still unclear whether genetic shifts (see Evolutionary responses to mismatches) will be fast and strong enough to prevent species extinctions under predicted climate change scenarios. Understanding the contexts in which evolution should be considered as a possible and plausible response vs. those in which it is not a likely response, remains a critical challenge for scientists studying ecological effects of climate change. Future research should aim at determining the capacity of adaptive, evolutionary changes in plant and pollinator species with contrasting life-histories, coupled with studies on the indirect evolutionary consequences of climate warming through changes in species interactions.

LONG-TERM STUDIES AND SIMULATION APPROACHES

Long-term monitoring programmes, specifically designed to track changes in pollination services and pollination interactions in time, are rare, expensive and time-consuming (Gordo and Sanz 2005). Ideally, such programmes should involve long-term monitoring, consisting of standardized sampling (Westphal *et al.* 2008) of flowering plants and pollinators, and their interactions. Such sampling schemes should fulfil certain criteria. To achieve reliable data on climate-driven changes in species assemblages, or the effects of mismatches, studies need to use a high taxonomic resolution, include data on abundance and demography and should preferably cover different climatic zones. An alternative to initiating new long-term monitoring studies would be to resample previous plant-pollinator interaction studies (Petanidou *et al.* 2008), and examine if observed changes may have been driven by recent climate change. It is important that such resampling procedures control for the large inter-annual variability in species abundance and link-structure that typically occur in these systems (Olesen *et al.* 2008).

Perhaps the most proactive research approach, which also could serve the need for rapid actions and changed conservation policies, would be to develop more advanced and realistic simulation models aimed at predicting future responses to climate change. Earlier simulation studies have shown that pollination networks may be quite resistant to perturbations (Memmott *et al.* 2004), but that they may also experience significant structural changes when perturbed (Aizen *et al.* 2008). Insight on the relative importance of various cues (see above) may also be used to validate assumptions made about climate-driven shifts in phonologies or distributions in simulation models (Devoto *et al.* 2007) or projections. In a recent study, Deutsch *et al.* (2008) used empirical fitness curves related to the thermal tolerance of insects across the globe and related this to the expected geographical variation in climate warming during the next century. Interestingly, they found that tropical insects were most likely to experience deleterious effects of warming due to their narrower thermal tolerance, despite the relatively lower temperature increase expected in tropical habitats. Identification of such fitness curves of thermal tolerance for plants and their pollinators, or potential niche spaces, could enable simulations of potential future mismatches among mutualistic partners. Simulations of altered nectar production under changed temperatures could also be a useful approach for a better understanding of the relationship between food availability and pollinator population growth.

ESTIMATING CONSEQUENCES OF MISMATCHES

Species may, as mentioned above, not only react directly to climate warming, but also indirectly via changes in the availability of their mutualistic partners. A prime priority for future research should be to examine whether climate driven temporal and spatial mismatches between plants and pollinators do occur and subsequently examine the potential ecological and evolutionary consequences of such mismatches. Elucidating the complex effects of climate warming, combined with other human-driven changes of habitats on species and their interactions, requires an awareness of the possibilities and limitations of such research approaches. When developing experimental protocols to assess climate-driven mismatches, a major challenge becomes the differences between plants and pollinators in their space use (plants are sessile, pollinators are mobile). The population dynamics of pollinators are probably controlled by resource availability such as floral resources and nesting sites at a landscape scale, whereas plants mainly are controlled by factors at the local patch scale (e.g., pollinators and D or nutrients). To overcome these scalerelated restrictions, a feasible approach would be to assess potential consequences of temporal and D or spatial mismatches on plant-pollinator mutualism, if they occur. For example, a temporal mismatch may be created by warming up plants to accelerate their flowering development; _forcing_ them to reach anthesis before their main pollinator is available, and thereafter track how their pollinator visitation, reproductive success and population dynamics is affected by such a mismatch. A similar approach would be to transplant flowering plants along altitudinal gradients to simulate both flowering advancement and delay. It should be kept in mind that the effective population size, representing mate availability, will likely be reduced in such experiments causing a confounding factor that is not directly related to climate.

Because many plants and pollinators are generalists (Waser *et al.* 1996), studying the outcome of a single interaction between two mutualistic partners exposed to a mismatch, where the partners operate on different spatial scales, may be problematic and unrealistic. We can envision one situation where manipulation would be efficient, albeit ethically questionable due to the rarity of such interactions and the involved species. In highly specialized symmetric interactions, where one plant species is pollinated by one pollinator species and where the pollinator has a restricted home range (e.g., some solitary bees), one could speculate that simultaneous experimental manipulation of both plant and pollinator densities would be achievable. Such an experiment could focus on altering the factors that are predicted to change in a warmer climate, and measure the population responses of both partners.

As for many studies of biological responses to climate change, effects of temperature-mediated mismatches on plant-pollinator interactions often have to be studied through observational data (Parmesan & Yohe 2003). Observations along natural gradients of climate conditions may be one potentially powerful tool to study effects of climate change on ecological interactions, particularly if they are combined with experiments designed to elucidate possible underlying mechanisms for the responses observed. For example, one could study how the magnitude of pollen limitation in plants (as a proxy for pollinator availability) changes along altitudinal gradients (as a proxy for climate change) (Totland 2001). Alternatively, one could manipulate the availability of pollinators (e.g., by using cages that exclude pollinators, completely or partially, from flowers) along natural gradients of climate conditions. Such an approach could enable an assessment of how altered abundance or composition of pollinators, for example as a simulation of a mismatch, may affect plant reproduction, recruitment and subsequent population and community dynamics under different climate conditions.

Manipulating the availability of flowers to assess how that may impact populations of pollinators is very time and cost intensive because it requires manipulations of flower availability over large spatial scales. This might still be possible in species-poor systems with low flower abundance, or where pollinators have highly restricted foraging ranges. Manipulation of resource availability and subsequent assessment of population dynamics of pollinators may be one way of estimating potential consequences of mismatches. Comparing demographic processes of pollinator populations under different resource conditions, for example different types of natural or cultivated landscapes, may be an observational approach to improve knowledge on population dynamics of pollinators.

It is also important that we improve the way mismatches are quantified. Several studies of phenology use first appearance dates (both flowering and flight) as indications of mismatch. However, this variable only represents a subset of the individuals in a population, whereas the mean advancement of phenology might matter more for how climate warming affects the persistence of mutualistic interactions. Likewise, it is not necessarily the change of distributional extremes of species geographical ranges that matter for their interactions with other species, but rather the change of their optimum or mean distribution (Lenoir *et al.* 2008).

CLIMATE CHANGE COULD AFFECT BEES THROUGH THEIR NATURAL ENEMIES

Honeybees are susceptible to several pathogens, parasites and certain specific pests and predators. Changing climate scenario may have profound effects in the spread and virulence of these diseases and parasites. These pathogens tend to have different haplotypes of varying virulence. Climate change can encourage the transfer of these haplotypes to honey bee populations (Le Conte and Navajas, 2008). Climate change induced movements of honey bees of different species and races would, bring them into contact with pathogens with which they have never co-evolved. The case of *Varroa destructor* and *Apis mellifera* can be one such example. In the span of a few decades, two extremely homogeneous haplotypes of this parasite were sufficient to invade virtually the entire *A. Mellifera* distribution range.

ENDANGERED MUTUALISMS: WHAT HAPPENS WHEN A PLANT LOSES ITS POLLINATOR ?

Poor reproduction observed in several rare plants has been linked to the loss of their specialized pollinators. Examples are populations of a snapdragon relative in South Africa and bird-pollinated vines in Hawaii. Highly specialized relationships occur between fig tree species and their pollinator, fig wasps, which can have dramatic effects on ecosystems when "keystone" species such as figs lose their specialized pollinators. However, most pollination systems can be characterized as "somewhat generalized". In exploiting each other's resources, it is in the interest of both pollinators and plants needing pollination services to remain at least somewhat flexible. Pollination systems are thus reasonably "robust"- most flowers attract and can be pollinated by a range of pollinators that often vary under different climatic conditions. Throughout the range of pollinators, however, some will be much more effective than others. Thus flowers usually will continue to experience visitation even if the most effective pollinators are for some reason eliminated. Pollinators will still visit flowers, but less quantities of pollen may be deposited, or may be deposited at the wrong place on the plant, or the visits may occur at times when the flower is less receptive to receiving pollen.

Possible Measures to Conserve/Enhance Pollinators (FAO 2009)

- Giving consideration to the season-long resources needed by pollinators, both before and after crop flowering.
- Ensuring connectivity of natural habitats in farming areas so that pollinators can more easily disperse and make needed range shifts in response to changing climates.

- Measures to promote pollinators include providing more non-crop fl owering resources in fields, such as cover crops, strip crops or hedgerows.
- In addition, the FAO compilation by Kjohl *et al.* (2011) suggests that generating data on the following aspects, pertaining to both crops and pollinators, is essential to assess the vulnerability of a nation or region to pollinator loss due to climate change.

Crop Information

- Important crop species and cultivars
- Main system of farming; small scale versus large scale
- The value of pollinator-dependent crops by using FAO's tool for national valuation of pollination services at a national level (http://www.internationalpollinatorsinitiative.org/jsp/documents/documents.jsp)
- Number of hectares planted with pollinatordependent crops
- Pollen and nectar flowers
- Temperature sensitivity of the most important pollinator-dependent crops obtained from
- http://ecocrop.fao.org/ecocrop/srv/en/home
- The metric for the risk assessment: the number of crops in the top 20 that have an upper maximum temperature of ³ 30° C.
- Important environmental cues controlling the phenology of the crop plants (e.g. degree days, day length or other factors important in controlling flowering time)

Beekeeping

- Beehive stocks (FAO estimates)
- Honeybee subspecies
- Thermal tolerance of managed honeybees
- Assessment of the potential of introducing alternative pollinators better suited for novel climates
- Understanding the biology and ecology of alternative pollinators

Wild/Native Pollinators

- Knowledge of the most common wild pollinators of important crops
- Thermal tolerance of native pollinators derived from distributions (http://www.discoverlife. org/mp/20m?act = make_map)
- Upper and lower temperature averages for the locations where the wild pollinators have been collected
- Identification of groups of bees above and below the body mass limit capable of endothermic heating – 35 mg

- Important environmental cues controlling the phenology of the most important pollinators (e.g. degree days, day length, snow cover or other factors important in controlling insect activity)
- Periods of activity
- Status of surrounding vegetation, including diversity and abundance of alternative floral resources and nesting sites for wild pollinators
- Proximity to natural surroundings
- Parasites and diseases
- Trends in pesticide use

CONCLUSION

The consequences of climate change are of recent realization, and hence the effect of this global phenomenon on pollinator activity and their interaction with crop plants need to be understood before formulating mitigation strategies. Though concern has been raised about the potential negative impact of climate change, there is paucity of scientific literature on how exactly pollinators are going to be affected, especially in crop plants. There is a lack of knowledge on temperature sensitivity of crop plants and their pollinators especially in the tropics where the diversity of entomophilous crops is expected to be highest. The socioeconomic consequences of reduced pollination service can be severe both in highly industrialized agro ecosystems depending on large-scale pollinator farming (managed honeybees) and in more diverse small-scale agro ecosystems depending on wild pollinators. Hence, there is a need for more studies to increase our knowledge on the basic ecology of crop pollination under climate change to secure food production for an increasing human population.

REFERENCES

Abrol DP (2009) Plant-pollinator Interactions in the Context of Climate Change – An Endangered Mutualism. J Palynology 45: 1-25.

Afik O. and Shafir S (2007) Effect of Ambient Temperature on Crop Loading in the Honey Bee, *Apis mellifera* (Hymenoptera: Apidae). Entomologia Generalis 29: 135-148.

Aizen MA, Garibaldi LA, Cunningham SA, Klein AM (2008) Long-term Global Trends in Crop yield and Production Reveal no Current Pollination Shortage but Increasing Pollinator Dependency. Curr Biol 18: 1572-1575.

Aizen MA, Harder LD (2009) The Global Stock of Domesticated Honey Bees is Growing Slower than Agricultural Demand for Pollination. Curr Biol 19: 915-918.

Ashman TL, Knight TM, Steets JA, Amarasekare P, Burd M, Campbell DR (2004) Pollen Limitation of Plant Reproduction: Ecological and Evolutionary causes and Consequences. Ecology 85: 2408-2421.

Bascompte J, Jordano P, Melian CJ, Olesen JM (2003) The Nested Assembly of Plant-animal Mutualistic Networks. Proc. Natl Acad. Sci. USA, 100: 9383-9387.

Bascompte J, Jordano P, Olesen, JM (2006) Asymmetric Coevolutionary Networks Facilitate Biodiversity Maintenance. Science 312: 431-433.

Bazzaz FA (1998) Tropical Forests in' a Future Climate: Changes in the Biological Diversity and Impact on the Global Carbon Cycle. Clim Chang 39: 317-336.

Biesmeijer JC, Roberts SPM, Reemer M, Ohlemuller R, Edwards M, Peeters T, Schaffers AP, Potts SG, Kleukers R, Kunin WE (2006) Parallel Declines in Pollinators and Insect-pollinated Plants in Britain and the Netherlands. Science 313(5785): 351-354.

Bishop JA, Armbruster WS (1999) Thermoregulatory of Alaskan Bees: Effects of Size, Phylogeny and Ecology. Funct Ecol 13: 711-724.

Boggs CL, Ross CL (1993) The Effect of Adult Food Limitation on Life-history Traits in Speyeria mormonia (Lepidoptera, Nymphalidae). Ecology 74: 433-441.

Bond WJ (1994) Do Mutualisms matter-assessing the Impact of Pollinator and Disperser Disruption on Plant Extinction. Philosophical Transactions of the Royal Society of London Series. B-Biological Sciences 344: 83-90.

Coope GR (1995) Insect Faunas in Ice Age Environments: Why so Little Extinction? In: Lawton J, May R (eds) Extinction rates. Oxford University Press, Oxford, UK.

Corbet SA (2000) Conserving Compartments in Pollination webs. *Conservation Biology* 14, 1229-1231.

Corbet SA, Williams IH, Osborne JL (1991) Bees and the Pollination of Crops and Wild Flowers in the European Community Bee World 72: 47-59.

Davis MB, Shaw, RG and Etterson JR (2005) Evolutionary Responses to Changing Climate Ecology 86: 1704-1714.

Delaplane KS and Mayer DF (2000) Crop Pollination by Bees. New York, CABI.

Deutsch CA, Tewksbury JJ, Huey RB, Sheldon KS, Ghalambor CK, Haak DC, Martin PR (2008) Impacts of Climate Warming on Terrestrial Ectotherms Across Latitude. Proc Natl Acad Sci U S A 105: 6668-6672.

Devoto M, Zimmerman M and Medan D (2007). Robustness of Plant-flower visitor webs to Simulated Climate Change. Ecol. Aust 17: 37-50.

Dormann CF, Schweiget O, Arens P, Augenstein I, Avirun S, Zobel M, Zobel M (2008) Prediction Uncertainty of Environmental Change Effects on Temperate European Biodiversity. Ecol Lett 11: 235-244.

Durant JM, Hjermann DO, Ottersen and Stenseth NC (2007) Climate and the Match or Mismatch between Predator Requirements and Resource Availability. Clin. Res 33: 271-283.

FAO (2009) Global Action on Pollination Services for Sustainable Agriculture. Food and Agriculture Organization of the United Nations. Viale delle Terme di Caracalla, 00153, Rome.

Fleming TH, Sahley CT, Holland JN, Nason JD Hamrick JL (2001) Sonoran Desert Columnar cacti and the Evolution of Generalized Pollination Systems. Ecological Monographs 71: 511-530.

Fontaine C, Dajoz I, Meriguet J, Loreau M (2006) Functional Diversity of Plant-pollinator Interaction webs Enhances the Persistence of Plant Communities. Plos Biol 4: 129-135.

Fortuna MA, Bascompte J (2006) Habitat Loss and the Structure of Plant-animal Mutualistic Networks. Ecol. Lett 9: 281-286.

Franks SJ, Sim S, Weis AE (2007) Rapid Evolution of Flowering time by an Annual Plant in Response to a Climate Fluctuation. Proc. Natl Acad. Sci. USA 104: 1278-1282.

Gallai N, salles J, Settle J, Bernard EV (2009) Economic Valuation of the Vulnerability of World Agriculture Confronted with Pollinator Decline. Ecol Econ 68: 810-821.

Gillooly JF, Brown JH, West GB, Savage VM Charnov EL (2001) Effects of Size and Temperature on Metabolic Rate. Science 293: 2248-2251.

Golubov J, Eguiarte LE, Mandujano MC, Lopez-Portillo J Montana C (1999) Why be a Honeyless Honey Mesquite? Reproduction and Mating System of Nectarful and Nectarless Individuals. American Journal of Botany 86: 955-963.

Gordo O Sanz JJ (2006) Temporal Trends in Phenology of the Honey Bee Apis mellifera (L.) and the Small White Pieris rapae (L.) in the Iberian peninsula (1952-2004). Ecol. Entomol 31: 261-268.

Heard TA (1999) The Role of Stingless Bees in Crop Pollination. *Annu Rev Entomol,* 44: 183-206.

Hegland SJ, Totland O (2005) Relationships between species Floral Traits and Pollinator Visitation in a Temperate Grassland. Oecologia, 145: 586-594.

Hegland SJ, Nielsen A, Lázaro A, Bjerknes AL, Totland O (2009) How does Climate Warming affect Plantpollinator Interactions? Ecol Lett 12: 184-195.

Inouye DW (2009) The Effects of Climate Change on the Phenological Interactions of Plants and Pollinators. Presented at the 2009 Ecological Society of America Meeting, Albuquerque.

IPCC (2007). Intergovernmental Panel on Climate Change, Fourth Assessment Report, Climate Change 2007: Syntheses Report. UNEP, Geneva.

Jordano P, Bascompte J, Olesen JM (2003) Invariant Properties in Coevolutionary Networks of Plant-animal Interactions. Ecol. Lett 6: 69-81.

Kjohl M, Nielson A, Stenseth NC (2011) Potential Effects of Climate Change on Crop Pollination. FAO, Rome.

Kleijn D, Raemakers I (2008) A Retrospective Analysis of Pollen Host Plant use by Stable and Declining Bumble Bee species. Ecology 89: 1811-1823.

Klein AM, Vaissiere BE, Cane JH, Steffan-Dewenter I, Cunningham SA, Kremen C (2007) Importance of Pollinators in Changing Landscapes for World Crops. Proc. R. Soc. B-Biol. Sci 274: 303-313.

Konvicka M, Maradova M, Benes J, Fric Z, Kepka P (2003). Uphill Shifts in Distribution of Butterflies in the Czech Republic: Effects of Changing Climate detected on a Regional Scale. Global Ecol Biogeography 12: 403-410.

Kudo G, Nishikawa Y, Kasagi T, Kosuge, S (2004) Does Seed Production of Spring Ephemerals Decrease when Spring comes Early? Ecol. Res 19: 255-259.

Le Conte Y, Navajas M (2008) Climate Change: Impact on Honey Bee Populations and Diseases. Revue Scientifique et Technique-Office International des Epizooties 27: 499-510.

Lenoir J, Gegout JC, Marquet PA, de Ruffray P, Brisse H (2008) A Significant upward Shift in Plant species Optimum Elevation during the 20th Century. Science 320: 1768-1771.

Maccagnani B, Ladurner E, Santi F, Burgio G (2003) Osmia cornuta (Hymenoptera, Megachilidae) as a Pollinator of Pear (Pyrus communis): Fruit- and Seed-set. Apidologie 34: 207-216.

Memmott J, Craze PG, Waser NM, Price MV (2007) Global Warming and the Disruption of Plant–pollinator Interactions. Ecol Lett 10: 710-717.

Memmott J, Waser NM, Price MV (2004) Tolerance of Pollination Networks to Species Extinctions. Proc. R. Soc. B-Biol. Sci 271: 2605-2611.

Morris WF, Pfister CA, Tuljapurkar S, Haridas CV, Boggs CL, Boyce MS (2008) Longevity can Buffer Plant and Animal Populations against Changing Climatic Variability. Ecology 89: 19-25.

Myer N (1992) Synergisms: Joint Effects of Climate Change and other Forms of Habitat Destruction. In: Lovejoy TE, Peters RL (eds) Global Warming and Biological Diversity. Yale University Press, Connecticut.

Olesen JM, Bascompte J, Elberling H, Jordano P (2008) Temporal Dynamics in a Pollination Network. Ecology 89: 1573-1582.

Parker I M (1997) Pollinator Limitation of *Cytisus scoparius* (Scotch broom), an invasive Exotic Shrub. Ecology 78, 1457-1470.

Parmesan C, Yohe G (2003) A Globally Coherent Fingerprint of Climate Change Impacts Across Natural Systems. Nature 421: 37-42.

Partap U, Shukla AN, Verma LR (2000) Impact of *Apis cerana* Pollination on Fruit Quality and yield in Peach and Plum in the Kathmandu Valley of Nepal. In: Matsuka M, Verma LR, Wongsiri S, Shrestha KK, Uma Partap (eds) Asian Bees and Beekeeping: Progress of Research and Development. Proceedings of the Fourth AAA International Conference, Kathmandu, 23-28 Mar 1998. Oxford and IBH Publishing Co. Pvt. Ltd., New Delhi, 274pp.

Petanidou T, Kallimanis AS, Tzanopoulos J, Sgardelis SP, Pantis JD (2008) Long-term Observation of a Pollination Network: Fluctuation in species and Interactions, Relative Invariance of Network Structure and Implications for Estimates of Specialization. Ecol. Lett 11: 564-575.

Petanidou T, Smets E (1996) Does Temperature Stress Induce Nectar Secretion in Mediterranean Plants? New Phytol 133: 513-518.

Potts SG, Jacobus CB, Kremen C, Neumann P, Schweiger O, William EK (2010) Global Pollinator Declines: Trends, Impacts and Drivers. Trends Ecol Evol 25(6): 345-353.

Price MV, Campbell DR, Waser NM, Brody AK (2008) Bridging the Generation Gap in Plants: Pollination, Parental Fecundity, and Offspring Demography. Ecology 89: 1596-1604.

Rosenzweig C, Karoly D, Vicareilli M, Neofotis P, Wu Q, Cassassa G (2008) Attributing Physical and Biological Impacts to Anthropogenic Climate Change. Nature 453: 353-357.

Rusterholz HP, Erhardt A (1998) Effects of Elevated CO_2 on Flowering Phenology and Nectar Production of Nectar Plants Important for Butter Flies of Calcareous Grasslands. Oecologia 113: 341-349.

Schweiger O, Biesmeijer JC, Bommarco R, Hickler T, Hulme P, Klotz S, Kuhn I, Moora M, Nielsen A, Ohlemuller R, Petandou T, Potts SG, Pysek P, Stout JC, Sykes M, Tscheulin T, Vila M, Wather GR, Westphal C (2010) Multiple Stressors on Biotic Interactions: How Climate Change and Alien species Interact to Affect Pollination. Biol Rev 85: 777-795.

Schweiger O, Settele J, Kudrna O, Klotz S, Kuhn I (2008) Climate change can cause Spatial mismatch of Trophically Interacting Species. Ecology 89: 3472-3479.

Skelly DK, Joseph LN, Possingham HP, Freidenburg LK, Farrugia TJ, Kinnison MT (2007) Evolutionary Responses to Climate Change. Conserv. Bio 21: 1353-1355.

Steffan-Dewenter I, Schiele S (2008) Do Resources or Natural Enemies Drive Bee Population Dynamics in Fragmented Habitats. Ecology 89: 1375-1387.

Thomas JA, Telfer MG (2004) Comparative Losses of British Butterflies, Birds, and Plants and the Global Extinction Crisis. Science 303: 1879-1881.

Velthuis HHW, van Doorn A (2006) A Century of Advances in Bumblebee Domestication and the Economic and Environmental Aspects of its Commercialization for Pollination. Apidologie 37: 421-451.

Visser ME, Both C (2005) Shifts in Phenology due to Global Climate Change: The need for a yardstick. Proc. R. Soc. B-Biol. Sci 272: 2561-2569.

Warren MS, Hill JK, Thomas J A, Asher J, Fox R, Huntley B, Roy DB, Telfer MG, Jeffcoate S, Harding P, Jeffcoate G, Willis SG,Greatorex-Davies J N, Moss D and Thomas CD (2001) Rapid Responses of British Butterflies to Opposing Forces of Climate and Habitat Change. Nature 414: 65-69.

Waser NM (1976) Food-supply and Nest Timing of Broad-tailed Hummingbirds in Rocky Mountains. Condor 78: 133-135.

Waser NM, Chittka L, Price MV, Williams NM, Ollerton J (1996) Generalization in Pollination Systems, and why it matters. Ecology 77: 1043-1060.

Westphal C, Bommarco R, Carre G, Lamborn E, Morison N, Petanidou T (2008) Measuring Bee Biodiversity in different European Habitats and Biogeographical Regions. Ecol. Monogr 78: 653-671.

Williams JW, Jackson ST, Kutzbacht JE (2007) Projected Distributions of Novel and Disappearing Climates by 2100 AD. Proceedings of the National Academy of Sciences of the United States of America 104: 5738-5742.

Williams NM, Minckley RL, Silveira FA (2001) Variation in Native Bee Faunas and its Implications for Detecting Community Changes. Conserv. Ecol., 5, 7. Available at: WWW document] http://www.consecol.org/vol5/iss1/art7. Last accessed on 21 November 2008.

Williams PH, Araujo MB, Rasmont P (2007) Can Vulnerability among British Bumblebee (Bombus) species be Explained by Niche Position and Breadth? Biol Conserv 138: 493-505.

Willmer P, Stone G (1997) Temperature and Water Relations in Desert Bees. J Therm Biol 22: 453-465.

Zuckerberg B, Woods AM, Porter WF (2009) Poleward Shifts in Breeding Bird Distributions in New York State. Global Change Biol 15: 1866-1883.

Pages: 58-70

Stress Tolerance and Plant Productivity
Edited by: Mr. Prasann Kumar and Dr. Pawan Kumar 'Bharti'
ISBN: 978-93-86841-56-8
Edition: 2018
Published by: Discovery Publishing House Pvt. Ltd., New Delhi (India)

4 Herbicide Selectivity and Resisitance with Special Reference Agricultural Crops

Prasann Kumar

ABSTRACT

Herbicides commonly known as weed killers, they are chemical substances used to control unwanted plants. Selective herbicides control specific weed species, while leaving thedesired crop relatively unaffected, while non-selective herbicides can be used to kill all plant material with which they come into contact. Apart from selective and non-selective, Other important differentiation include (1) Persistence - How long the product stays in place and remains active (2) Means of uptake - Whether it is absorbed by aboveground foliage only, through the roots, or by other means. (3) Mechanism of action - How it works.

Key words: Agriculture, Biotic, Crop, Density, Effect, Forage, Gap, Persistence

INTRODUCTION

Historically, products such as common salt and other metal salts were used as herbicides, however these have gradually fallen out of favor and in some countries a number of these are banned due to their presence in soil, toxic and groundwater contamination. Herbicides have also been used in warfare and conflict in ancient time. Modern herbicides are often synthetic mimic of natural plant hormones which interfere with the growth of the target plants. The term organic herbicide has come to mean herbicides for organic farming. Some plants also produce their own natural herbicides, such as the genus walnuts (the tree of heaven); such action of natural herbicides, and other related chemical interactions, are called allelopathy. Due to herbicide resistance, a number of products combine herbicides with different means of action. Integrated pest management may use herbicides

Department of Agronomy, School of Agriculture, Lovely Professional University, Jalandhar - 144 411 (Punjab) (India)

alongside other pest control methods. In the US in 2007, about 83% of all herbicide usage, determined by weight applied, was in agriculture. In 2007, world pesticide expenditures totaled about $39.4 billion; herbicides were about 40% of those sales and constituted the biggest portion, followed by insecticides, fungicides, and other types. Smaller quantities are used in forestry, pasture systems, and management of areas set aside as wildlife habitat. History Prior to the widespread use of chemical herbicides, cultural controls, such as altering soil pH, salinity, or fertility levels were used to control weeds. Mechanical control (including tillage) was also and still is, used to control weeds. First herbicides 2,4-D, was the first chemical herbicide, was discovered during the Second World War. Although research into chemical herbicides began in the early 20th century, the first major breakthrough was the result of research conducted in both the UK and the US during the Second World War into the potential use of agents as biological weapons. The first modern herbicide, 2,4-D, was first discovered and synthesized by W.G. Temple man at Imperial Chemical Industries. In 1940, he showed that "Growth substances applied appropriately would kill certain broad-leaved weeds in cereals without harming the crops." When 2,4-D was commercially released in 1946, it triggered a worldwide revolution in agricultural output and became the first successful selective herbicide. It allowed for greatly enhanced weed control in wheat, maize, rice, and similar grass crops, because it kills broadleaf plants, but not most monocots (grasses). The low cost of 2,4D h led to continued usage today, and it remains one of the most commonly used herbicides in the world. Like other acid herbicides, current formulations use either an amine salt (often trimethylamine) or one of many esters of the parent compound. These are easier to handle than the acid. Further discoveries The triazine family of herbicides, which includes atrazine, were introduced in the 1950s; they have the current distinction of being the herbicide family of greatest concern regarding groundwater contamination. Atrazine does not break down readily (within a few weeks) after being applied to soils of above neutral pH. Glyphosate (Roundup) was introduced in 1974 for nonselective weed control. Following the development of glyphosate-resistant crop plants, it is now used very extensively for selective weed control in growing crops. Many modern chemical herbicides used in agriculture and gardening are specifically formulated to decompose within a short period after application. This is desirable, as it allows crops and plants to be planted afterwards, which could otherwise be affected by the herbicide.

Types of herbicide: (1) Selectivity (a) Selective herbicides: They control or suppress certain plants without affecting the growth of other plant species. Selectivity may be due to translocation, differential absorption, physical (morphological) or physiological differences between plant species. 2,4-D, mecoprop, and dicamba control many broadleaf weeds,but remain ineffective against turf grasses. (b) Non-selective herbicides: These herbicides are not specific in acting against certain plant species and control all plant material with which they come into contact. They are used to clear industrial sites, waste ground, railways and railway embankments. Paraquat, glufosinate, glyphosate is non-selective herbicides.

Herbicide selectivity: In agriculture, chemical control of weeds is based on herbicide selectivity and it can be defined as the differential response level among species after the application of a particular molecule. Selectivity refers to the capacity of a particular herbicide to eliminate weeds in a crop, without affecting yield or quality of the final product or Selectivity is intrinsically related with the fact that plant species respond differently to the same herbicide. Despite the fact that herbicide selectivity has been long recognized in Weed Science, the concept is incomplete because it commonly excludes the importance of the mechanisms involved. Herbicide selectivity derived from differences among plants in interception and uptake of herbicides, in Metabolic pathways and rates; in targetenzyme sensitivity (site of action), and in tolerating product phytotoxicity. Further, herbicide selectivity can be based not only in biotic characters, but also in product characteristics; mode of application (in time and space), use of antidotes or safeners and genetic engineering. Herbicide selectivity should not be evaluated only by the product itself, but considering the interaction between other factors, including environment, rate, and crop aspects. Therefore, selectivity must be seen as several plant protection factors to minimize injuries. Among selectivity factors associated with plant species, The differential metabolism of herbicides is one of the most important factor, Thus, the objectives is to characterize herbicide selectivity by differential metabolism, to present the main metabolic pathways associated with selectivity, to define the phytotoxicity concept and the intrinsic potential of additional energy waste that might lead to yield losses and to propose experimental and practical alternatives to improve herbicide selectivity in crops. Terms evaluating herbicide selectivity: (a) Controls or checks: Trial conduction and experimental area homogeneity, the checks of a selectivity experiment must be permanently weeded, to avoid interference from weeds. The trials must be established under rigorous environmental control, either by increasing the number of replicates (which sometimes is not sufficient), or by adopting double, paired or lateral checks (b) Variables and data evaluation: Selectivity trials must include, besides visual evaluation of the damage, evaluations of crop yield, since there are herbicides that cause significant injuries but the growth recovery allows the re-establishment of potential yield known as temporary stress but there are herbicides that do not induce visual symptoms (hidden phytotoxicity), but affect the growth rate (permanent stress). (c) Use of less statistical tests: Tukey's test is rigorous, and, therefore, is appropriated to identify large differences. In selectivity experiments, the objective is to demonstrate the absence of difference, thus small differences are important to be detected. Less sensitive tests, such as the 't-test', the 'Duncan' test; or large probabilities would better fit the experimental goals. Point to be considered for herbicide selectivity (a) Follow recommendations of Good Agricultural Practices in terms of rate, product and mixtures, timing of application; cultivar or hybrid; and environmental conditions. (b) Exercise care in relation to product (chemicals) interaction, mainly herbicides and organo-phosphorate insecticides applied together or at short intervals between applications. (c) Use antidotes or safeners, always when recommended. (d) Whenever possible, rank herbicide applications according to selectivity, starting with products with enzymatic insensitivity, such as ACCase inhibitor in soybean, cotton and dry beans.e. Adopt genetically modified crops tolerant to herbicides (a) Factors affecting herbicide selectivity Before reaching the target (a) Drif (b) Volatility After reaching the target 1. Spray interception and retention (a) Leaf properties (b) Other plant characteristics (c) Characteristics of the spray solution 2. Environmental Factors a. Moisture/ rainfall/humidity (b) Temperature (c) Ligh. 5. Herbicide Resistance Weed resistance to herbicides has become a major concern in crop production worldwide. Resistance to herbicides is often attributed to lack of rotational programmes of herbicides and to continuous applications of herbicides with the same sites of action. Thus, a true understanding of the sites of action of herbicides is essential for strategic planning of herbicide-based weed control. Plants have developed resistance to atrazine and to ALS-inhibitors and more recently, to glyphosate herbicides. Marestail is one weed that has developed glyphosate resistance. Glyphosateresistant weeds are present in the vast majority of soybean, cotton and corn farms. Weeds that can resist multiple other herbicides are spreading. Few new herbicides are near commercialization, and none with a molecular mode of action for which there is no resistance. Because most herbicides could not kill all weeds, farmers rotated crops and herbicides to stop resistant weeds. During its initial years, glyphosate was not subject to resistance and allowed farmers to reduce the use of rotation. A family of weeds that includes water hemp (Amaranthus rudis) is the largest concern. A 2008-9 survey of 144 populations of water hemp in 41 Missouri counties revealed glyphosate resistance in 69%. Weeds from some 500 sites throughout Iowa in 2011 and 2012 revealed glyphosate resistance in approximately 64% of water hemp samples. The use of other killers to target "residual" weeds has become common, and may be sufficient to have stopped the spread of resistance from 2005 through 2010 researchers discovered 13 different weed species that had developed resistance to glyphosate. But since then only two more have been discovered. Weeds resistant to multiple herbicides with completely different biological action modes are on the rise. In Missouri, 43% of samples were resistant to two different herbicides; 6% resisted three; and 0.5% resisted four. In Iowa, 89% of water hemp samples resist two or more herbicides, 25% resist three, and 10% resist five (Figure 4.1 & 4.2).

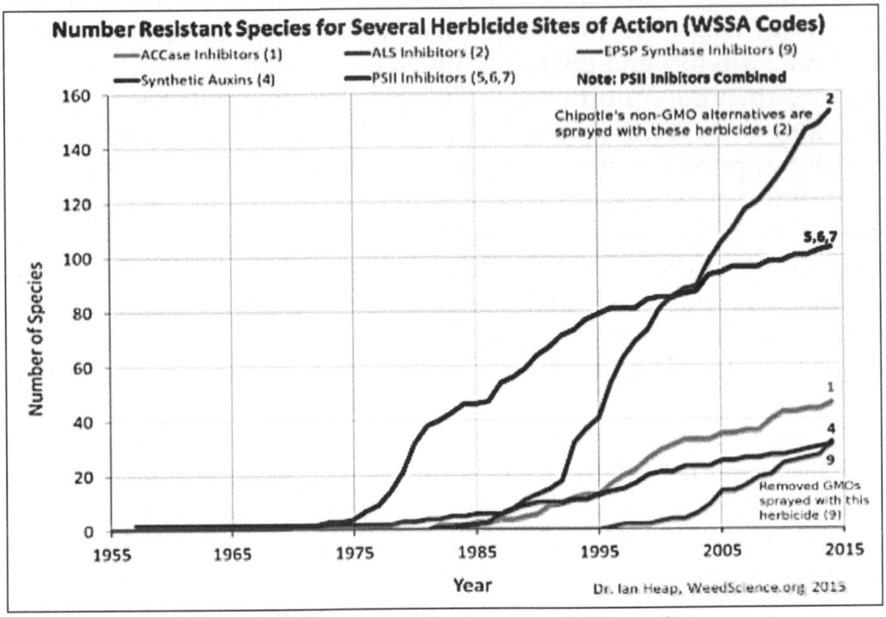

Fig. 4.1: Diagrammatic representation of crop resistance towards different herbicides

Source: Based on Review of Literature

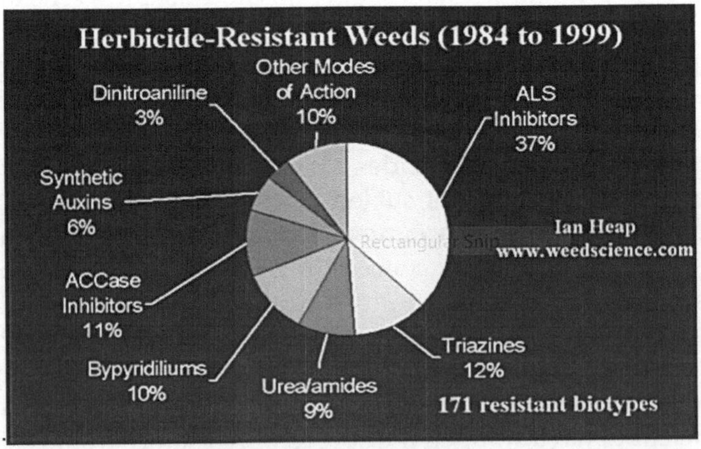

Fig. 4.2: Pi-chart of herbicide resistant weeds

Source: Based on Review of Literature

(a) Biochemistry of resistance Resistance to herbicides can be based on one of the following biochemical mechanisms. (1) Target-site resistance: This is due to a reduced or even lost ability of the herbicide to bind to its target protein. The effect usually relates to an enzyme with a crucial function in a metabolic pathway, or to a component of an electron-transport system. Target-site resistance may also be caused by an overexpression of the target Enzyme. (2) Non-target-site resistance: This is caused by mechanisms that reduce the amount of herbicidal active compound reaching the target site. One important mechanism is an enhanced metabolic detoxification of the herbicide in the weed, which leads to insufficient amounts of the active substance reaching the target site. A reduced uptake and translocation of the herbicide may also result in an insufficient herbicide transport to the target site. (3) Cross-resistance: In this case, a single resistance mechanism causes resistance to several herbicides. The term target-site crossresistance is used when the herbicides bind to the same target site, whereas non-target-site cross-resistance is due to a single non-target-site mechanism. (4) Multiple resistance: In this situation, two or more resistance mechanisms are present within individual plants, or within a plant population. (b) Resistance management Careful observation is important so that any reduction in herbicide efficacy can be detected. This may indicate evolving resistance. It is vital that resistance is detected at an early stage as if it becomes an acute, whole-farm problem, options are more limited and greater expense is almost inevitable. An essential pre-requisite for confirmation of resistance is a good diagnostic test. Ideally, this should be rapid, accurate, cheap and accessible. Many diagnostic tests have been developed, including glasshouse pot assays, petri dish assays and chlorophyll fluorescence. A key component of such tests is that the response of the suspect population to a herbicide can be compared with that of known susceptible and resistant standards under controlled conditions. An integrated weed management (IWM) approach is required, in which as many tactics as possible are used to combat weeds. In this way, less reliance is placed on herbicides and so selection pressure should be reduced. Optimising herbicide input to the economic threshold level should avoid the unnecessary use of herbicides and reduce selection pressure. Herbicides should be used to their greatest potential by ensuring that the timing, dose, application method, soil and climatic conditions are optimal for good activity. In the UK, partially resistant grass weeds such as Alopecurus myosuroides (black grass) and Avena spp. (Wild oat) can often be controlled adequately when herbicides are applied at the 2-3 leaf stage, whereas later applications at the 2-3 tiller stage can fail badly. The patch spraying, or applying herbicide to only the badly infested areas of fields, is another means of reducing total herbicide use. Rotate, crop types – Crop rotations allow for a rotation of herbicide types. Don't plant uncompetitive crops two years in a row in a field. Tank Mix herbicides with different modes of action. The tank mix can delay the development of resistant weeds it the components control the same weed with different modes of actions. The chemicals used should have acted against potentially herbicide resistant biotypes. Use herbicides with short residual activity Utilize post-harvest weed control - It reduces weed seed production, controls perennials and prevents worse infestations for the following year. Factor Low risk, high risk Cropping system Annual ploghing Continuous minimum tillage Weed control Cultural only Herbicide only Herbicide use Many modes of action Single mode of action Control in previous year Excellent Poor Weed infection Low High (Table 4.1).

Table 4.1: Agronomic factors influencing the risk of herbicide resistance development

Factor	Low Risk	High Risk
Cropping system	Annual ploghing	Continuous minimum tillage
Weed control	Cultural only	Herbicide only
Herbicide use	Many mode of action	Single mode of action
Control in previous year	Excellent	Poor
Weed infection	Low	High

Source: Based on Review of Literature

(c) Approaches to treating resistant weeds ? Alternative herbicides- When resistance is first suspected or confirmed, the efficacy of alternatives is likely to be the first consideration. The use of alternative herbicides, which remain effective on resistant populations can be a successful strategy, at least in the short term. The effectiveness of alternative herbicides will be highly dependent on the extent of crossresistance. If there is resistance to a single group of herbicides, then the use of herbicides from other groups may provide a simple and effective solution, at least in the short term. Mixtures and sequences- The use of two or more herbicides which have differing modes of action can reduce the selection for resistant genotypes. Ideally, each component in a mixture should: (a) Be active at different target sites, (b) Have a high level of efficacy (c) Be detoxified by different biochemical pathways (d) Have similar persistence in the soil (e) Exert negative cross-resistance ? Herbicide rotations- Rotation of herbicides from different chemical groups in successive years should reduce selection for resistance. This is a key element in most resistance prevention programmes. The value of this approach depends on the extent of cross-resistance, and whether multiple resistances occur owing to the presence of several different resistance mechanisms. A practical problem can be the lack of awareness by farmers of the different groups of herbicides that exist. In Australia a scheme has been introduced in which identifying letter are included on the product label as a means of enabling farmers to distinguish products with different modes of action. Mechanisms of herbicide resistance Herbicide resistance have become a major concern for grain producers across the world. Currently there are 41 weed species only in Australia with resistance to one or more of 11 herbicide modes of action. Management of herbicide resistance usually depends on an understanding of the biology of the weed species and the herbicides that are still effective for control. Every time a herbicide is used to kill weeds or stop their seed production it selects for resistance. How strongly herbicides select for resistance depends on the proportion of weeds that are controlled by each application and how frequently applications of the same mode of action are made. Generally mechanisms of herbicide resistance are divided into target site and non-target site mechanisms. (a) Target site resistance mechanisms Target site mechanisms involve a change to the protein that binds the herbicide resulting in a lack of inhibition of the biochemical pathway. The most obvious of these is where a mutation within the target protein reduces binding of the herbicide. This is the classic target site mutation and is typically seen as providing virtual immunity to the herbicide. However, that is not always the case and it is possible to have weak target site mutations as well as strong target site mutations. Target site mutations arise due to single point mutations in the underlying DNA that change an amino acid in the protein. This changed amino acid may either remove a bond required for binding the herbicide or change the shape of the binding site. For most target sites there is more than one possible mutation that will provide resistance to herbicides. In many cases, different mutations give different levels of resistance and patterns of cross-resistance. For example, resistance selected by sulfonylurea herbicides may not result in resistance to the imidazolinone herbicides. The data suggests that cross-resistance to imidazolinone herbicides occurs about 30% of the time with broadleaf weeds and 50% of the time with grass weeds. However, this is variable between species. The reasons of the area that the different groups of herbicides bind differently in the binding pocket, so different mutations affect only one or both types of herbicides The other type of target site resistance is where there are many more copies of the target site than would normally be present. In this type of resistance, the extra target sites act like a sponge soaking up the herbicide. This mechanism has so far only been seen with glyphosate resistant weeds. If this type of mechanism was to occur for another herbicide target site it would be expected to provide resistance to every herbicide in that mode of action. (b) Non-target site resistance mechanisms Non-target site resistance mechanisms allow plants to survive application of the herbicide by not allowing sufficient herbicide to reach the target site. The weed may be initially affected by the herbicide application, but will survive and set seed. The most common example of non-target site resistance is due to increased herbicide detoxification. With this resistance mechanism, there is more rapid breakdown of the herbicide inside the plant and less of the active herbicide reaches the target site to kill the plant. With this mechanism, the species has to start with some ability to metabolism the herbicide, but that becomes greatly enhanced in the resistant individuals. For this reason, enhanced metabolism is typically observed in herbicides that can be used selectively in the crop; such as Groups A, B, C, D and I.The exact nature of the mutation that results in resistance due to enhanced herbicide degradation has not been identified. However, evidence points to the increased activity of several enzymes, rather than a single enzyme. One outcome of this type of mechanism is that it frequently leads to cross-resistance to herbicides of different modes of action. A variant on herbicide detoxification is reduced activation of the herbicide. Several herbicides are applied as pro-herbicides and rely on the plant metabolizing them to the active compound. If the plant fails to do this, the herbicide will not work. A second non-target site mechanism involves changes to the translocation of herbicides within the plant. In this mechanism, the herbicide becomes trapped in the leaf tips and reduced amounts are present in the meristem and other parts of the plant. Where the herbicide has to be present in the growing tissue to kill the plant, reducing translocation will reduce the concentration of herbicide at the target site in these key tissues. There are several mechanisms whereby a plant can reduce the translocation of herbicides. The main mechanism seems to be through pumping the herbicide into the cell vacuole. As this involves specific transporters for the herbicide, resistance usually occurs to a single herbicide. An alternative type of reduced translocation is where the herbicide is trapped in tissues that are then shed from the plant. This 'rapid necrosis' resistance resembles the plant response to pathogen attack, but on a massive scale where the whole leaves rapidly die and fall off taking the herbicide with them. Two other types of non-target site resistance are theoretically possible, but have not been well documented. Reducing the absorption of the herbicide into the plant will reduce the concentration of the herbicide at the target site. The other type of mechanism is where the plant is able to avoid the detrimental effect of the herbicide action, usually through increased capacity to deal with oxygen radicals. This has been proposed as a mechanism of paraquat resistance, for example, but is only a practical mechanism if the plant also has the ability to rapidly remove the herbicide from the target site (Figure 4.3).

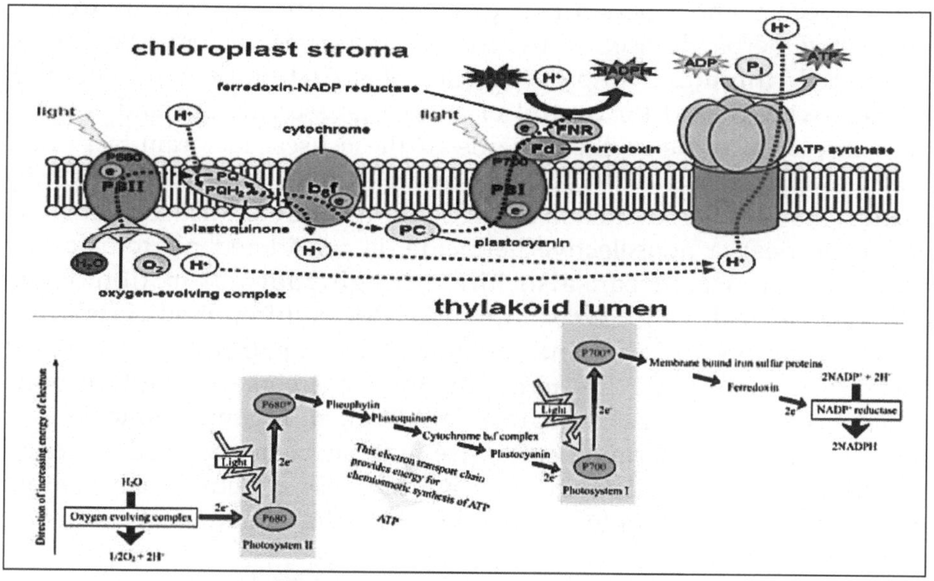

Fig. 4.3: Effects of herbicides on photosynthesis

Source: Based on Review of Literature

List of common herbicides: (a) Synthetic herbicides 2,4-D is a broadleaf herbicide in the phenoxy group used in turf and notill field crop production. Now, it is mainly used in a blend with other herbicides to allow lower rates of herbicides to be used; it is the most widely used herbicides in the world, and third most commonly used in the United States. It is an example of the synthetic auxin (plant hormone). Aminopyralid is a broadleaf herbicide in the pyridine group, used to control weeds on grassland, such as docks, thistles and nettles. It is notorious for its ability to persist in compost. Atrazine, a triazine herbicide, is used in corn and sorghum for control of broadleaf weeds and grasses. Still used because of its low cost and because it works well on a broad spectrum of weeds common in the US corn belt, atrazine is commonly used with other herbicides to reduce the overall rate of atrazine and to lower the potential for groundwater contamination; it is a photosystem II inhibitor. Clopyralid is a broadleaf herbicide in the pyridine group, used mainly in turf, rangeland, and for control of noxious thistles. Notorious for its ability to persist in compost, it is another example of synthetic auxin. Dicamba, a postemergent broadleaf herbicide with some soil activity, is used on turf and field corn. It is another example of a synthetic auxin. Glufosinate ammonium, a broad-spectrum contact herbicide, is used to control weeds after the crop emerges or for total vegetation control on land not used for cultivation. Imazapyr a nonselective herbicide is used for the control of a broad range of weeds, including terrestrial annual and perennial grasses and broadleaf herbs, woody species, and riparian and emergent aquatic species. Linuron is a nonselective herbicide used in the control of grasses and broadleaf weeds. It works by inhibiting photosynthesis. Metolachlor is a pre-emergent herbicide widely used for control of annual grasses in corn and sorghum; it has displaced some of the atrazine in these uses. Picloram, a pyridine herbicide, mainly is used to control unwanted trees in pastures and edges of fields. It is another synthetic auxin Sodium chlorate (disused/banned in some countries), a nonselective herbicide, is considered phytotoxic to all green plant parts. It can also kill through root absorption.Several sulfonylureas, including Flazasulfuron and Metsulfuron-methyl, which act as ALS inhibitors and in some cases are taken up from the soil via the roots. Organic herbicide The term "organic" has come to imply products used in organic farming. Under this definition, an organic herbicide is one that can be used in a farming enterprise that has been classified as organic. Depending on the application, they may be less effective than synthetic herbicides and are generally used along with cultural and mechanical weed control practices.

Homemade herbicides include:

Corn gluten meal (CGM): It is a natural pre-emergence weed control used in turfgrass, which reduces germination of many broadleaf and grass weeds. Vinegar: it is effective, for 5-20% solutions of acetic acid, with higher concentrations most effective, but it mainly destroys surface growth. Steam: it has been applied commercially, but is now considered uneconomical and inadequate. It controls surface growth but not underground growth. Flame: it is considered more effective than steam, but suffers from the same difficulties.

D-limonene (citrus oil): It is a natural degreasing agent that strips the waxy skin or cuticle from weeds, causing dehydration and ultimately death. Saltwater or salt applied in appropriate strengths to the root zone will kill most plants. Monocerin produced by certain fungi will kill certain weeds such as Johnson grass. Resent work on herbicide resistance Dow, Bayer Crop Science, Syngenta and Monsanto are all developing seed varieties resistant to herbicides other than glyphosate, which will make it easier for farmers to use alternative weed killers. Even though weeds have already evolved some resistance to those herbicides, Powles says the new seed-and-herbicide combos should work well if used with proper rotation. Conclusion due to constantlyraise in social pressure to increase in food, fiber and energy production, sometimes the concept of selectivity has not been carefully applied, while the rational should be just the opposite. Herbicide selectivity is an agricultural technology that has been widely exploited in chemical weed control strategies, but it may also be seen as a major aspect that can result in yield losses (Figure 4.4).

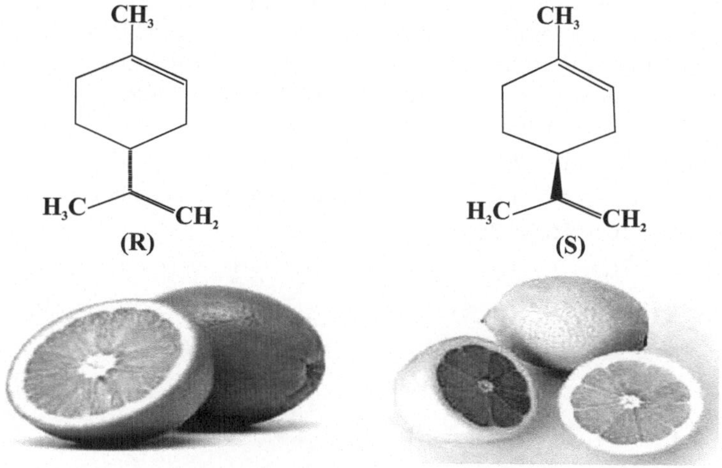

Fig. 4.4: Citrus oil

CONCLUSION

Herbicide metabolism is related to energy disposal, and hence, phytotoxicity symptoms characterize a second energy expenditure that should not be accepted as a natural physiological response, that might result in crop yield losses.Weeds, when interfering with the crop, reduce quality and yield. The herbicides, however, are tools used to avoid these losses, and thus, it is not reasonable that when herbicides are applied, they also might represent risks to yield losses. To avoid or reduce crop losses and injuries, it is necessary that herbicide recommendations are based on selectivity assays conducted under rigorous experimental procedures, as well as, it is important to increase growers' awareness about the best use for each product.

REFERENCES

http://onlinelibrary.wiley.com/10.1111/j.1469X

http://onlinelibrary.wiley.com/doi/10.1002/ps.2780290304/full

http://www.tandfonline.com/doi/abs/10.1080

http://www.sciencedirect.com/science/article/pii ?

http://onlinelibrary.wiley.com/doi/10.1111/j.1365

https://www.degruyter.com/view/j/dmdi.1995.12.3

https://msu.edu/course/css/292/Lecture%208.pdf

http://www.scielo.br/scielo.php?script=sci_arttext&pid=S0103

WSSA Herbicide Site of Action (SOA) Classification List

Herbicide Resistance: Toward an Understanding of Resistance Development and the Impact of Herbicide-Resistant crops (Vencill *et al.*, Weed Sci. 2012, Special Issue: 2-30)

Reducing the Risks of Herbicide Resistance: Best Management Practices and Recommendations (Norsworthy et al., Weed Sci. 2012, Special Issue: 31-62). University of California Agriculture and natural resource, ANR publication 8493, July 13.

http://www.weedscience.org/Summary/UniqueCountry.asp?lstCountryID=7&FmCountry=Go

Herbicide Selectivity and Performance. by P. Miller and P. Westra

Herbicide Resistant Weeds: The Technology and Weed Management by Jamal R. Qasem http://dx.doi.org/10.5772/56036

Pages: 71-85

Stress Tolerance and Plant Productivity

Edited by: Mr. Prasann Kumar and Dr. Pawan Kumar 'Bharti'

ISBN: 978-93-86841-56-8

Edition: 2018

Published by: Discovery Publishing House Pvt. Ltd., New Delhi (India)

5 Impact of Road Side Pollution on Physiological Behaviour of Road Side Plant

Abhishek Swami[1] and Deepika Chauhan[2]

INTRODUCTION

The life support system on this planet consists of air, water, land, flora and fauna. Normally these are mutually interconnected and also interdependent. The activities of man constitute one single factor, which often disrupt the intricate balance among the foregoing constituents of the life support system. In his eagerness to urbanize and industrialize, man has not only destroyed plant cover built up meticulously by nature over millions of years, but also polluted air, water and land, so much so that development has become synonymous with deforestation and desertification and progressed with pollution.

Developmental activities carry with them the seeds of environmental damage, assisted and abetted by both needs and greed of man. Activities such as manufacturing, processing, transportation and consumption not only deplete the stock of natural resources but also add stress to the environmental system by accumulating the stock of wastes. The productivity of the economic system, however, depends on the supply and quality of natural and environmental resources. While water, soil, air, forest and fisheries resources are productive assets, the pollution of water, air, atmosphere and noise are the by-products of economic development. The term pollution is derived from the Latin word *'pollutioneum'* which means to defile or make dirty. According to National Environmental Research Council, "Pollution is viewed as the release of substances and energy as waste products of human activities, which result in harmful changes within the natural environment".

1 Department of Applied Science, Dronacharya Group of Institutions, Greater Noida, (UP) (India)

2 Department of Botany, Garg (PG) College, Laksar, Haridwar (Uttarakhand) (India)

The presence of one or more contaminant such as dust, gas, mist, odors, smoke, smog or vapors in the outdoor atmosphere, in quantity of characteristics and duration so as to be injurious to human beings, plants or animal life or to property or which unreasonably interferes with the comfortable enjoyment of life and property is known as Air Pollution. Air Pollution may be personal, occupational or community air pollution. Exposure of individual to dust, fumes, smoke, smog and gases may be regarded as personal air pollution. The type of exposure of an individual to potentially hazardous concentration of aerosols, vapors and gases in his working environment is known as occupational air pollution. Community air pollution involves pollution from a variety of sources and contaminants and factors, which cause adverse social, economic and health effects. The community air pollution not only affects many individuals but it can also exert a significant impact on man's total environment including plants, animals, buildings, property and even the wealth.

Air pollution is a global problem and can affect the physical environment, human health and vegetation. There are many types and sources of air pollutants. They can be broken down into general categories such as mobile and fixed sources and natural sources. Examples of mobile sources include cars, trucks, buses, trains and aircrafts. Examples of fixed sources would be large industrial operations, refineries, numerous small industries, which produce pollutant precursors, agricultural burning, dairy and cattle industries, and fertilizer production processes.

Natural sources can also play a significant role in pollutant production. For example, volcanic activity can release significant amounts of pollutants into the atmosphere, which can be distributed globally. Fugitive dust from non-vegetated areas or from agricultural operations is also an important environmental concern.

Finally, emission of organic compounds from trees and plants themselves are termed "biogenic emissions" and can contribute to formation of pollution in certain areas. Although there are naturally occurring atmospheric pollutants, human activities account for a significant proportion of these pollutants.

Air pollutants, which come out directly from their sources are called as primary air pollutants. There are five primary pollutants, which together contribute more than 90% of global air pollution. These are carbon monoxide, nitrogen oxides, hydrocarbons, sulphur oxides and particulates. Secondary pollutants are formed in the atmosphere when chemical components are fueled by sunlight. These 'photochemical' reactions result in the production of various compounds including oxides of nitrogen (NO_x), peroxyacylnitrates (PAN), sulfur oxides and aerosols, polyaromatic hydrocarbons (PAH), ozone and multitudes of other chemical species.

Transportation is one of the most important sources of air pollution. The pollution from automobiles may be highly significant, particularly in congested and poorly ventilated roads. Congestion intensifies air pollution problems, increases commuting times, and raises vehicles operating costs. The major pollutants generated by the automobiles are hydrocarbons (HC), oxides of nitrogen (NO_x), carbon monoxide (CO), smoke and lead (Trivedi and Goel, 1995).

Analytical Methods

The chlorophyll 'a', 'b' and total chlorophyll and carotenoids in the leaves of selected plant species were determined as per Arnon (1949) method.

Ascorbic acid was determined by the method of Sadasivam and Manikam (1991). Six samples of each of the tree species were analyzed on each sampling date. Similarly replicate samples and analytical blank were also analyzed to check the reliability of data.

Air pollution tolerance index (APTI) was estimated using the method of by Singh and Rao (1983).

RESULTS

The total number of vehicles passing through the study area (eight hour duration) were counted on each sampling date. Vehicles count helped in understanding the vehicular load on the study area. The average density of vehicles flowing through the study area was noted as 1816 vehicle per hour (average of 8 hours). This number also increased to 1200% on certain special occasions such as on somwati amavas, when two to three million people from different parts of country come to take a holy dip in river Gang at Har Ki Pauri.

Commonly two types of effects were recorded on the selected plant species during the study period i.e. visible effects, which were visibly with naked eyes and the biochemical effects.

Visible Effects

The selected plant species showed some of the common visible effects due to auto exhaust pollution. Most frequent effects noted were necrosis and chlorosis. Necrosis started form development of small irregular shaped grayish green areas with water soaked appearances which was due to collapse of mesophyll cells. These areas subsequently became dry to form brownish-red to black colored spots fruits also developed necrotic patches due to air pollutants. Chlorosis was also noted in the leaves of trees, which were exposed to road side pollution due to automobiles. This is due to the effect of Sulphur dioxide. Sulphur dioxide enters the leaves through stomata attacking the spongy parenchymatus tissue and then spreading to the plastid layer. Since the cells near the vein are rarely affected, damaged leaves often show a network of green veins on discolored background.

Physiological Effects

Variations in various physiological characteristics of the selected plant species exposed to automobile emissions are given in Tables 5.1, 5.2, 5.3 and 5.4.

Monthly data on physico-chemical and physiological parameters of leafsamples of *Holoptelea integrifolia*collected from polluted and control areas of site 4 are given in Table 5.1, 5.2, 5.3 and 5.4.

Dust content: During the first year of study, dust content in the leaves of *Holoptelea integrifolia* at polluted area ranged between 0.08±0.02 mg (Nov.) to 0.25±0.09 mg (June) and at control area it was ranged between 0.01±0.005 mg (May, Aug., and Nov.) to 0.08±0.02 mg (July). Thus increase in dust content in the leaf samples collected from polluted area in comparison to leaf samples of control area was recorded and it was ranged between 65.21% (July) to 95.65% (Aug.).

In the second year of study, dust content at polluted area ranged between 0.02±0.005 mg (May) to 0.14±0.05 mg (Dec.), whereas dust content at control area ranged between 0.01±0.005 mg (Feb. and May) to 0.07±0.02 mg (March). Higher amount of dust was recorded in the leaf samples collected from polluted area and it ranged between 22.22% (July) to 80.00% (Feb.).

Relative water content (%): During the first year of study, relative water content of leaves of *H. integrifolia* collected from polluted area ranged between 51.13±1.27% (Jan.) to 79.15±1.60% (Oct.), whereas relative water content of leaves collected from control area ranged between 55.55±2.27% (Dec.) to 86.18±1.77% (Oct.).

Thus there was a reduction in relative water content in the leaf samples collected from polluted area in comparison to leaf samples collected from control area, which ranged between 0.75% (March) to 22.37% (May).

During the second year of the study, relative water content ranged between 54.61±1.29% (March) to 75.08±1.18% (Dec.) at polluted area and between 58.71±1.81% (Sept.) to 79.74±1.60% (Dec.) at control area. A reduction in relative water content in the leaf samples collected from polluted area was recorded, which ranged between 1.06% (Jan.) to 8.44% (Feb.).

pH: pH value of extract of leaves sampled from polluted area ranged between 5.30±0.08 (Oct.) to 6.23±0.14 (Jan), whereas at control area, pH varied between 6.25±0.20 (Dec.) to 6.69±0.20 (Feb.) in the first year of study.

Thus reduction of pH value towards the acidic side in the leaf samples of polluted area was recorded, which ranged between 2.22% (April) to 18.46% (Oct.) during the first year of study.

Table 5.1: Monthly variation in physico-chemical and physiological parameters of leaf samples of *H. integrifolia* collected from polluted and control areas at the site- 4 during 2003-04. (Mean of 6 samples)

Months	Parameters														
	Dust Content (mg)			Relative Water Content (%)			pH			Ascorbic Acid mg/g			Carotenoids mg/g		
	P	C	I%	P	C	D%	P	C	D%	P	C	D%	P	C	D%
2003-04															
December	0.10±0.03	0.03±0.01	70.00	54.56±1.67	55.55±2.27	1.81	5.95±0.11	6.25±0.20	4.80	1.25±0.11	1.44±0.22	13.19	1.62±0.22	1.78±0.14	8.98
January	0.14±0.04	0.02±0.005	87.71	51.13±1.27	56.28±2.00	9.15	6.23±0.14	6.49±0.17	4.00	1.23±0.13	1.87±0.19	34.22	1.80±0.30	2.11±0.17	14.69
February	0.18±0.05	0.04±0.01	77.77	54.00±1.33	61.00±1.82	11.47	6.11±0.09	6.69±0.20	8.66	1.39±0.17	1.69±0.21	17.75	1.32±0.29	1.50±0.13	12.00
March	0.20±0.05	0.04±0.01	80.00	63.32±1.77	63.80±1.77	0.75	6.17±0.10	6.52±0.17	5.36	1.77±0.20	2.02±0.17	12.37	1.42±0.24	1.61±0.20	11.80
April	0.17±0.07	0.04±0.01	76.47	68.05±1.11	78.77±1.86	13.60	6.16±0.12	6.30±0.16	2.22	1.49±0.11	1.71±0.22	14.76	1.57±0.24	1.60±0.22	1.87
May	0.17±0.06	0.01±0.005	94.11	54.39±1.89	70.07±1.86	22.37	6.23±0.07	6.45±0.11	3.41	1.05±0.20	1.81±0.16	41.98	1.12±0.21	1.66±0.19	32.53
June	0.25±0.09	0.05±0.02	80.00	54.77±2.12	63.55±1.89	13.76	5.80±0.09	6.34±0.10	8.51	1.45±0.11	2.28±0.27	36.41	1.54±0.26	2.37±0.17	35.02
July	0.23±0.06	0.08±0.02	65.21	56.42±1.16	65.58±2.09	13.96	5.60±0.12	6.50±0.12	13.84	1.13±0.13	1.85±0.20	38.91	1.22±0.31	1.91±0.19	36.12
August	0.23±0.08	0.01±0.005	95.65	66.03±1.37	72.89±1.16	9.41	5.50±0.12	6.30±0.16	12.69	1.20±0.19	1.65±0.26	27.27	1.15±0.14	1.80±0.22	36.11
September	0.18±0.10	0.03±0.01	83.33	77.45±1.14	81.36±1.63	4.80	5.60±0.12	6.50±0.19	13.84	1.17±0.13	1.63±0.27	28.12	1.30±0.15	1.63±0.14	20.24
October	0.19±0.11	0.02±0.01	89.42	79.15±1.60	86.18±1.77	8.15	5.30±0.08	6.50±0.16	18.46	1.25±0.17	1.79±0.16	30.16	1.38±0.20	1.75±0.19	21.14
November	0.08±0.02	0.01±0.005	87.50	73.67±1.33	76.66±2.19	3.90	5.50±0.09	6.50±0.11	15.38	1.52±0.15	1.77±0.27	14.12	1.17±0.17	1.39±0.20	15.82

Where: P = Polluted area, C = Control area, D =% Decrease, I =% Increase

Table 5.2: Monthly variation in physico- chemical and physiological parameters of leaf samples of sample of sample of *H. integrifolia* collectedfrom polluted and control areas at the site- 4 during 2003-04. (Mean of 6 samples)

Months	Parameters									
	Chlorophyll 'a' mg/g			Chlorophyll 'b' mg/g			Total Chlorophyll mg/g			APTI
	P	C	D%	P	C	D%	P	C	D%	P
2003-04										
December 2003	1.33±0.19	1.49±0.29	10.73	0.88±0.17	1.05±0.11	16.19	2.21±0.22	2.54±0.13	11.81	6.47
January	1.44±0.22	1.55±0.25	7.09	1.00±0.13	1.11±0.17	9.90	2.44±0.19	2.66±0.17	8.27	6.17
February 2004	1.48±0.21	1.70±0.22	12.94	0.90±0.11	1.08±0.13	16.66	2.38±0.19	2.78±0.19	14.38	6.58
March 2004	1.70±0.22	1.88±0.19	9.54	1.00±0.17	1.11±0.11	9.90	2.70±0.24	2.99±0.17	9.69	7.90
April 2004	1.68±0.27	1.92±0.17	40.63	0.85±0.20	1.03±0.11	17.47	2.53±0.23	2.95±0.22	14.23	8.09
May 2004	1.26±0.20	1.66±0.16	32.32	1.08±0.14	1.15±0.15	6.08	2.34±0.27	2.81±0.25	16.72	6.33
June 2004	1.70±0.19	1.89±0.19	43.70	1.28±0.11	1.29±0.10	0.77	2.98±0.20	3.18±0.14	6.28	6.75
July 2004	1.34±0.19	2.00±0.22	33.00	1.14±0.13	1.16±0.20	1.72	2.48±0.19	3.16±0.13	21.51	6.55
August 2004	1.30±0.22	1.66±0.13	21.68	0.83±0.19	1.11±0.16	25.22	2.13±0.18	2.77±0.12	23.10	7.51
September 2004	1.51±0.17	1.98±0.19	23.73	0.82±0.17	1.16±0.22	29.31	2.33±0.14	3.14±0.14	25.79	8.87
October 2004	1.27±0.19	1.66±0.19	31.72	0.89±0.16	1.15±0.20	22.60	2.16±0.16	2.81±0.18	23.13	8.84
November 2004	1.11±0.25	1.43±0.27	22.37	0.55±0.10	0.82±0.17	32.92	1.66±0.17	2.25±0.22	26.22	8.54

Where: P = Polluted area, C = Control area, D =% Decrease, APTI = Air pollution tolerance index

Table 5.3: Monthly variation in physico- chemical and physiological parameters of leaf samples of *H. integrifolia* collected from polluted and control areas at the site - 4 2004-05. (Mean of 6 samples)

Months	Parameters														
	Dust content (mg)			Relative water content (%)			pH			Ascorbic acid mg/g			Carotenoids mg/g		
	P	C	I%	P	C	D%	P	C	D%	P	C	D%	P	C	D%
2004-05															
December	0.14±0.05	0.06±0.02	57.14	75.08±1.18	79.74±1.60	5.84	6.25±0.11	6.50±0.12	3.84	1.45±0.17	1.70±0.17	14.70	1.67±1.16	1.74±0.29	4.02
January	0.14±0.03	0.07±0.02	50.00	74.25±1.70	75.05±1.32	1.06	6.30±0.10	6.50±0.11	3.07	1.24±0.19	1.75±0.19	29.14	1.32±0.13	1.87±0.11	29.41
February	0.05±0.01	0.01±0.005	80.00	71.05±1.61	77.60±1.72	8.44	6.02±0.08	6.65±0.15	9.47	1.63±0.20	2.55±0.11	36.07	1.73±0.28	2.32±0.11	25.43
March	0.12±0.04	0.07±0.03	41.66	54.61±1.29	59.35±1.81	7.98	5.95±0.08	6.27±0.17	5.10	1.17±0.22	1.45±0.22	19.31	1.69±0.22	2.27±0.20	25.55
April	0.11±0.04	0.05±0.01	54.54	55.61±1.61	60.36±1.69	7.86	6.44±0.11	6.70±0.11	3.88	1.26±0.19	1.92±0.27	34.37	1.20±0.21	1.78±0.16	32.58
May	0.02±0.005	0.01±0.005	50.00	58.12±1.81	61.50±1.22	5.49	6.21±0.13	6.50±0.16	4.46	1.29±0.12	1.98±0.20	34.84	1.12±0.20	1.58±0.19	29.11
June	0.09±0.02	0.04±0.01	55.55	58.06±1.19	62.96±1.50	7.78	6.21±0.12	6.50±0.13	4.46	1.51±0.21	1.58± 0.17	4.43	1.15±0.16	1.51±0.13	23.84
July	0.09±0.03	0.07±0.02	22.22	58.12±1.59	59.80±1.22	2.80	6.00±0.09	6.50±0.13	7.69	1.59±0.26	2.11±0.15	24.64	1.24±0.11	1.48±0.16	16.21
August	0.10±0.04	0.04±0.01	60.00	57.15±1.20	59.62±1.07	4.14	6.25±0.08	6.40±0.09	2.34	1.33±0.19	1.51±0.12	11.92	1.23±0.13	1.45±0.14	15.17
September	0.13±0.03	0.05±0.01	61.53	55.33±2.00	58.71±1.81	5.75	6.08±0.11	6.50±0.11	6.46	1.23±0.16	1.71±0.25	28.07	1.29±0.16	1.65±0.11	21.81
October	0.11±0.06	0.03±0.01	72.72	56.66±1.54	59.60±1.20	4.93	5.95±0.07	6.42±0.17	7.32	1.53±0.22	1.96±0.19	21.93	1.25±0.27	1.84±0.17	32.06
November	0.11±0.04	0.04±0.01	63.63	56.80±1.81	59.77±1.20	4.96	6.00±0.13	6.43±0.15	6.68	1.24±0.20	1.61±0.17	22.98	1.24±0.24	1.63±0.12	23.92

Where: P = Polluted area, C = Control area, D =% Decrease, I =% Increase

Table 5.4: Monthly variation in physico-chemical I and physiological parameters of leaf samples of *H. integrifolia* collected from polluted and control areas at the site- 4 during 2004-05. (Mean of 6 samples)

Months	Parameters									
	Chlorophyll 'a' mg/g			Chlorophyll 'b' mg/g			Total Chlorophyll mg/g			APTI
	P	C	D%	P	C	D%	P	C	D%	P
2004-05										
December	1.18±0.21	1.52±0.14	22.36	0.66±0.12	1.04±0.19	36.53	1.84±0.29	2.56±0.22	28.12	8.68
January	1.33±0.20	1.79±0.14	25.69	0.43±0.19	1.04±0.11	58.53	1.76±0.22	2.83±0.20	37.80	8.24
February	1.25±0.27	1.96±0.15	36.22	0.76±0.16	1.51±0.14	49.66	2.01±0.25	3.47±0.13	42.07	8.41
March	1.26±0.19	1.96±0.11	35.71	1.05±0.17	1.40±0.15	25.00	2.31±0.24	3.36±0.15	31.25	8.42
April	1.32±0.14	2.10±0.19	37.14	0.77±0.23	1.18±0.20	34.74	2.09±0.19	3.28±0.19	36.28	6.63
May	1.18±0.11	1.78±0.17	33.70	0.66±0.19	1.37±0.24	51.82	1.84±0.17	2.15±0.12	14.41	6.85
June	1.16±0.11	1.75±0.19	33.71	0.61±0.20	1.38±0.13	55.79	1.77±0.20	3.13±0.11	43.45	7.01
July	1.10±0.20	1.59±0.22	30.81	0.12±0.05	0.62±0.14	40.54	1.72±0.19	2.70±0.19	36.29	7.03
August	1.17±0.19	1.61±0.12	27.32	0.59±0.12	1.35±0.21	56.29	1.76±0.25	2.96±0.27	40.54	6.78
September	1.25±0.13	1.50±0.19	16.66	0.83±0.12	1.25±0.24	33.60	2.08±0.16	2.75±0.75	24.36	6.53
October	1.08±0.17	1.63±0.13	33.74	0.95±0.20	1.25±0.24	24.00	2.03±0.16	2.88±0.19	29.51	6.88
November	1.21±0.21	1.53±0.15	20.91	0.60±0.20	1.08±0.17	44.44	1.81±0.23	2.61±0.12	30.51	6.64

Where: P = Polluted area, C = Control area, D =% Decrease, I =% Increase, APTI = Air pollution tolerance index

During the second year of study period, pH at polluted area ranged between 5.95±0.08 (March) to 6.44±0.11 (Jan.) and at control area, it was ranged between 6.27±0.11 (March) to 6.70±0.11 (April). The reduction in pH value towards acidic side was recorded in the samples from polluted area, which ranged between 2.34% (Aug.) to 9.47% (Feb.).

Ascorbic acid: During the first year of the study period, ascorbic acid in the leaf samples of *H. integrifolia* collected from polluted area ranged between 1.05±0.20 mg/g (May) to 1.77±0.20 mg/g (March) whereas ascorbic acid content at control area ranged between 1.44±0.22 mg/g (Dec.) to 2.28±0.27 mg/g (June). There was reduction in the ascorbic acid in the leaf samples of polluted area in comparison to leaf samples of control area, and it was ranged between 12.37% (March) to 41.98% (May).

During the second year of study, ascorbic acid at polluted area ranged between 1.17±0.22 mg/g (March) to 1.63±0.20 mg/g (Feb.), whereas ascorbic acid in the leaves collected from control area ranged between 1.45±0.22 mg/g (March) to 2.55±0.11 mg/g (Feb.). Thus reduction in ascorbic acid in the leaf samples collected from polluted area ranged between 4.43% (June) to 36.07% (Feb.).

Carotenoid contents: Carotenoid contents at polluted area ranged between 1.12±0.21 mg/g (May) to 1.80±0.30 mg/g (Jan.), whereas carotenoid contents of leaves collected from control area varied from 1.39±0.20 mg/g (Nov.) to 2.37±0.17 mg/g (June) during 2003-04. There was a reduction in carotenoid contents in the leaf samples of polluted area in comparison to leaf samples of control area, which ranged between 1.87% (April) to 36.12% (July).

During the second year of the study, carotenoid content at polluted area ranged between 1.12±0.20 mg/g (May) to 1.73±0.26 mg/g (Feb.) and at control area it was ranged between 1.45±0.14 mg/g (Aug.) to 2.32±0.11 mg/g (Feb.). A reduction in the concentration of carotenoid pigments in the leaf samples of polluted area was recorded, which ranged between 4.02% (Dec.) to 32.58% (April).

Chlorophyll 'a': During the study period 2003-04, chlorophyll 'a' content of leaves sampled from polluted area ranged between 1.11±0.25 mg/g (Nov.) to 1.70±0.20 mg/g (March) and at control area it was ranged between 1.43±0.27 mg/g (Nov.) to 2.0±0.22 mg/g (July). Reduction in chlorophyll 'a' in the sample collected from polluted area was thus noted, which ranged between 7.09% (Jan.) to 43.70% (June).

During the second year of study, chlorophyll 'a' content of leaves collected from polluted area ranged from 1.08±0.17 mg/g (Oct.) to 1.33±0.20 mg/g (Jan.), whereas at control area it was ranged between 1.50±0.19 mg/g (Sept.) to 2.10±0.19 mg/g (April). Thus there was a reduction in chlorophyll 'a' content in the leaf samples collected from polluted area, which varied from 16.66% (Sept.) to 37.14% (April).

Chlorophyll 'b': The concentration of chlorophyll 'b' content of leaves sampled from polluted area ranged between 0.55±0.10 mg/g (Nov.) to 1.28±0.11 mg/g (June), whereas chlorophyll 'b' concentration of leaves collected from control area ranged between 0.82±0.17 mg/g (Nov.) to 1.29±0.10 mg/g (June). Thus reduction in chlorophyll 'b' content in the leaf samples collected from polluted area ranged between 0.77% (June) to 32.92% (Nov.) during the first year of study.

During the study period 2004-05, chlorophyll 'b' content of leaves collected from polluted area ranged between 0.12±0.05 mg/g (July) to 1.05±0.17 mg/g (March), whereas at control area it ranged between 0.62±0.14 mg/g (July) to 1.51±0.14 mg/g (Feb.). Reduction in chlorophyll 'b' in the samples collected from polluted area was thus noted, which ranged between 24.0% (Oct.) to 58.53% (Jan.).

Total Chlorophyll: Total chlorophyll in the leaves of *H. integrifolia* at polluted area ranged between 1.66±0.17 mg/g (Nov.) to 2.98±0.20 mg/g (June), whereas total chlorophyll of leaves collected from control area ranged between 2.25±0.22 mg/g (Nov.) to 3.18±0.14 mg/g (June). The reduction of total chlorophyll concentration in the samples collected from polluted area ranged between 6.28% (June) to 26.22% (Nov.) in the first year of study period.

During the second year of study, total chlorophyll contents of leaves collected from polluted area ranged between 1.72±0.19 mg/g (July) to 2.31±0.24 mg/g (March), whereas total chlorophyll of leaves collected from control area ranged between 2.15±0.12 mg/g (May) to 3.47±0.13 mg/g (Feb.). Thus a significant reduction was recorded in the concentration of total chlorophyll contents in the leaf samples collected from polluted area, which ranged between 14.41% (May) to 43.45% (June).

Air Pollution Tolerance Index (APTI): Air pollution tolerance index of *H. integrifolia* during the first year of study ranged between 6.17 (Jan.) to 8.87 (Sept.), whereas during the second year of the study, it ranged between 6.53 (Sept.) to 8.68 (Dec.).

It has been observed that due to continuous exposure of the plants growing at road side to different pollutants like roadside dust, smoke, soot and other pollutants, the leaf surface remain covered with these pollutants. As a result, clogging of stomata occurs and gaseous exchange becomes very low and inception of light energy is poor, which finally reduces photosynthetic rate and energy concentration in plants (Pajenkomp, 1961; Larman, 1972; Borka, 1980). Garg *et al.* (2000) have noted maximum concentration of dust on 'Safeda' and 'Mahua' leaves due to rough upper surface and vertical deposition of the leaves. Wagela *et al.* (2002) reported maximum deposition of lead on *Dalbergia sissoo* leaves and minimum on *Polyalthia longifolia* in the same area and explained that higher particulate contents on the leaves of former were due to its rough upper surface, with emergent veins and prominent curvature, which supported particulate deposition and least drifting, while the low dust contents in the later case were due to pendulous habit and glabrous leaf surface that do not allow particulate to stay over the surface. Flanagn *et al.*, (1980) Lebel *et al.*, (1992), Patil *et al.*, (1992) and Joshi *et al.*, (1993) have also reported similar observations with different plant species. Present study reveals that highest amount of dust was deposited in the leaf samples of *Holoptelea integrifolia* (June, 2004), it may be due to their sticky surface, which adhere the dust blown by the automobiles.

Large quantities of water maintain the physiological balance under stress conditions especially during the air pollution (Dedio, 1975 and Lewis, 1976). Amount of moisture loss and moisture retaining capability is related with size and number of the stomata. Smaller size and less number of stomata result into higher moisture retaining capacity and less moisture loss. Larger the size and higher the number of stomata, lower is the moisture retaining capacity. The present investigation reveals that leaf samples collected from polluted sites have less amount of moisture retaining capacity, which may be due to size and number of stomata damaged by road side automobile stress. Ramadrishnaiah and Somasheker (2003) have also reported reduction in the water content in the leaves of *Vernonia cinerea, Lagascea mollis, Tridax procumbens, Vinca rosea, Euphorbia hirta, Amaranthus spinosus* and *Ageratum conyzoides* due to their exposure to vehicular pollution. The reduction in relative water content observed in most of the species growing along the roadside indicates their disturbed physiological status due to auto exhaust pollution.

The moisture content of the leaves at polluted area was less in comparison to control area. Under normal conditions due to transpiration, the layers of air in immediate contact with leaf surface get saturated with the vapours. This decreases the vapour pressure gradient between the outside and the inside of the leaves, but when dust is deposited on the leaves, it absorbs water, as a result the vapour pressure gradient becomes more steep and the water from inside the leaf is lost to the outside dust at a fast rate coupled by the capillary action. Not only these dust particles get saturated form water vapours coming from the leaves, but also there is a loss of water to the atmosphere. The surface area for water loss also gets increased greatly. This may be the possible reason for lower moisture content of leaves in polluted areas. In the present study, relative water content in the leaf samples from all four selected trees species decreased at polluted area and highest reduction in relative water content was observed in the *T. grandis,* which was 26.28% (Feb, 2005).

According to Mapson (1958), sulphur dioxide causes imbalance between ascorbic acid and dehydro- ascorbic acid. This further suggests that poisoning of specific enzyme by SO_2 may decrease ascorbic acid and increase dehydroascorbic acid. It is possible that reduction in ascorbic acid content of SO_2 exposed plants might be due to the enzyme poisoning and Sulphonation of their –SH group. Some time higher reduction in ascorbic acid at relatively low levels of pollutants accumulation may also be observed, which may be due to decline in the resistance of plants in scavenging toxic radicals, under prolonged exposures of air pollutants.

The rate of production of free radicals, active oxygen and sulphate levels must have increased at faster rate than the equivalent process involved in the production of free radical scavengers. This could affect the production of precursors of ascorbic acid, i.e. sugar leading to the decline of ascorbic acid under low sulphate levels. Lower amount of ascorbic acid in the plants of polluted area than non-polluted area was also reported by Aberg (1958). Chaudhary and Rao (1977) observed pollution tolerance of plants with their ascorbic acid level and concluded that higher the level of ascorbic acid the greater the tolerance.

Ascorbic acid, a natural antioxidant in plants has been shown to play an important role in pollution tolerance (Chen *et al.*, 1990).Sharma (1991) have studied amelioration effect of ascorbic acid against the phytotoxicity of SO_2 in wheat plants. It was observed that the plants sprayed with ascorbic acid exhibited better growth yield and less foliar injury in comparison to those exposed to SO_2 only. Present investigation also reveals that there was a reduction in ascorbic acid content in plant samples of all four species collected from polluted area of different sites and highest reduction was found in *H. integrifolia*, which was 41.98% (May, 2004).

Tiwari and Bansal (1993) have reported the effect of NO_2 on evergreen tree species and reported a decrease in ascorbic acid content in the plants, which were exposed to NO_2. Ramakrishnaiah and Somasekhar (2003) studied ascorbic acid content in road side plants, exposed to varying degree of traffic pollution. They observed significant inverse relationship with traffic density and ascorbic acid content. Rao and Le Blanc (1966) have also reported reduction of chlorophyll content brought by acidic pollutants like SO_2 which causes phaeophythin formation by acidification of chlorophyll. These injuries further retard net assimilation rate of the plants (Weinstein and McCune, 1990).

Capron and Mansfield (1976) proposed that gaseous and many particulate pollutants cause chlorosis in leaves and other green parts. In the present study, a decreasing trend in chlorophyll 'a', 'b', total chlorophyll and carotenoid content in the leaf samples from polluted area was observed, which was significant in comparison to control area. Highest reduction of 43.70% (June, 2004) and 56.29% (August, 2005) was found in chlorophyll 'a' and chlorophyll 'b' contents, respectively in *H. integrifolia*, whereas highest reduction 45.32% (April, 2005) in total chlorophyll was obserbed in *T. grandis*. Highest reduction 36.12% (July), 2004 in carotenoid content was recorded in *H. integrifolia*.

A considerable reduction in chlorophyll 'a', 'b' and total chlorophyll, in the leaves of these plants growing on the roadside, supports the argument that the chloroplast is the primary site of attack by air pollutants such as SPM, SO_2 and NO_x. This view has further been supported by the studies of Furukawa *et al.* (1980).

Chlorophyll contents are essential for the photosynthetic activity. Reduction in chlorophyll has been used as an indicator of air pollution (Pawar and Dubey, 1985). Reduction in chlorophyll contents of a variety of crop plant due to SO_2 and O_3 exposure have also been reported by Agarwal (1985). Agarwal (1984-85) and Sharma (1984) have also studied the effect of air pollution on plants like *Cassia fistula,Dalbergia sissoo, Bauhinia purpurea, Bougainvillea spectabilis, Cassia siama, Mangifera indica* and *Pongamia pinnaata*. They found that the concentration of chlorophyll 'a' and Chlorophyll 'b' were lower in polluted sites as compared to control sites.

It was suggested by Borka (1986) that air pollutants make their entrance into tissues through the stomata and cause partial destruction of chloroplast and decrease pigment contents in the cells of polluted leaves. Sulphur dioxide plays an important role in the reduction of chlorophyll pigments (Mandloi and Dubey, 1988; Rao and Dubey, 1985). The depletion of chlorophyll content of the plant species is in the support of earlier findings of Prasad and Inamdar (1990) and Bansal *et al.* (1991). Mishra and Gupta (1993) reported that dusted or encrusted leaf surface is responsible for reduced photosynthesis and thereby causing reduction in chlorophyll content. Bala (2005) has reported that size of leaves and stomata get highly reduced due to exposure of plant species *Ipomoea cairica* and *Polyalthia longifolla* to vehicular pollution.

SO_x get dissolved in water in the leaf tissues, and causes local injury by germinating toxic ions (Malhotra and Hocking, 1976, Manninen *et al.* 1996). Reduction of chlorophyll may be due to the increase of chlorophyllase enzyme activities, which in turn affects the chlorophyll concentration in plants (Mandal and Mukherji, 2000).

Singh *et al.* (1985) have reported that photosynthetic pigments were degraded and leaf extract, pH and protein content declined in SO_2 treated plants. Plants on the basis of their responses to pollutants under field conditions have been classified into sensitive and tolerant species (Jacobson and Hill, 1970). The degree of sensitivity of plants depends on their developmental stage, nutritional status and other ecological factors. The level of injury will be high in sensitive species and low in tolerant ones, which also help in abatement of air pollution. Singh and Rao (1983) used parameters viz. pH, ascorbic acid content, chlorophyll a, b, carotenoid and relative water content of leaf samples to get air pollution tolerance index (APTI).

Tiwari and Bansal (1994) have studied air pollution tolerance indicies of some planted trees in urban area of Bhopal. APTI values of twenty five species growing in various localities in Bhopal were determined. They found that air pollution tolerance level of each plant was different and plants sharing more APTI value are more tolerant to air pollution than those having low APTI values. Similarly, an experiment was conducted by Madan (1998) for getting the APTI value of eight plant species and found a highest APTI value for *Aesculus indicus* (96.23) and lowest for *Jacaranda mimosaefolia* (20.38). Mashitha and Pise (2001) analysed selected plants from Nagpur city for air pollution tolerance index (APTI) to monitor the level of air pollution and found that around 50% of the plants to be sensitive, out of which 10% being highly sensitive. They observed that very few plants were able to tolerant the pollution viz. *Haloptelea spp.* and *Cassia spp.* with a high APTI index. Karthyiyayini *et al.*,(2005) determined the air pollution tolerance index (APTI) of 27 species growing in the natural conditions adjacent to Coimbatore –Ooty highways by calculating ascorbic acid, total chlorophyll, leaf pH and relative water content and observed that *Azadirachta indica* trees, *Ricinus communisis, Bougainvillea spectabilis, Calotropis gigantia* among shrubs, *Amaranthus virids, Datura stamonium* amongst herbs, *Cucuribita pepo* amongst climbers, have high degree of tolerance and can be used as bioindicators and also be grown as bioaccumulators. In the present investigation, highest APTI value, 8.87 (Sept., 2004) has been obtained for *H. integrifolia* followed by *S. robusta* (8.60), *T. grandis* (6.97) and *M. indica* (5.98).

REFERENCES

Arnon, D.I. (1949). Copper Enzyme in Isolated Chloroplasts. Polyphenoloxidase in Beta vulgaris Plant Phsysiology, 24, 1-15.

Agrawal, M. (1985). Plant Factors as Indicator of SO2 and O3 Pollutants. Proc. International Symposium on Biological Monitoring of the State Environment (Bio- indicator), pp. 225-231. Indian National Science Academy, New Delhi.

Chen, Y.M. Lucas, P.W. and Wellburn, A.R. (1990) Relative Relationship between Foliar Injury and Change in Antioxidants Levels in Red and Norway Spruce Exposed to Acidic Mists. *Environ. Pollut.* 69: 1-15.

Farmer, J.C and T.D.B. Lyon (1977). Lead in Glasgow Street Dirt and Soil. Sci. *Total Environ*, 8, 89-93.

Fuji. S. (1973). The Current Damage of Plant Damage by Air Pollution in the Ckayama Prefecture, *Shokbutsu Boeki* 27: 249-252.

Gupta, M.C. and A.K.M Ghouse (1987): The Effects of Coal – Smoke Pollutants on the Leaf Epidermal Architecture in Solanum molengena L variety Pusa Purble Long. *Environ. Pollut.* 41, 315-321.

Jacob, M.B and Hochheiser, S. (1958). Continuous Sampling and Untra-micro Determination of Nitrogen dioxide in Air. *Anal. Chem.* 30: 426.

Lone., P.M, Khan, A.A and Shah., S.A. (2005). Study of Dust Pollution caused by Traffic in Aligarh City. *Indian J. Environ Hlth.* Vol. (47), 4, 33-36.

Madhumanjari Mandal and S. Mukherji *(2000).*: Changes in Chlorophyll Content, Chlorophllase Activity, Hill Reaction, Photosynthetic CO_2 uptake, Sugar and Starch Content in Five Dicotyledonous Plants Exposed to Automobile Exhaust Pollution. *J.Environ.Biol.* 21 (1), 37-41.

Malhotra, S.S. and Hocking, D. (1976). Biochemical and Cytological Effects of SO_2 on Plant Metabolism. *New Phytol.* 76: 229-237.

Manninen, S., Huttunen, S., Rautio, P. and Paramaki, P. (1996). Assessing the Critical Level of SO_2 for Scots Pine. *Environ. Pollut.* 93: 27-38.

Mandloi, B.L. and P.S. Dubey (1988). The Industrial Emission and Plant Response at Pithanpur (M.P). *Int. J. Ecol. Environ. Sci.*,14, 75-99.

Oman, J., A.S. Cnik and B. Dejonovi (2001). Influence of Lignite Composition on Thermal Power Plant Performance. *Energy Conversion and management,* 42(3), 265-271.

Pawar, K. and P.S. Dubey (1985). Effects of Air Pollution on the Photosynthetic Pigments of *Ipomea fistulosa* and *Phoenix sylvestris*. All India Seminar on Air Pollution Control, Indore, Abs. 19-21, 4 (1985).

Rao, D.N. and F.Leblance. (1966) Effect of Sulphur Dioxide on Lichen Alga with Special Reference to Chloroplast. *Bryologist,* 69, 69-72.

Rao. M.V. and P.S. Dubey (1985). Plant Response against SO2 in Field Conditions. *Asian Environ.,* 10, 1-9.

Sarkar, P.K., Baherjee, A., and Mukherji, S. (1986): Accelereation of Peroxide and Catalase Activity in Leaves of Wild Dicotyledonous Plants, as an Indication of Automobile Exhaust pollution. Environmental Pollution (Series A) 42: 189-295.

Seinfeld, J.H. (1975). Air Pollution (Physical and Chemical fundamentals), Mc. Graw-Hill Book Company, New York (1975).

Siefermann-Harms, D. (1987). The Light Harvesting and Protective Function of Carotenoids in Photosynthetic Memberanes. *Physiol. Plant.* 69: 561-568.

Singh, S.K. and Rao, D.N. (1983). Evaluation of Plants for their Tolerance to Air Pollution. Proceedings of Symposium on Air Pollution Control. Vol. 1., *Indian Assoc. for Air Pollution Control, New Delhi.*

Weinstein, L.H and McCune, D.C. (1990). Implication of Air Pollution for Plant Life. *Proc. Amer. Phil.Soc.* 114: 18-21.

West, P.W., and Gaeke, G.C., (1956). Fixation of Sulphur Dioxide as Sufitomercurate III and Subsequent Colorimetric Determination, *Anal. Chem.,* 28, 1816.

Woolhouse, H. (1986). Plant Senescences. *In*: Procesa and Control of Plant Senescence (Eds: Y.Y. Leshem, A.W. Halvey and C.Frankel). Elsevier Science Publisher, Netherlands, 3-20 pp.

Pages: 86-104

Stress Tolerance and Plant Productivity
Edited by: Mr. Prasann Kumar and Dr. Pawan Kumar 'Bharti'
ISBN: 978-93-86841-56-8
Edition: 2018
Published by: Discovery Publishing House Pvt. Ltd., New Delhi (India)

6 Role of Rhizobium in Enhancing the Yield and Yield Attributes of Crops with Special Reference to Chickpea

Prasann Kumar

ABSTRACT

Role of pulses in Indian agriculture needs hardly any emphasis. The pulses are an integral part of the cropping system of the farmers all over the country because these crops fit in well in the crop rotation and crop mixtures followed by them. Pulse crops, besides being rich in protein and some of the essential amino acids, enrich the soil through symbiotic nitrogen fixation from atmosphere.

Key words: Amino acid, Biotic, Crops, Desi, Esential, Forage, Gap

INTRODUCTION

Chickpea is cultivated for its seeds. They are rich source of protein and chickpea seeds contain 17-20% of protein. Chickpea is an important rabi crop mainly sown in September-November and harvested in February. Crop duration is 90-120 days, depending on the variety. Desi varieties are short duration while Kabuli varieties take relatively longer period, to mature. Similarly cooler like northern India take longer period compared to relatively warm weather in southern parts of India. It is best suited to areas having low to moderate rainfall and a mid cold weather.Excessive rains soon after sowing or at flowering stage are harmful for the crop.It is best suited to area having moderate rainfall of 60-90 cm per annum. It has an indeterminate growth habit, which means that the growth cycle extends as long as available. G.S. Tagore & S.L. Namdeo reported that Pulses are the second most important group of crops after cereals. Developing countries contribute about 74% to the global pulses production and the remaining comes from developed countries. India, China, brazil, Canada, Myanmar,

Department of Agronomy, School of Agriculture, Lovely Professional University
Jalandhar - 144 411 (Punjab) (India)

and Australia are the major pulse producing countries with relative share of 25%, 10%, 5%, 5%, and 4% respectively. In 2009, the global pulses production was 61.5 million tonnes from an area of 70.6 million hectares with an average yield of 871kg/ha. Dry beans contributed about 32% to global pulses production followed by dry peas (17%), Chickpea (15.9%), broad bean (7.5%), lentil (5.7), cowpea (6%) and pigeon pea (4.0%). India is the largest producer and consumer of pulses in the world contributing around 25-28% of the total global production. About 75% of the global chickpea (cicer arietinum L.) area falls in India. Chickpea is the third most important pulse crop. It accounts for 20 per cent of the world pulse production. Major producers of chickpea include India, Pakistan and Mexico. Global production, as per the latest available estimates of Food and Agricultural Organization (FAO), is about 12 million metric tons in 2011. India is the largest producer, with about 8 million tons, accounting about 70 per cent of total world production. Six countries including India, Australia, Turkey, Myanmar, Pakistan and Ethiopia account for about 90 per cent of world chickpea production. According to the latest available estimates by the FAO, Pakistan is the largest importer while Australia is the largest exporter in the world in 2011. However, India is a net – importer for most of the period and hence any fluctuation in world production may have an impact on domestic prices.

PRODUCTION STATISTICS OF CHICKPEA

Production of chickpea is concentrated in central and southern parts of India. Production trends during the past 15 years indicated that except for a few years in the early 2000s, the output of chickpea fluctuated at around 6 million tonnes for over a decade till 2007-08. However, production has steady increased thereafter and largely in tune with the trends in yield levels and reached about 8.8 million tonnes in 2012-13. This increase in production is possible due to development of high yielding disease resistant varieties, matching production and production technologies in chickpea growing areas. Incidentally, the period the steep rise in production is in perfect line with the rise in minimum support prices (MSP) announced by the Govt. of India along with a significant expansion in the area under cultivation. Madhya Pradesh is the single largest producer in the country, accounting for over 40 per cent of total production. Rajasthan, Maharashtra, Uttar Pradesh and Andhra Pradesh contributed about 14%, 10%, 9% and 7%, respectively. On the other hand, the share of Andhra Pradesh and Karnataka has consistently been rising during the past 10 years. Further, states like Jharkhand and Chhattisgarh are expanding their area and production of chickpea crop. During 2012-13, highest production of chickpea (3551 thousand tones) was recorded in Madhya Pradesh with productivity of 435 kg/ha. In Rajasthan, production of 1265 thousand tones was achieved with productivity of 1010 kg/ha. In Maharashtra, production of 1058 thousand tones was recorded with productivity of 844kg/ha. Highest productivity of 1430 kg/ha was recorded in Bihar state. In Andhra Pradesh, 759 thousand tonnes of chickpea was produced with productivity of 1115 kg/ha (Figure 6.1) (Table 6.1).

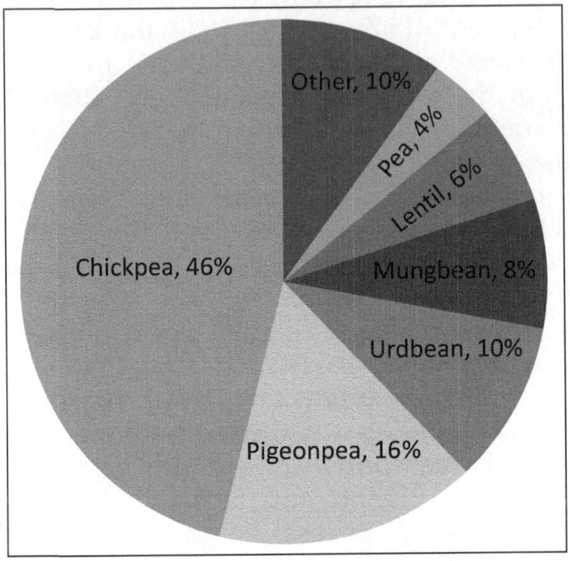

Fig. 6.1: Indian pulse production

Source: Based on review of literature

Table 6.1: Production of pulse

Year	Area		Production		Yield		% Coverage Under Irrigation
2005-06	22.39	-1.6	13.39	2.0	598	3.6	15.0
2006-07	23.76	6.1	14.11	5.4	594	-0.7	15.4
2007-08	23.63	-0.5	14.76	4.6	625	5.2	16.2
2008-09	22.09	-6.5	14.57	-1.3	660	5.6	16.0
2009-10	23.28	5.4	14.66	0.6	630	-4.5	16.2
2010-11	26.4	13.4	18.24	24.4	691	9.7	14.8
2011-12	24.46	-7.3	17.09	-6.3	699	1.2	16.1
2012-13	23.26	-4.9	18.34	7.3	788	12.7	18.6
2013-14	25.23	8.5	19.27	5.1	764	-3.0	N.A
2014-15	23.10	-8.4		-10.9		-2.7	N.A

Note: The yield rates given above have been worked out on the basis of Production area taken in 000units. Green revolution period, N.A. not available.

Source: Agricultural Statistics at a Glance, 2013. Directorate of Economics and Statistics, Ministry of Agriculture, Govt. of India)

Growth Rate of Total Pulses.

A-Million ha, P-Million Tonnes, Y-kg/ha, Growth rate- Percent (%)) (Dr.A.K. Tiwari)

BOTANICAL DESCRIPTION

Chickpea belongs to family Leguminoseae. It is a small, much branched herbaceous plant rarely exceeding 60 centimeter height. Chickpea has a well developed root system. The roots usually include a central strong tap root, with numerous lateral branches that spread out in all directions in the upper layer of soils. There are numerous nodules on roots. The rhizobium bacteria present in these nodules fix up atmospheric nitrogen.Stem is generally greyish in appearance. The stem is branched with granular hairs on it. The main branch in gram usually produces not more than one secondary shoot, but in some types the main branches may produce numerous lateral branches. The leaves are pinnately compound, usually with one terminal leaflet. There are 9-15 pairs of leaflets. The leaflets of the pinnate leaves are small, and have serrated edges. The flower are typical papilionaceous consisting of five sepals, five petals comprised of one standard, two wings and two keels, ten stamens, nine fused to form one staminal column and one free, and a carpel with the style borne laterally on the ovary. The pod is about 2 cm long and usually contain two seeds. A single plant produces about 50 to 150 pods. The seeds are spherical in shape, wrinkled and with a pointed beak. Colour of seed may vary from white, light fawn, yellowish-orange, brown, dark brownish and with a little bluish tinge. The cotyledons are thick and yellowish in colour. Chickpea is a winter season crop but sever cold and frost are injurious to it. Frost at the time of flowering results in the failure of the flowers to develop seeds or in the killing of the seeds inside the pod. Excessive rains soon after sowing or at flowering and hailstorms at ripening cause heavy loss. It is best suited to areas having moderate rainfall. Chickpea is grown on a wide range of soils in India. In the north, gram is generally grown on moderately heavysoils. Light soils, mostly sandy loams are preferred in Punjab, Uttar Pradesh, Haryana and Rajasthan. The best type of soil for chickpea is one that is well drained and not too heavy. On dry and light soils, the plants remain short while on heavy soils having high after retention capacity, the vegetative growth is abundant, light becomes limiting and fruiting is retarded. However, chickpea is not suited to soils having a pH higher than 8.5. High yielding photo-insensitive cultivar are not available in pulses and this appears to be the most important reason for low productivity of pulse crops in the country. Chickpea is highly sensitive to soil aeration. So, very fine and compact seedbed is not suitable for chickpea it requires a loose and well aerated seedbed. Sowing dates is the most important for crops All India Co-ordinated Pulse Improvement Project conduct and experiment at different centres over last several years have amply demonstared that second fortnight of October is the optimum time for sowing chickpea in most of the chickpea growing areas of northern India. Delay beyond this period results in conspicuous reduction in yield. Early sowing of chickpea results in excessive vegetative growth and poor setting of pods. The early sown crops suffers more from wilt owing to high temperature at that time. The crop may be sown at a row spacing of 30-40 centimetres. The seed should be placed with 8-10 centimetres deep. Chickpea being a leguminous crop fulfils the major part of its nitrogen requirement (about 75%) through the process of symbolic nitrogen fixation which work effectively from three to four weeks after sowing. However, if the soils have low organic matter and poor nitrogen supply may require 20-25 kg per hectare of nitrogen as starter doses which can meet plant requirement before the formulation of nodules. Chickpea require a light irrigation because heavy irrigation is always harmful to gram crop. Excess of irrigation enhances vegetative growth and depresses chickpea yield. Chick being a stature crop suffers severely by infestation of weeds. Hand weeding or inter culture with the help of hoe is always better than herbicides because inter culture operations improve aeration in the soil. Some important diseases of chickpea are Wilt, sclerotinia blight, grey mold, rust and Ascochyta blight and the important insect pests of chickpea are cutworms and gram pod borer. Chickpea has the potential to yield far higher than the national average. A well managed crop yields about 20-25 quintals of grain per hectare which is about three to four times higher than the national average (Figure 6.2).

Fig. 6.2: Seeds of Chickpea
Source: Based on review of literature

Rhizobia can survive and reproduce in the soil, but they are best known for fixing N_2 inside the nodules that develop on legume plants whose roots they have infected. A single founding rhizobium may produce a billion or more descendants inside a nodule. Respiration in support of N_2 fixation consumes reduced carbon compounds that rhizobia could otherwise have used to support their own current or future reproduction. For example Instead of fixing N_2, rhizobia could use carbon received from the plant to synthesize energy-rich storage molecules like polyhydroxybutyrate (PHB), which could enhance rhizobium survival and reproduction after they return to the soil. Rhizobia range from mutualists, which supply their host with nitrogen at a reasonable carbon cost, to parasites, which infect legumes plants but then fix little or no N_2 inside their nodules. Even at a single location, different strains of Rhizobia can vary 10 fold in the net benefits they provide their host, an measured by growth of test plant (R.F. Denison and E.T. Kiers). "Rhizobia are small bacteria that fix nitrogen once they found a base inside root nodules of legumes". In order terms, they can be defined as legume root-nodules bacteria. Fixation of nitrogen cannot be done independently. That is rhizobia require a plant host. It represents a vital source of N input in agricultural soils including those in arid regions. That is they convert dinitrogen into ammonia. Ammonia is toxic in nature. Hence they are rapidly absorbed into organic compounds. Nitrogen fixation helps in increasing productivity of low –N soils and soil fertility. The various behavioural factors such as drought stress, nutrient deficiency, salt stress, fertilizers and pesticides are reviewed. These major stress factors suppress the growth and symbiotic characteristics of most rhizobia; however, several strains, distributed among various species of rhizobia, are tolerant to stress effect. The Rhizobium – legume symbiosis is suggested to be the ideal solution to the improvement of the soil fertility and the rehabilitation of arid lands (HH Zahran). Nitrogen- Fixing Bacteria belongs to the group of prokaryotes. Their main functionis the conversion of stable nitrogen gas in the atmosphere to a biologically useful form. Nitrogenase is an enzyme complex that reduces dinitrogen to ammonia. A huge amount of nitrogen is consumed during the nitrogen fixation and the nitrogenise enzymes are irreversibly inactivated by oxygen. Acetylene reduction assay is used to measure the Nitrogenase activity. A very less portion of species is capable of carrying out nitrogen fixation. That is around two genera of cyanobacteria and much more. Nodulation in chickpeas start at 10-12 days after planting. The active nodules are pink in colour due to the presence of leghaemolobin, and are capable of fixing atmospheric nitrogen. The nitrogen fixing process continues up to 40-50 days after sowing in warm climates. In cooler climates, it may continue more than 100 days depending on soil moisture and temperature (Dart 1947). Rhizobia are aerobic, rod shaped, motile, gram negative, heterotropic, and non-spore forming bacteria, which live freely in soil and in the root region of leguminous and non leguminous plants. Rhizobia fix atmospheric nitrogen and thus, not only increase the production of inoculated crops but also leave a fair amount of nitrogen in the soil, which benefit the subsequent crops (Agarwal 1998). Most of these bacteria are very sensitive to soil water deficit, which adversely affect their nitrogen fixation capacity and hence the productivity of whole legume plant (Miller and Wood 1996). They are also sensitive to higher salt concentration (Wilson 1994) and are capable of growing at 200 mM salt concentration, but the growth is more abundant at lower salt concentration (Rafiq 1997). Shreeyaa reported that plants require a lot of nitrogen to make protein. After the harvest, the soil becomes deficient in nitrogen. Even though nitrogen gas is available in abundance in the air, plants cannot utilize in the manner they can do with carbon-dioxide. They need nitrogen in a soluble form. The bacterium called Rhizobium take atmospheric nitrogen and convert it into soluble from for the plants to utilize. But Rhizobium cannot make its own food. So, it lives in the root of leguminous plants such as gram, moong, peas, beans and provide them with nitrogen. In return, the plants provide food and shelter to the bacteria. Thus, they have a symbiotic relationship. This is a great advantages to farmers as they do not need to add nitrogen fertilizer in which leguminous plants are grown. S.G. Khattak and T. Khan conduct an experiment to evaluate the effect of Rhizobial inoculation and nitrogen application. They found that rhizobial inoculation improve nodulation on the root system of the crop however, nitrogen application at sowing could not affect the nodulation status of the crop. Inoculation and fertilizer nitrogen individually and in combination significantly increased the grain yield of the crop. The inoculated treatment receiving 30kg N ha^{-1} produced the highest grain yield. There was no significant difference in between the nitrogen treated and inoculated. Legume-rhizobia (Rhizobium/Bradyrhizobium/Mesorhizobium) symbiosis is an effectives agronomic practice ensuring adequate supply of N than the application of fertilizer-N. However, various environmental factors limit nitrogen fixation, such as soil moisture deficiency, osmotic stress, extremes of temperature, soil salinity, soil acidity, alkalinity nutrients deficiency, overdoses of fertilizers and pesticides, affect the survival and infectivity rate of rhizobia (Zahran 1999). G.W.O' Hara and R.M. Daniel reported the productivity of chickpea is poor; it is mainly due to imbalance application of nutrients and use of traditional varieties. Under such situation use of Rhizobium has shown advantages in enhancing chickpea productivity. Rhizobium assumes a great importance on account of their vital role in N_2-fixation. The root nodules bacteria, Rhizobium spp, in a symbiotic relationship with leguminous plants, make an important contribution to nitrogen input in soils. The symbiotic nitrogen fixation carried out by rhizobia, and this process is benefit for agricultural. Rhizobium play a very important role in agriculture by inducing nitrogen-fixing nodules on the roots of legumes such as peas, beans, clover and alfalfa. The symbiosis can relieve the requirements for added nitrogenous fertilizer during the growth of leguminous crop. The Rhizobium group study the bacterial and legume genes involved in establishing and maintaining the symbiosis. The expression of "nodulation" genes in the bacteria is activated by signals from plants roots and as a result the bacteria synthesise signals that induce a nodule meristem and enable the bacteria to enter this merisrem via a plant made infection thread. The chemical signals synthesised by the bacteria are based on a modified amino acid (homoserine lactone) carring a variable acyl chain substituent, and are called acyl transduction lactones (AHLs). By detecting and reacting to these chemicals, individual cells can sense how many cells surrounded them, and whether are enough bacteria, i.e. a quorum, to initiate the change towards acting in a multicellular fashion. This is known as 'quorum sensing' and this laboratory is Coordinating an EU consortium on 'Rhizosphere Communication' to investigate the extent to which specific plant growth-promoting bacteria use AHL - based quorum sensing regulation of important physiological traits, and degree of cross – talk with plant pathogens (Allan Downie & Nick Brewin). P.H. Graham; Rhizobia gain entry to leguminous roots, form nodules, and fix atmospheric nitrogen through a complex process. Nodulation beings when a suitable strain of Rhizobium encounters a leguminous root system. The Rhizobium multiplies, in the process producing substantial amounts of IIA and other as yet unidentified but specific substances. These substances cause deformation and curling of the plant root hairs. The root hair invaginates at the apical portion, and some rhizobia pass into the invaginated section. This reaction is very localized and in many plants is also acid sensitive. A fungus-like infection thread is formed by the plant, and the rhizobia are contained within this thread even as they move down the root hair and into the cortex of the plant. When the infection thread penetrates a tetraploid cell, it begins to break up, and the rhizobia, still surrounded by a plant mucilage, are released into the plant cell cytoplasm. They begin to multiply, and the IAA produced causes multiplication of the tetraploid and surrounding diploid cells. This multiplication leads to the structure we cell a "nodule". When released into the plant cell, the rhizobia are still bacillary in shape. They quickly lose this cylindrical appearance, becoming "bacteroids," and in this from begin N_2 fixation. During active fixation, there are usually four distinct nodular zones: an outer cortical tissue uninfected by bacteria, an inner zone where the cells are infected but the rhizobia are still in the bacillary form, the central tissue containing N_2- fixing but generally nonviable Rhizobium "bacteroids," and an area of degenerating nodule tissue. C.A. Napoli and H. Hubbel; the legume, the bacteria, and the nodule constitute the system for this type of nitrogen fixation. It is a process where both the bacteria and the plant benefit by the association. The bacteria convert atmospheric nitrogen to fixed nitrogen which is available to the plants, and in turn, the bacteria derive nutrients from the tissue of the plant. Not all species of Rhizobium produce nodulation and nitrogen fixation with any legume. There is a degree of specificity between the bacteria and legumes. For purpose of inoculation with commercial preparations of these bacteria, legumes are divided into seven major categories as follows: alfalfa, clover, peas and vetch, cowpeas, beans, lupines, and soybeans. Rhizobium species or strains effective for one group are less effective or ineffective for other groups. Even within a species, certain strains are more effective than others with a given host plant. Inoculation of seeds before planting is a desirable practice, since not all agricultural soils contain the right kinds of bacteria for optimum symbiotic nitrogen fixation with legume crops. Most of the commercial preparations consist of selected strains of bacteria dispensed in moist humus. Rhizobia is the group of soil bacteria that infect the roots of legumes to form root nodules. Rhizobia are found in the soil and after infection, produce nodules in the legumes where they fix nitrogen gas(N_2) from the atmosphere turning it into a more readily useful from of nitrogen. From here, the nitrogen is exported from the nodules and used for growth in the legume. Once the legume dies, the nodules breaks down and releases the rhizobia back into the soil wherecan live individually or reinfect a new legume host. Specific strain of rhizobia are required to make functional nodules on the roots able to fix the N_2. Having this specific rhizobia present is beneficial to the legume, as the N_2 fixation can increase crop yield. Inoculation with rhizobia tends to increase yield. Legume inoculation has been an agriculture practice for many years and has continuously improve over time. It has also been stated that"cereals were healthier and higher yielding when grown after a legume". Cereals are the another major crop, so if integrated in a crop rotation with legumes, then rhizobium inoculation can be very beneficial to crops other than legumes. Increasing the possible amount of yield for multiple crops would help farmers very much in growing their current food production as well to help close the gap between current yield and potential yield. A.Namvar reported that Rhizobium inoculation continued to have positive effect on growth indices and yield components of chickpea. Non-inoculated plants showed less growth indices including total dry matter(TDM), leaf are index(LAI), crop growth rate (CGR), relative growth rate (RGR) and net assimilation rate (NAR) while the highest values of these indices were observed at the high inoculated plants. The highest plant height, number of primary and secondary branches, number of pods per plants and number of grain per plants were obtained from the highest Rhizobium inoculation. The inoculation of seeds with Rhizobium is known to increase nodulation, N uptake, growth and yield parameters of legume crops. Albay rak *et.al* (2006) studied the effect of inoculation with Rh. Leguminosarum on seed yield and yield components. Rhizobium bacteria synthesized Phythohormons like auxin as secondary metabolites in inoculated plants. Phytohormones are known to play a key role in plant growth regulation. They promotes seed germination, root elongation and stimulation of leaf expansion. In addition, great root development and proliferation of plants in response to Rhizobium activities enhance water and nutrients uptakes (Werner, Newton2005: Erman *et al* 2011).

Plant growth promotion by Rhizobia can be both direct as well as indirect. N is required for synthesis of nucleic acids, enzymes, proteins and chlorophyll and hence it is a vital elements for plant growth. N is used for enhancing agricultural productivity. Biological nitrogen fixation is a process of converting atmospheric N into ammonia through cascade of reactions between prokaryotes and plants with the use of comples enzyme system. Major part of the N fixed by legumes is harvested as grain while the soil and the succeeding crops in the form of root and shoot residues (Wilson and Burris 1947). Nitrogen fixation has two components: dinitrogenase reductase, the iron protein and dinitrogenase (metal sofactor). The iron protein provides the electrons with a high reducing power to dinitrogenase which in turn reduces N_2 to NH_3. Depending on the availability of metal cofactor, three types of N fixing systems have been identified: Mo-nitrogenise, Fe- nitrogenise(Laranjo *et al* 2004). Legume nitrogen fixation start with the formation of a nodule. A common soil bacterium, Rhizobium, invades the root and multiplies within the cortex cells. The plant supplies all the necessary nutrients and energy for the bacteria. Small nodules can be seen 2-3 weeks after planting, depending on legume species and germination conditions. When nodules are young and not yet fixing nitrogen, they are usually white or grey inside. As nodules grow in size they gradually turn pink or reddish in colour, indicating nitrogen fixation has started. The pink or red colour is caused by leghemoglobin (similar to haemoglobin in blood) that controls oxygen flow to the bacteria. The entire nodule is generally ½ inch in diameter. Nodule on perennial are long-lived and will fix nitrogen through the entire growing season, as long as condition are favourable.Where as nodules on annuals are short-lived and will be replaced constantly during the growing season. At the time of pods fill, nodules on legumes generally lose their ability to fix nitrogen because the plant feeds the developing seed rather than the nodules. Legume nodules are no longer fixing nitrogen usually turn green, and may actually be discarded by the plants. If white, grey or green nodules predominate, little nitrogen fixation is occurring as a result of an inefficient Rhizobium strain, poor plant nutrition, pod filling, or other plant stress. The nitrogen fixed is not free. The plant must contribute a significant amount of energy in the form of photosynthate (photosynthesis derived sugar) and other nutrientional factor for the bacteria. Any stress that reduce plant activity will reduce nitrogen fixation. Factor like temperature and water may not be under the control of the farmer. But the nutritional stress (especially phosphorus, potassium, zinc, iron, molybdenum and cobalt) can be corrected with fertilizers. The legume responds directly to the nutrient, and indirectly to the increased nitrogen nutrition resulting from enhanced nitrogen fixation. Poor nitrogen fixation in the field can be easily corrected by inoculation, fertilization, or other management practice (W.C. Lindemann and C.R. Glover). D. Dutt conducted an experiment during the winter season to evaluate the performance of chick pea to application of phosphorous and bio-fertilizer. In this phosphorous and bio-fertilizer application influenced significantly the growth attributes, nodulation, leghaemoglobin contain, nitrogenise activity, yield components seeds and stover yields, harvest index and phosphorous uptake of chickpea, except test weight. Seed inoculated with Rhizobium and phosphobacterin was significantly superior over no inoculation or phosphobacterin inoculation. Combined application of phosphorous and bio-fertilizers (Rhizobium and phosphobacterin) enhanced significantly. Nodule formation by Rhizobium on legume plants. The first stage is the establishment of the Rhizobium legume N_2-fixing symbiosis is the infection of the host legume by the appropriate Rhizombium species. Root hairs are the site of infection.The first microscopically visible indication of the bacteria-plant interaction is deformation and curling of the normally straight root hairs. Aseptically culture clover seedling with undeformed root hairs. A clover seedling inoculated with Rhizobium trifolii. The bacteria are in clumps (floes) in the rhizosphere. A characteristic deformation is curling at the root hairs tip to produce a "shepherd's crook" (C). The bacteria enter the root hair and are enclosed in a tubular structure the infection thread which is the first microscopically visible sign of a successful infection. The bacteria appear to enter the root hair by a process of invagination. Root hair cell-wall growth is redirected at a localized point resulting in the wall growing back into the root hair to formthe tubular infection thread. There is no direct penetration through the root hair cell wall, and bacteria remain extracellular within the infection thread. A serial section sequence through a root hair which had a shepherd's crook at the origin of the infection thread (C.A. Napoli and H.Hubbell). Leguminous plants are able to fix atmospheric N_2 through the association with rhizobia. The legume plant supplies the carbohydrate for bacterial growth while the bacteria fix atmospheric N_2 into NH_4^+, to be converted into amino acids that can be used by the plant to synthesize proteins for its growth and development (Russell 2008). Symbiotic association is a highly specified relationship between the host plant and the bacteria. Rhizobium-legume symbiosis involves the interaction between the plants and the bacteria leading to initiation and development of the root nodules. Soil bacteria like Rhizobium live in nodules as nitrogen fixing bacteroids. A single rhizobial cell that infects a root hairs can increases the progeny by 10^{10} within few weeks. Rhizobia require a plant host; therefore, they cannot independently fix nitrogen. These bacteria are located around root hair and fix atmospheric nitrogen using particular enzyme called nitrogenise. Rhizobia use plant resources for this own reproduction whereas fixed atmospheric nitrogen is used to meet nitrogen requirement of both itself and the host plants (Eutropia V.Tairo and Patrick A Nd akidemi).Soil bacteria are very important in biochemical cycles and have been used for crop production for decades. Free living soil bacteria beneficial to plant growth, usually referred to as plant growth promoting rhizobacteria (PGPR), are capable of promoting plant growth by colonizing the plant root. Symbiotic nitrogen-fixing bacteria include the cyanobacteria of all the genera Rhizobium, Bradyrhizobium, Azorhizobium and Sinorhizobium. Free living nitrogen-fixing bacteria are associative nitrogen fixers. E.J. Patriarca and M. Iaccarino reported that symbiotic nitrogen fixation is carried out in specialized organs, the nodules, whose formation is induced on leguminous host plants by bacteria belonging to the family Rhizobiaceae. Nodules development is a complex multistep process, which requires continued interaction between the two partners and thus the exchange of different signals and metabolites. NH_4^+ is not only the primary product but also the main regulator of the symbiosis: either as ammonium and after conversion into organic compounds, it regulates most stages of the interaction, from the production of nodules inducers to the growth, function, and maintenance of nodules. The adaptation of bacterial NH_4^+ metabolism to the variable environment generated by the plants, which actively controls and restricts bacteria growth by affecting oxygen and nutrients availability, thereby allowing a proficient interaction and at the same time preventing parasitic invasion.R. Parveen, M. Sadiq and M. Saleem conduct an experiment to evaluate the role of Rhizobium Inoculation in Chichpea (Cicer arietinum L.) under water stress conditions. In this Rhizobium inoculation enhanced yield under both normal and stressed conditions, but its performance was better under normal than under stress. Rhizobium inoculation proved ineffective to recover loss caused by water stress. Gwata *et al* reported that plant treated with Rhizobium inoculation had significant effects on nodulation, emergence percentage, time of maturity, chlorophyll content, plant height, seed protein, pods per plant and grain yield because the plants were grown in a nitrogen- free medium, the available nitrogen as indicated by the dark green leaves was derived from the N_2- fixation process. Nitrogenous compounds resulting from N_2- fixation are exported from root nodules in the formof ureides (aalantoin and allantoic acids) and translocated to the leaves where they are catabolised and used for the biosynthesis of chlorophyll and other protein essential for photosynthesis. Concentration of chlorophyll dyes is a reliable index of physiological plant conditions, through frequently it is not duly appreciated in agricultural sciences.

A. Senberga reported that Legume seed inoculation prior to sowing is well-known practices in agriculture. Nitrogen fixation, due to the symbiotic relationship between legumes and rhizobia, improves the productivity of legumes. Rhizobia strain specificity leading to differences in the total protein content. Plant cultivar appeared to have a decisive role in the formation of protein content when inoculated with Rhizobium sp. When choosing Rhizobium sp. Strains for legume inoculation, soil type also should be consider. Rhizobia has the potential to be used as a commercial preparation intended for increasing legume protein content, alongside with increased legume yield; however, different rhizobia strains should be mixed together to achieve the optimal result. The legume- Rhizobium symbiosis is a typical example of mutualism. Because several unrelated strains infects each individual plant, any one strain could redirect resources from N_2 fixation to its own reproduction without killing the host plant upon which they all depend. It turns out that legume plants guide the evolution of rhizobia towards greater mutualism by reducing the oxygen supply to nodules that fix less N_2 thereby reducing the frequency of cheaters in the next generation. Symbiotic N_2 – fixation has been studied widely and exploited as a means of increasing crop yields (Boholool, 1990; Sharma *et al* 1993). The fixed N_2 is released when the plants die, making it available to other plants and this helps in fertilizing the soil. The great majority of legumes have this association, but a few genera do not. N. Bidyarani reported that the use of Rhizobium inoculants in chickpea is well establish; however, meagre efforts have been directed towards the use of other microbial supplements for improving nutrient uptake and yields. Soil chlorophyll, nitrogen-fixation and available N possessed high positive direct effects on grain yield through positive-correlations and- high direct effects and also had high positive indirect effects through other component traits. The cumulative effects of improved plant growth and nutrient uptake exhibited a positive correlation with microbiological activity, especially nitrogen fixation, soil chlorophyll and soil available nitrogen. This may account for the significantly higher yields as compared to control.Rhizobium are soil bacteria that fix nitrogen once they found a base inside root nodules of legumes. It helps the plants grow and gives them nutrients. Its helps in increasing productivity of low-N soils and soil fertility. They help in increased plant growth through soil nutrients enrichment by nitrogen fixation, phosphate solubilisation, siderphore production. They increased plant protection by influencing cellulose, protease and lipase production and enhance plant defense by triggering induced systemic resistance through lipopolysaccharides, flagella, homoserine, lactose, acetoin and butanediol against pests and pathogens(A. Sathya and Lakshmanan).

MICRO-ORGANISM ASSISTED METAL EXTRACTION FROM CONTAMINATED SOIL

Some microorganism reduce the metal toxicity for plants by [1] Decreasing their accumulation into the plants while some others increase the amount of metal extracted by plants or [2] By increasing either the biomass of plants (diluting effects) or the concentration of metals accumulated in plants. Microorganisms just minimize the stress produced due to accumulation of excess metal in the plants.

$$+\textit{Increase in Biomass of Plant} = \frac{1}{\textit{Concentration of metals per unit biomass}}$$

Source: Drawn by the author

Enhancement of Metal Accumulation by Plants

[A] Bioavailability of metals

Low availability of the metals in the soil solution is the one of the major significant factor for the lower amount of metals extracted by plants from the soil. In general, scientist reported that, they oftenaccount for less than 1% of the total metal in soil (Whiting *et al.*, 2001; Braud *et al.*, 2006b) and the rate of availability is influenced by the several soil physical and chemical characteristics such as pH, CEC and organic matter (Kayser *et al.*, 2001). Scientist reported that, the positive effects will be observed if we apply soil-bioaugmentation. It is happens due to more fraction of metal present in the soil solution. Braud *et al.*, 2006b have shown that, if we take *Pseudomonas aeruginosa* and *Pseudomonas fluorescens* for remediation purpose of heavy metal especially lead, then it increases the available lead concentration in the soil solution by the 11.3%. So naturally it remediation will enhanced due to bio-augmentation of plants. It is observed that, the boundation of lead occurs with Fe-Mn oxides and organic matter. Abou-Shanab *et al.*, (2006) have shown an increase of extractable Ni with *Microbacterium arabinogalactanolyticum* by a factor up to 15 with respect to the Ni concentration in the soil. The availability of metals also affected with the nature of metal itself and physio-chemical properties of the soil. The pH has inverse relation with the availability of metals in the soil whereas the acidity shows positive relation with the availability of the metals. In a soil bio-augmented with the ecotomycorrhizal fungus *Paxillusinvolutus*, the concentration in NH_4NO_3-extractable Cd, Cu, Pb and Zn were, respectively, up to 1.22, 1.11, 1.33 and 1.33 fold higher than those recorded in the non-bioaugmented soil depending on the soil composition (Baum *et al.*, 2006). Microbial performances cannot be compared with each other because the methods used to estimate the bioavailable fractions of metals vary from one experiment to other experiment. Indeed several extractants are used such as water (Chen *et al.*, 2005; Di Gregorio *et al.*, 2006; Wu Q.T. *et al.*, 2006; Wu S.C. *et al.*, 2006b), $MgCl_2$ (Braud *et al.*, 2006b),

NH_4NO_3 (Baum *et al.*, 2006), DTPA (Chen *et al.*, 2004a; Di Gregorio *et al.*, 2006b), KNO_3 (Di Gregorio *et al.*, 2006) and HCl (Wang *et al.*, 2007b). Bioavailability of metals is even divided into three different pools (Cao *et al.*, 2007): immediately soluble metals (with water), exchangeable metal forms (with KNO_3) and complexes or adsorbed metal form (with EDTA).

Microbial siderophores, manly localized in the rhizosphere (Bossier *et al.*, 1988), enhance the Fe (III) mobility and also various other cations (Hofte *et al.*, 1993; Diels *et al.*, 2002). Principle component analysis (PCA) shows close positive relationships between the microorganisms that produce siderophores and the amount of Cr and Pb in the exchangeable fraction (Braud *et al.*, 2006b). Bacteria such as *Azotobacterchroococcum* (N-fixing bacteria), *Bacillusmegaterium* (P-solubilizer) and *Bacillusmunilaginosus* (K-solubilizer) (Wu Q.T. *et al.*, 2006; Wu S.C. *et al.*, 2006b) and *Bacillus* sp. RJ 16 (Sheng and Xia 2006) can decrease the pH value, probably by excreting low molecular weight organic acids, enhancing the bioavailability of Cd, Pb and Zn (Chen *et al.*, 2005). The metal concentrations in the majority simply extractable fractions have been showing to amplify in the bio-augmentation (Braud *et al.*, 2000b; Sheng and Xia 2006). Subsequent to six months, the concentrations of accessible metals are still elevated within the bio-augmented soil compared on the way to the non-bioaugmented ones (Baum *et al.*, 2006) signifying with the intention of inoculated microorganisms does stay alive and be metabolically active. A number of other studies have made known, nevertheless, the opposing, i.e., bio-augmentation has refusal consequence on metal speciation. Meant for instance, *Glomuscaledonium* (Chen *et al.*, 2004a) and *Glomusmosseae* (Citterio *et al.*, 2005) have no effect on the speciation of Cd and Zn, Cr and Ni, respectively. No effect of bio-augmentation by these microorganisms on the rate of phytoextraction has been observed to confirm these results.

[B] Metal extraction by plants

The metal concentration in plants has been shown to be higher or lower compared to the control (non-bioaugmented soil), depending on the metal (Bi *et al.*, 2003a; Baum *et al.*, 2006) and/or its concentration in the soil (Chen *et al.*, 2003). Nevertheless bio-augmentation almost always increases the rate of metal extracted by plants. I am giving the root morphology, which acts an important role in the bioaugmentation of contaminated soil of hazardous waste site. Most often metal concentration in microorganisms-assisted plant is higher than the control (non-bioaugmented soil). Bacteria, mainly PGPR and fungi, mainly AMF are used as pure cultures or as co-cultures. Whether the soil is bioaugmented or not, metal concentration in roots are generally higher than in shoots, by a factor exceeding 10 for most experiments. When the concentration of metals accumulated by plants increase with bioaugmentation, this increase most of the time is proportionally higher in roots than in shoots. Some experiments have, however, show the contrary with bacteria (de Souza *et al.*, 1996b) and fungi (Liao *et al.*, 2003; Malcova *et al.*, 2003; Leung *et al.*, 2006). PGPR such as *Agrobacterium, Alcaligenes, Arthrobacter, Azospirillum, Azotobacter, Bacillus, Burkholderia, Serratia, Pseudomonas* and *Rhizobium* (O'Sullivn and O'Gara 1992; Hoflich *et al.*, 1994; Carlot *et al.*, 2002; Glick 2003) are particularly interesting for metal extraction by plants since they increase both the rate of metals accumulated by plants and the plant biomass. Pseudomonads are well-known producers of siderophores involved in the modification of metal speciation in soils. Siderophores synthesized by *P. fluorescens* improve Fe uptake by tomatoes (Duss *et al.*, 1986), carnations and oats (Dujiff *et al.*, 1991), vine and maize (Sharma and Johri 2003a, b) with the disappearance of the chlorosis phenomena in peanut (Jurkevitch *et al.*, 1988). Few hydroxamate siderophores, such as desferrioxamine B, can complex with Pb (Dubbin and Louise Ander 2003) and potentially helping Pb uptake by plants. However, complexation of Cd, Cu and Zn is much higher with nitrilotria-complexation of Cd, Cu and Zn is much higher with nitrilotriacetate compared to desferrioxamine B (Neubauer *et al.*, 2000). PGPR lowers the metal toxicity by reducing ethylene produced by plant in response to heavy metals. Conversely the most common auxin, indole-3-acetic acid (IAA) synthesized by rhizobacteria has been shown to be involved in the metal uptake. IAA produced by *Bacillussubtilis* SJ-101 increases Ni concentration in *B. juncea* by a factor of 1.5 (Zaidi *et al.*, 2006). In hydroponic conditions, simultaneous addition of EDTA and IAA synthesized by rhizobacteria increase Pb extraction by plant by a factor of 28 against 6 with EDTA (Lopez *et al.*, 2005). AMF can also enhance metal extraction by plants, e.g., Cd in bean and maize (Guo *et al.*, 1996), alfalfa (El- Kherbawy *et al.*, 1989), clover (Joner and Leyval 1997) and soyabean (Heggo *et al.*, 1990) depending on the soil characteristic.

CONCLUSION

Rhizobium bacteria also synthesized Phythohormons like auxin as secondary metabolites in inoculated plants. Phytohormones are known to play a key role in plant growth regulation. They promotes seed germination, root elongation and stimulation of leaf expansion. It also play a very important role in agricultural by inducing nitrogen fixing nodules on the roots of legumes. Usually crops require a lot of nitrogen to make proteins. They cannot utilize the atmospheric nitrogen. They can use in soluble form. The Rhizobium bacteria convert atmospheric nitrogen into soluble form. In this way Rhizobium play an important role for farmers because it helps farmers to save fertilizers and manures.

REFERENCES

Abou-Shanab RAI., Angle JS., Chaney RL (2006). Bacterial Inoculants Affecting Nickel uptake by *Alyssum murale* from Low, Moderate and High Ni Soils. Soil Biol. Biochem., 38: 2882-2889.

Agropedia.iitk.ac.in.node.

All India Coordinate Pulse Improvement Project.

Baum C, Hrynkiewicz K, Leinweber P, Meissner R (2006). Heavy-metal Mobilization and uptake by Mycorrhizal and Nonmycorrhizal Willows (*Salixdasyclados*). J Plant Nut. Soil Sci., 169: 516-522.

BB Bohlool, JK Ladha, DP Garrity, T George- for Sustainable Agriculture, 1992-Springer.

Bi YL, Li XL, Christie P (2003a). Influence of Early Stages of Arbuscular mycorrhiza on uptake of Zinc and Phosphorus by Red Clover from a Low Phosphorus Soil Amended with Zinc and Phosphorus. Chemosphere, 50: 831-837.

Bijus.com.biology.rhizobium.

Bossier P, Hofte M, Verstraete W (1988). Ecological Significance of Siderophores in Soil. Adv. Microbiol. Ecol., 10: 385-414.

Braud A, Jezequel K, Vieille E, Tritter A, Lebeau T (2006b). Changes in Extractability of Cr and Pb in a Polycontaminated Soil after Bioaugmentation with Microbial Producers of Biosurfactants, Organic Acids and Siderophores. Water, Air and Soil Pollu., 6: 261-279.

Byjus.com.biology.rhizobium.

Cao A, Carucci A, Lai T, La Colla P, Tamburini E (2007). Effect of Biodegradable Chelating Agents on Heavy Metals Phytoextraction with *Mirabilis jalapa* and on its Associated Bacteria. Europ. J Soil Biol., 43: 200-206.

Carlot M, Giacomini A, Casella S (2002). Aspects of Plant Microbe Interactions in Heavy Metal Polluted Soil. Acta Biotechno., 22: 13-20.

Chen B, Shen H, Li X, Feng G, Christie P (2004a). Effects of EDTA Application and Arbuscular Mycorrhizal Colonization on Growth and Zinc uptake by Maize (*Zea mays* L.) in Soil Experimentally Contaminated with Zinc. Plant and Soil, 261: 219-229.

Chen B, Shen H, Li X, Feng G, Christie P (2004a). Effects of EDTA Application and Arbuscular Mycorrhizal Colonization on Growth and Zinc Uptake by Maize (*Zea mays* L.) in Soil Experimentally Contaminated with Zinc. Plant and Soil, 261: 219-229.

Chen BD, Li X., Tao HQ, Christie P, Wong MH (2003). The Role of Arbuscular Mycorrhiza in Zinc uptake by Red Clover Growing in a Calcareous Soil Spiked with Various Quantities of zinc. Chemosphere, 50: 839-846.

Chen YX, Wang YP, Lin Q, Luo YM (2005). Effect of Copper-tolerant Rhizosphere Bacteria on Mobility of Copper in Soil and Copper Accumulation by *Elsholtzia splendens*. Environ. Intl., 31: 861-866.

Citesurx..ist..pus.edu/viewdoc/download.

Citterio S, Prato N, Fumagalli P, Aina R, Massa N, Santagostino A, Sgorbati S, Berta G (2005). The Arbuscular Mycorrhizal Fungus *Glomus mosseae* Induces Growth and Metal Accumulation Changes in *Cannabissativa* L. Chemosphere, 59: 21-29.

Di Gregorio S, Barbafieri M, Lampis S, Sanangelantoni AM, Tassi E, Vallini G (2006). Combined Application of Triton X-100 and Sinorhizobium sp. Pb002 inoculum for the Improvement of Lead Phytoextraction by *Brassica juncea* in EDTA Amended Soil. Chemosphere, 63: 293-299.

Di Simine CD, Sayer JA, Gadd GM (1998). Solubilization of Zinc Phosphate by a Strain of *Pseudomonas Fluorescens* Isolated from a Forest Soil. Biology and Fertility of Soils, 28: 87-94.

Dubbin WE, Louise Ander E (2003). Influence of Microbial Hydroxamate Siderophores on Pb(II) Desorption from a-FeOOH. Appl. Geochem., 18: 1751-1756.

Duijff BJ, Bakker PAHM, Schippers B (1991). Influence of Pseudobactin- 358 on the Iron Nutrition of Plants. In: Sixth International Fe Symposium.

Duss F, Mozafar A, Oertli JJ, Jaeggi W (1986). Effect of Bacteria on the Iron uptake by Axenically-cultured Roots of Fe-efficient and Fe-inefficient Tomatoes (*Lycopersiconesculentum* Mill.). J Plant Nut., 9: 587-598.

El-Kherbawy M, Angle JS, Heggo A, Chaney RL (1989). Soil pH, Rhizobia, and Vesicular-arbuscular Mycorrhizae Inoculation Effects on Growth and Heavy Metal uptake of Alfalfa (*Medicago sativa* L.). Biol. Fert. Soils, 8: 61-65.

Glick BR (2003). Phytoremediation: Synergistic use of Plants and Bacteria to Clean up the Environment. Biotechnol. Adv., 21: 383-393.

Guo Y, George E, Marschner H (1996). Contribution of an Arbuscular Mycorrhizal Fungus to the uptake of Cadmium and Nickel in Bean and Maize Plants. Plant and Soil, 184: 195-205.

GWO'hara. RM Daniel- Soil Biology and Biochemistry, 1985-Elsevier.

Heggo A, Angle JS, Chaney RL (1990). Effects of Vesicular Arbuscular Mycorrhizal Fungi on Heavy Metal uptake by Soybean. Soil Biol. Biochem., 22: 856-869.

HH Zahra-Microbiology and Molecular Biology Reviews,1999-Am Soc Microbiol.

Hoflich G, Wiehe W, Kuhn G (1994). Plant Growth Stimulation by Inoculation with Symbiotic and Association Rhizosphere Microorganisms. Experientia 50.

Hofte M, Buysens S, Koedam N, Cornelis P (1993). Zinc Affects Siderophore - Mediated High Affinity Iron uptake Systems in the Rhizosphere *Pseudomonas aeruginosa* 7NSK2. BioMetals 6: 85-91.

https://brainly.in.Secondary school.Science.

https://www.hindawi.com.journals.ija.

https://www.ncbi.nlm.nih.gov.articles.

Joner EJ, Leyval C (1997). Uptake of 109Cd by Roots and Hyphae of a *Glomusmosseae/ Trifoliumsubterraneum* Mycorrhiza from Soil Amended with High and Low Concentrations. New Phytologist., 135: 353-360.

Jurkevitch E, Hadar Y, Chen Y (1988). Involvement of Bacterial Siderophores in the Remedy of Lime-induced Chlorosis in Peanut. Soil Sci. Soc. Amer. J., 52: 1032-1037.

Kayser G, Korckritz T, Markert B (2001). Bioleaching for the Decontamination of Heavy Metals. Wasser and Boden., 53: 54-58.

Leung HM, Ye ZH, Wong MH. (2006). Interactions of Mycorrhizal Fungi with *Pteris vittata* (As hyperaccumulator) in As-contaminated Soils. Environ. Poll., 139: 1-8.

Liao JP, Lin XG, Cao ZH, Shi YQ, Wong MH (2003). Interactions between Arbuscular Mycorrhizae and Heavy Metals under Sand Culture Experiment. Chemosphere, 50: 847-853.

Lopez ML, Peralta-Videa JR, Benitez T, Gardea-Torresdey JL (2005). Enhancement of Lead uptake by Alfalfa (*Medicagosativa*) using EDTA and a Plant Growth Promoter. Chemosphere, 61: 595-98.

Malcova R, Vosatka M, Gryndler M (2003). Effects of Inoculation with *Glomus intraradices* on Lead uptake by *Zea mays* L. and *Agrostiscapillaris* L. Appl. Soil Ecol., 23: 55-67.

Mmbr.asm.org.content.

Modern Techniques of Raising Field Crops.

Neubauer U, Nowack B, Furrer G, Schulin R (2000). Heavy Metal Sorption on Clay Minerals affected by the Siderophore desferrioxamine B. Environ. Sci. Technol., 34: 2749-2755.

Nfsm.gov.in.PulsesStatus2016.

O'Sullivan DJ, O'Gara F (1992). Traits of Fluorescent Pseudomonas spp. Involved in Suppression of Plant Root Pathogens. Microbiol. Rev., 56: 662-676.

Sc.org.pk/file.Download.aspk.archived papered.28.

Sharma A, Johri BN (2003a). Combat of Iron-deprivation through a Plant Growth Promoting Fluorescent Pseudomonas Strain GRP3A in Mung Bean (*Vigna radiata* L. Wilzeck). Microbiol. Res., 158.

Sharma A, Johri BN (2003b). Growth Promoting Influence of Siderophore-producing *Pseudomonas* Strains GRP3A and PRS9 in Maize (*Zea mays* L.) under Iron Limiting Conditions. Microbiol. Res., 158: 243-248.

Sheng XF, Xia JJ (2006). Improvement of Rape (*Brassica napus*) Plant Growth and Cadmium uptake by Cadmium-resistant Bacteria. Chemosphere, 64: 1036-1042.

Wang FY, Lin XG, Yin R (2007b). Role of Microbial Inoculation and Chitosan in Phytoextraction of Cu, Zn, Pb and Cd by *Elsholtzia splendense* a Field Case. Enviro. Pollu., 147: 248-255.

Web.inflibnet.ac.in/ojs/index. kJAS/articles.

Whiting SN, de Souza MP, Terry N (2001). Rhizosphere Bacteria Mobilize Zn for Hyperaccumulation by *Thlaspi caerulescens*. Enviro. Sci. Technol., 35: 3144-3150.

Wu QT, Deng JC, Long XX, Morel JL, Schwartz C (2006). Selection of Appropriate Organic Additives for Enhancing Zn and Cd phytoextraction by hyperaccumulators. J Environ. Sci., 18: 1113-1118.

Wu SC, Luo YM, Cheung KC, Wong MH (2006b). Influence of Bacteria on Pb and Zn Speciation, Mobility and Bioavailability in Soil: A Laboratory Study. Environ. Poll., 144.

www.csum.edu/hcbio27/biotechinology/lec10/lindemanhtml.

www.ncbi.nlm.nih.gov.articles.

www.ncbi.nlm.nih.gov.NCBI.Literature.Pub Med Central(PMC).

www.researchgate.net/file.Post Loader.html?id....assetkey.

www.scholarresearchlibry.com.articles.

www.sciencedirect.com/science/articles/pii.

www.scoop.it.rhizobium-catabollism.

www.tandfonline.com/doi/abs.

www.usa.journals.com/wp-content.

Zaidi S, Usmani S, Singh BR, Musarrat J (2006). Significance of Bacillus Subtilis Strain SJ-101 as a Bioinoculant for Concurrent Plant Growth Promotion and Nickel Accumulation in *Brassicajuncea*. Chemosphere, 64: 991-997.

Pages: 105-125

Stress Tolerance and Plant Productivity

Edited by: Mr. Prasann Kumar and Dr. Pawan Kumar 'Bharti'

ISBN: 978-93-86841-56-8

Edition: 2018

Published by: Discovery Publishing House Pvt. Ltd., New Delhi (India)

7 Arsenic Induced Toxicity in Plants with Special Reference to their Oxidative Damage

Prasann Kumar

ABSTRACT

Arsenic is a chemical element with symbol As and atomic number 33. Arsenic occurs in many minerals, usually in combination with sulfur and metals, but also as a pure elemental crystal. Arsenic is a metalloid. It has various allotropes, but only the gray form is important to the industry.

Key words: Arsenic, Chemical, Density, Elemental

INTRODUCTION

The primary use of metallic arsenic is in alloys of lead (for example, in car batteries and ammunition). Arsenic is a common n type dopant in semi-conductor electronic devices, and the opto electronic compound gallium arsenide is the second most commonly used semi-conductor after doped silicon. Arsenic and its compounds, especially the trioxide, are used in the production of pesticides, treated wood products, herbicides, and insecticides. These applications are declining, however. A few species of bacteria are able to use arsenic compounds as respiratory metabolites. Trace quantities of arsenic are an essential dietary element in rats, hamsters, goats, chickens, and presumably many other species, including humans. However, arsenic poisoning occurs in multicellular life if quantities are larger than needed. Arsenic contamination of groundwater is a problem that affects millions of people across the world.One of the simplest arsenic compounds is the trihydride, the highly toxic, flammable, pyrophoric arsine (AsH_3). This compound is generally regarded as stable, since at room temperature, it decomposes only slowly. At temperatures of 250-300°C decomposition to

Department of Agronomy, School of Agriculture, Lovely Professional University
Jalandhar - 144 411 (Punjab) (India)

arsenic and hydrogen is rapid. Several factors, such as humidity, presence of light and certain catalysts (namely aluminium) facilitate the rate of decomposition. It oxidizes readily in air to form arsenic trioxide and water, and analogous reactions take place with sulfurand selenium instead of oxygen (figure 7.1). Compounds of arsenic resemble in some respects those of phosphorus, which occupies the same group (column) of the periodic table. The most common oxidation states for arsenic are: –3 in the arsenides, which are alloy-like intermetallic compounds, +3 in the arsenites, and +5 in the arsenates and most organoarsenic compounds. Arsenic also bonds readily to itself as seen in the square As_3^{-}4 ions in the mineral skutterudite. In the +3 oxidation state, arsenic is typically pyramidal owing to the influence of the lone pair of electrons (figures 7.1, 7.2, 7.3, 7.4 & 7.5).

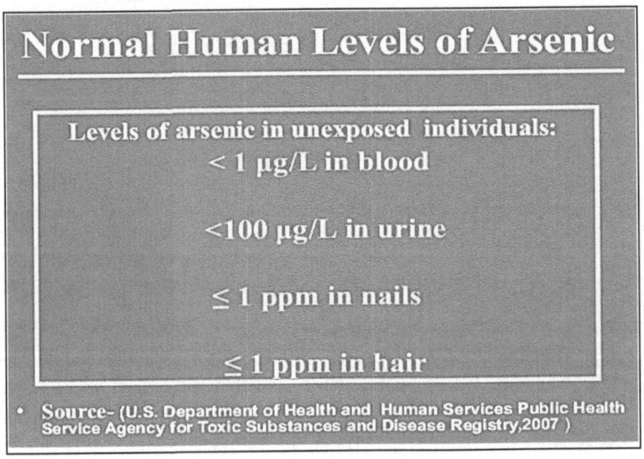

Fig. 7.1: Normal Human Levels of Arsenic

Source: Based on review of literature

Arsenic in the periodic table

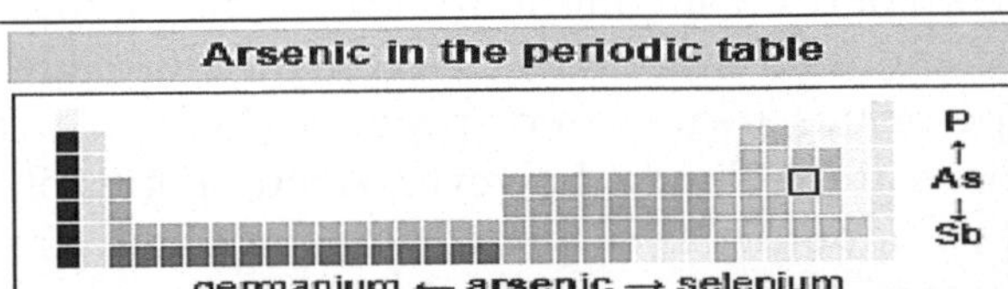

Atomic number (Z)	33
Group, period	group 15 (pnictogens), period 4
Block	p-block
Element category	metalloid
Electron configuration	[Ar] $3d^{10}$ $4s^2$ $4p^3$
Electrons per shell	2, 8, 18, 5

Fig. 7.2: Arsenic in the periodic table

Source: Based on the review of literature

Fig. 7.3: Arsenic and its symbol, atomic number and atomic weight

Source: Based on review of literature

Atomic properties	
Oxidation states	5, 4, 3, 2, 1,[3] −1, −2, −3 (a mildly acidic oxide)
Electronegativity	Pauling scale: 2.18
Ionization energies	1st: 947.0 kJ/mol 2nd: 1798 kJ/mol 3rd: 2735 kJ/mol (more)
Atomic radius	empirical: 119 pm
Covalent radius	119±4 pm
Van der Waals radius	185 pm

Spectral lines

Fig. 7.4: Atomic properties of arsenic

Source: Based on the review of literature

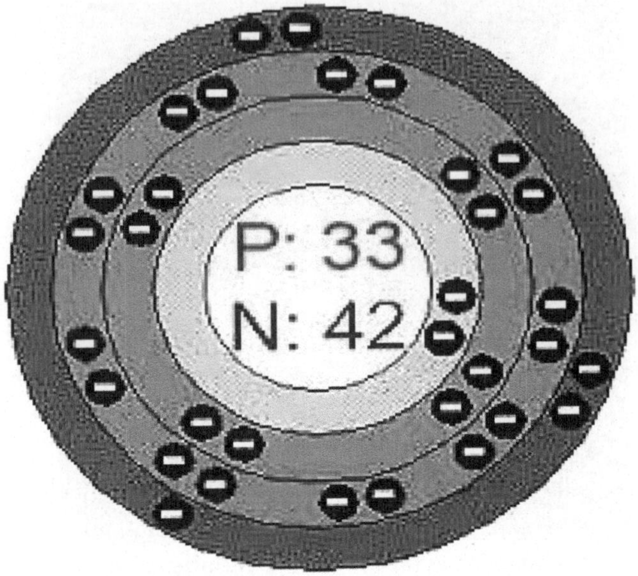

Fig. 7.5: Atomic spectra of the Arsenic

Source: Based on review of literature

Arsenic has a similar electronegativity and ionization energies to its lighter congener phosphorus and as such readily forms covalent molecules with most of the nonmetals. Though stable in dry air, arsenic forms a golden-bronze tarnish upon exposure to humidity which eventually becomes a black surface layer. When heated in air, arsenic oxidizes to arsenic trioxide; the fumes from this reaction have an odor resembling garlic. This odor can be detected on striking arsenide minerals such as arsenopyrite with a hammer. It burns in oxygen to form arsenic trioxide and arsenic pentoxide, which have the same structure as the more well-known phosphorus compounds, and in fluorine to give arsenic pentafluoride. Arsenic (and some arsenic compounds) sublimes upon heating at atmospheric pressure, converting directly to a gaseous form without an intervening liquid state at 887 K (614°C). The triple point is 3.63 MPa and 1,090 K (820°C). Arsenic makes arsenic acid with concentrated nitric acid, arsenous acid with dilute nitric acid, and arsenic trioxide with concentrated sulfuric acid; however, it does not react with water, alkalis, or non-oxidising acids. Arsenic reacts with metals to form arsenides, though these are not ionic compounds containing the As_3^- ion as the formation of such an anion would be highly endothermic and even the group 1 arsenides have properties of intermetallic compounds. Like germanium, selenium, and bromine, which like arsenic succeed the 3d transition series, arsenic is much less stable in the group oxidation state of +5 than its vertical neighbor's phosphorus and antimony, and hence arsenic pentoxide and arsenic acid are potent oxidizers.The two forms of inorganic arsenic, arsenate (AsV) and arsenite

(AsIII), are easily taken up by the cells of the plant root. Once in the cell, AsV can be readily converted to AsIII, the more toxic of the two forms. AsV and AsIII both disrupt plant metabolism, but through distinct mechanisms. AsV is a chemical analog of phosphate that can disrupt at least some phosphate-dependent aspects of metabolism. AsV can be translocated across cellular membranes by phosphate transport proteins, leading to imbalances in phosphate supply. It can compete with phosphate during phosphorylation reactions, leading to the formation of AsV adducts that are often unstable and short-lived. As an example, the formation and rapid autohydrolysis of AsV-ADP sets in place a futile cycle that uncouples photophosphorylation and oxidative phosphorylation, decreasing the ability of cells to produce ATP and carry out normal metabolism. AsIII is a dithiol reactive compound that binds to and potentially inactivates enzymes containing closely spaced cysteine residues or dithiol co-factors. Arsenic exposure generally induces the production of reactive oxygen species that can lead to the production of antioxidant metabolites and numerous enzymes involved in antioxidant defense. Oxidative carbon metabolism, amino acid and protein relationships, and nitrogen and sulfur assimilation pathways are also impacted by As exposure. Readjustment of several metabolic pathways, such as glutathione production, has been shown to lead to increased arsenic tolerance in plants. Species- and cultivar-dependent variation in arsenic sensitivity and the remodeling of metabolite pools that occurs in response to As exposure gives hope that additionalmetabolic pathways associated with As tolerance will be identified (Figure 7.6).

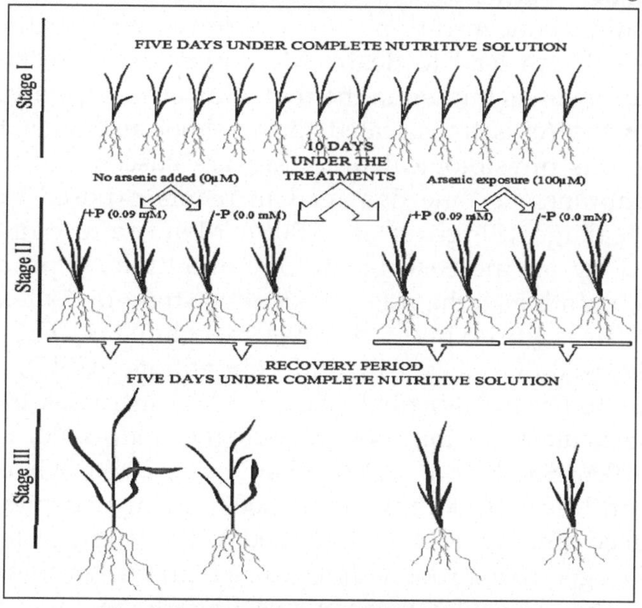

Fig. 7.6: Arsenic exposure in plants

Source: Based on the review of literature

The element arsenic (As) is an environmental toxin that is found naturally in all soils (Cullen and Reimer, 1989; Smedley and Kinniburgh, 2002). The main environmental exposure to As for humans is through contaminated drinking water, for example on the Indian sub-continent (Nordstrom, 2002). Arsenic becomes part of the human solid food chain when crops and fodder become contaminated. The metalloid enters into farming systems through a variety of means that include natural geochemical processes (Smedley and Kinniburgh, 2002), the past and present use of As-based pesticides, mining operations, irrigation with As-contaminated groundwater, and fertilization with municipal solid wastes (Meharg *et al.*, 2009). Arsenic contamination of the human food chain is a world-wide concern that is not restricted by economic boundaries. Rice grain has been identified as a major source of human As outside of contaminated drinking water (Meharg *et al.*, 2009). In rice samples collected from around the world, As was found to be normally distributed in samples from developing economies, but strongly skewed toward high As contents in samples from developed economies (Meharg *et al.*, 2009). Thus, the elimination of As accumulation in grain, especially rice, is a major research goal.Arsenic is non-essential and generally toxic to plants. Roots are usually the first tissue to be exposed to As, where the metalloid inhibits root extension and proliferation. Upon translocation to the shoot, As can severely inhibit plant growth by slowing or arresting expansion and biomass accumulation, as well as compromising plant reproductive capacity through losses in fertility, yield, and fruit production (reviewed by Garg and Singla, 2011). At sufficiently high concentrations, As interferes with critical metabolic processes, which can lead to death. Most plants possess mechanisms to retain much of their As burden in the root. However, a genotype-dependent proportion of the As is translocated to the shoot and other tissues of the plant. Numerous physiological processes are susceptible to As toxicity. Cellular membranes become damaged in plants exposed to As, causing electrolyte leakage (Singh *et al.*, 2006). Membrane damage is often accompanied by an increase in malondialdehyde, a product of lipid peroxidation, pointing to the role of oxidative stress in As toxicity. Arsenic exposure induces antioxidant defense mechanisms. The synthesis of ascorbate, the γ-Glu-Cys-Gly tripeptide glutathione (GSH), and the GSH oligomer ([γ-Glu-Cys]n-Gly) phytochelatin (PC) increases throughout the plant, but particularly in the roots (Schmöger *et al.*, 2000; Li *et al.*, 2004; Geng *et al.*, 2006; Singh *et al.*, 2006; Khan *et al.*, 2009), while anthocyanin accumulates in leaves (Catarecha *et al.*, 2007). Plant transpiration intensity can be reduced (Stoeva and Bineva, 2003). Low As burden causes the number of nitrogen-fixing root nodules to be repressed in soybean (Vázquez *et al.*, 2008). The molecular mechanisms underlying these physiological responses to As exposure are not clear, but have recently attracted increased attention.One of the manyinteresting paradoxes related to As toxicity is that plant growth is stimulated at low As concentrations (Woolson *et al.*, 1971; Carbonell-Barrachina *et al.*, 1997, 1998b; Miteva, 2002; Garg and Singla, 2011). The fact that this phenomena occurs under axenic conditions in cultured plants, such as Arabidopsis thaliana (Chen *et al.*, 2010), indicates that the trait is not based on As disrupting plant-biotic interactions. Instead, it results either from a direct interaction of As with plant metabolism, or from an interaction of As with plant nutrients. While the mechanism is unknown, it has been suggested that the growth benefit arises from As stimulation of Pi uptake (Tu and Ma, 2003) (Figure 7.7).

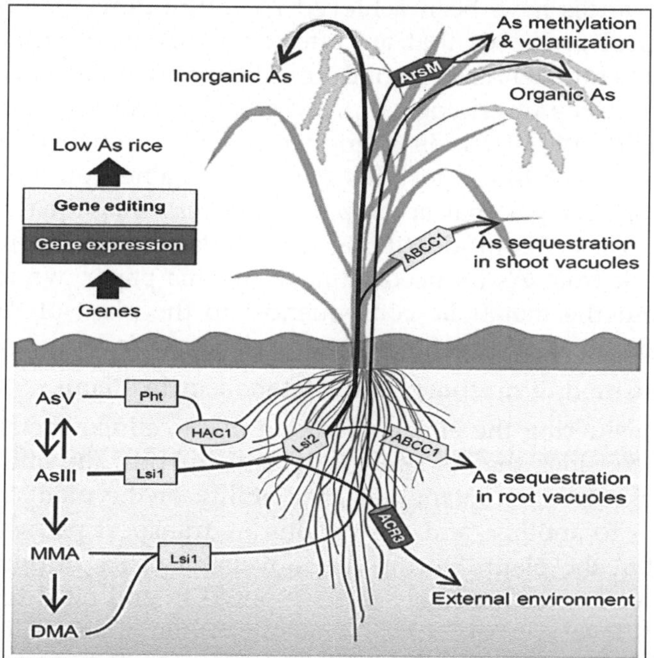

Fig. 7.7: Arsenic mobilization in plants
Source: Based on Review of Literature

There are relatively few species of plants that are naturally As tolerant. Among these are a group of plants including Pteris vittata and other members of the Pteridaceae that hyperaccumulate As (Ma *et al.*, 2001; Visoottiviseth *et al.*, 2002; Ellis *et al.*, 2006; Pickering *et al.*, 2006; Zhao *et al.*, 2009). The growth of these plants is not compromised during times when they are accumulating extremely high levels of As. In contrast to as non-hyperaccumulating plants, hyperaccumulators tend not to restrict as to the roots, instead allowing transfer of the toxicant immediately to the shoots. This is likely to be an important aspect of the hyperaccumulation phenotype. The mechanisms by which these plants are able to hyperaccumulate. As are being elucidated, but it is not entirely clear how they are able to avoid As toxicity while As is actively accumulating to extremely high levels in the leaves. A better understanding of the mechanisms responsible for As resistance and toxicity in plants is needed. A potential outcome of a better understanding would be the production of As-resistant plants for phytoremediation and safe cropping. For soil remediation and contaminated site rehabilitation, a diverse group of resistant plants suitable for growth in a wide-range of environments and able to (hyper) accumulate as in harvestable biomass are needed. In contrast, for safe cropping in areas where land and/or groundwater are contaminated, As-resistant plants that prevent as accumulation in the harvested plant product are required. Significant advances have been achieved recently in our understanding of the physiological processes that are affected by as exposure. We are also making progress unraveling some of the biochemical mechanisms underlying the disruption of key physiological processes. Our understanding of As an inducer of oxidative stress is a good example of such a biochemical mechanism. In recent times, insights have been gained on identifying the gene expression changes that accompany As stress. One area where much remains to be learned is in identifying the cellular metabolic processes that are most at risk from As-induced damage. In this paper, we review what is known about the metabolic consequences to the plant of As exposure, identifying key areas where further research is needed.

Arsenic Acquisition, Transport, and Metabolism in Plants

When considering the effects of As on plant cellular metabolism, it is important to consider the As species present in soils, the ability of these chemical species to enter plant cells, the ability of the plant to transform one As species to another, and the various As transport pathways that are available within the plant. During the movement of As through the plant tissues, some cell types are likely to be exposed to and need to respond to relatively high levels of particular As species, while others will be exposed to only low levels of the metalloid. The cell types that are exposed to high levels of particular As species is a defining difference between As hyperaccumulators and non-accumulators. While non-accumulators tend to retain As in root cells, with much lower concentrations of As in shoot cells, the hyperaccumulators have incredibly high concentrations of As in the cells of aerial tissues compared to the root. Understanding the responses of different cell types to the various As species to which they are exposed and internalize will likely be important in designing ways of producing plants that are better suited to deal with high environmental As burdens. The speciation, acquisition, transport, and metabolism of As have been extensively reviewed recently (Zhao *et al.*, 2009, 2010; Zhu and Rosen, 2009; Mendoza-Cózatl *et al.*, 2011), so only a brief overview of these topics will be given here to provide a context for the discussion on the consequences of As exposure to cellular metabolism (Figure 7.8).

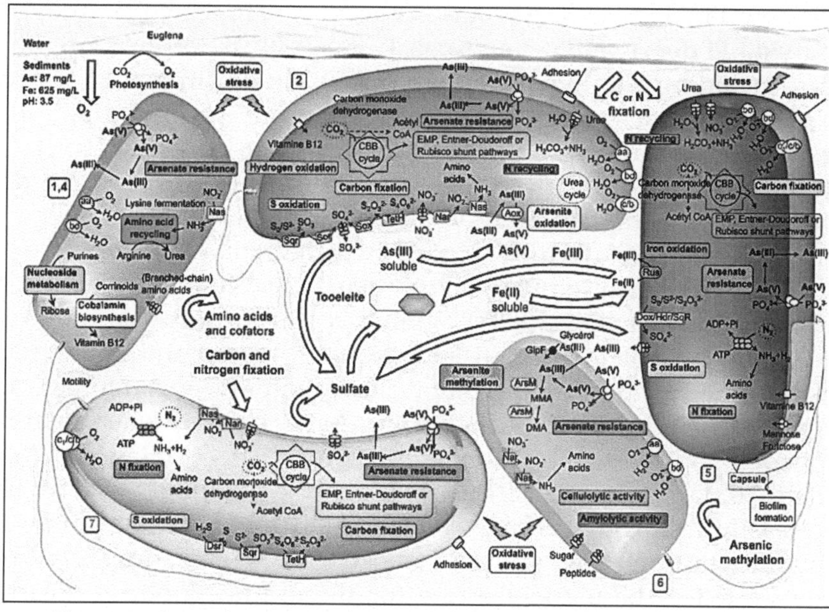

Fig. 7.8: Arsenic acquisition and transportation in plants

Source: Based on review of literature

Arsenic Acquisition and Transport

In the environment, As can exist as inorganic or organic species. Of the two inorganic forms, the more highly oxidized arsenate (AsV) predominates in aerobic environments, while the more highly reduced arsenite (AsIII) is the predominant form in anaerobic environments, such as flooded rice paddy fields. Microbes are able to biotransform inorganic As to organic forms (Zhao *et al.*, 2010). The organic species of AsV that are found at low concentrations in most soils include monomethylarsonic acid (MMAV – superscript denotes As oxidation state), dimethylarsinic acid (DMAV) and trimethylarsine oxide (TMAOV). The concentrations of the methylated species are higher in anaerobic soils than in aerobic soils (Abedin *et al.*, 2002). The corresponding mono-, di-, and trimethylated derivatives of AsIII (MMAIII, DMAIII, TMAIII) are volatile. They are produced in the soil through processes likely to be limited by the availability of MMAV (Mestrot *et al.*, 2011). Like AsV and AsIII, the methylated forms of As are phytotoxic (Zhao *et al.*, 2010).AsV is an analog of inorganic phosphate (Pi) and is easily transported across the plasmalemma by Pi transporter (PHT) proteins (Ullrich-Eberius *et al.*, 1989; Meharg and Macnair, 1990, 1991, 1992; Wu *et al.*, 2011). AsV and Pi compete for uptake through the same transport systems in As hyperaccumulators (Wang *et al.*, 2002; Tu and Ma, 2003), As-tolerant non-hyperaccumulators (Meharg and Macnair, 1992; Bleeker *et al.*, 2003) and As-sensitive non-accumulators (Abedin *et al.*, 2002; Esteban *et al.*, 2003).

Under low Pi conditions, AsV may outcompete Pi for entry into the plant, amplifying Pi deprivation symptoms. Conversely, Pi fertilization can protect plants, including the hyperaccumulator P. vittata, from AsV toxicity (Tu and Ma, 2003). Increasing or decreasing the rate of Pi and As uptake by increasing or decreasing PHT protein amount or activity at the plasmamembrane through genetic means can also increase or decrease, respectively, the toxicity of AsV (Shin *et al.*, 2004; González *et al.*, 2005; Catarecha *et al.*, 2007; Wu *et al.*, 2011). In the Arabidopsis pht1–3 mutant, which has a compromised Pi uptake system, As accumulates without causing toxicity (Catarecha *et al.*, 2007), similar to the Pi fertilization effect in P. vittata. The lack of toxicity in such non-hyperaccumulating systems has been explained by postulating that a slower rate of As accumulation allows the plant to detoxify the incoming As before defense systems are overloaded and the toxicant can exert its toxic effects (Hartley-Whitaker *et al.*, 2001a; Catarecha *et al.*, 2007).Once inside the plant cell, AsV can probably move easily from one cellular compartment to another, crossing internal membranes through the various Pi transporters. For example, AsV has been demonstrated to be a co-substrate for three mitochondrial dicarboxylate transporters, proteins localized to the inner mitochondrial membrane and responsible for dicarboxylate exchange with co-substrates such as Pi, between the cytosol and the organelle matrix (Palmieri *et al.*, 2008). The outcome of this rapid movement would be the rapid equilibrium of As throughout the cell, exposing all parts of cellular metabolism to the toxicant.AsV can be found in the xylem, having most likely been loaded into the xylem vessels by PHT proteins (Catarecha *et al.*, 2007; Zhao *et al.*, 2010; Mendoza-Cózatl *et al.*, 2011; Wu *et al.*, 2011). However, roots of As non-hyperaccumulators have the ability to strongly retain As. In Arabidopsis, only about 3% of the As taken up by the root was translocated to the shoot (Quaghebeur and Rengel, 2003). Similar results have been found for other plants (Lomax *et al.*, 2012). Of the small portion of As that is translocated, no more than 40% would be expected to be in the form of AsV, based on As speciation determinations in a number of species (Zhao *et al.*, 2009). AsIII is able to enter root cells through nodulin26-like intrinsic proteins (NIPs, Meharg and Jardine, 2003; Bienert *et al.*, 2008; Isayenkov and Maathuis, 2008; Ma *et al.*, 2008). These proteins belong to the aquaporin family of major intrinsic proteins. In rice roots, the OsNIP2;1/OsLsi1 silicon transporter has been implicated as the major AsIII uptake protein, while AsIII efflux from rice root cells to the xylem is through the OsLsi2 silicon transporter (Ma *et al.*, 2008). The localization of OsLsi2 to the proximal side of epidermal and endodermal cells (Ma *et al.*, 2007), and OsLsi1 to the distal side of the same cells (Ma *et al.*, 2006) is an elegant example of the heterogeneous distribution of proteins in a membrane providing directionality to solute transport across cells and tissues. Other types of proteins may facilitate the transport AsIII into cells. In yeast, the majority of AsIII uptake occurs through hexose permeases (Liu *et al.*, 2004). While plants have proteins with strong homology to the yeast hexose permeases, it is not known if they provide a path for AsIII entry into plant cells (Figure 7.9).

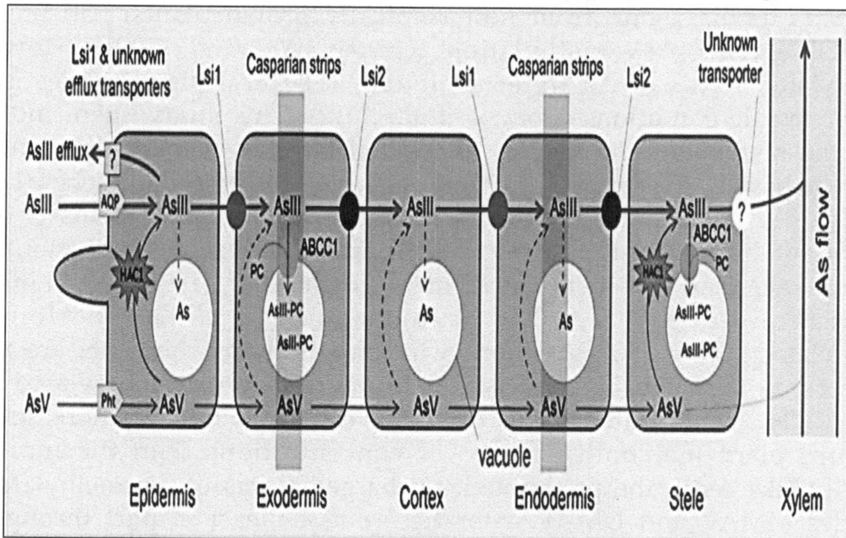

Fig. 7.9: Accumulation of Arsenic in plants sample

Source: Based on the review of literature

In As hyperaccumulating species, such as P. vittata, As is not immobilized in the roots, but is instead rapidly transported as AsIII through the xylem to the fronds (Lombi *et al.*, 2002; Pickering *et al.*, 2006; Su *et al.*, 2008). In the fronds, AsIII is sequestered as free AsIII in the vacuole (Lombi *et al.*, 2002; Pickering *et al.*, 2006), where it accumulates to extremely high levels (Zhao *et al.*, 2009). It has been shown that PvACR3 is involved in the vacuolar sequestration of AsIII (Indriolo *et al.*, 2010). This protein is a homolog of the yeast ScACR3p protein, a plasmamembrane protein responsible for the efflux of AsIII from the yeast cell. In P. vittata, the PvACR3 protein still acts to efflux AsIII from the cytosol, but instead of delivering the AsIII to the outside of the cell, PvACR3 resides on the vacuolar membrane and transports the AsIII into the vacuole. Single-copy ACR3 genes are found in moss, lycophytes, ferns, and gymnosperms, but not in angiosperms, which may help explain the lack of As hyperaccumulators among the angiosperms (Indriolo *et al.*, 2010). Plants have been found to contain methylated As species (Marin *et al.*, 1992; Quaghebeur and Rengel, 2003; Raab *et al.*, 2005, 2007b; Xu *et al.*, 2007). For example, when fed AsIII or AsV, roots of Helianthus annuus (sunflower) contained up to 14 extractable and separable forms of As, of which eight were identified (Raab *et al.*, 2005). Among these forms were MMAV and DMAV and a MMAIII-PC complex. The finding of methylated As species inside plant tissues brought the question of their origins to recent attention. Several reports using non-axenically grown plants concluded that plants were able to methylate AsV to form MMAV and DMAV (Raab *et al.*, 2005, 2007b; Xu *et al.*, 2007). Moreover, it was reported that leaf extracts of Agrostis tenuis, again from non-axenically grown plants, had an AsV-inducible AsIII/AsV methylation activity (Wu *et al.*, 2002). However, methylated forms of As were not found in several plant species grown under axenic conditions (Lomax *et al.*, 2012). This study, then, indicates that the methylated derivatives of As that have been found in plants are likely to have been acquired after biotransformation by soil microbes (Lomax *et al.*, 2012). The question of the source of methylated forms of As is important, as methylated forms of AsIII are more reactive and cytotoxic to animal cells than non-methylated forms (Styblo *et al.*, 1997, 2000; Lin *et al.*, 1999; Schwerdtle *et al.*, 2003; Naranmandura *et al.*, 2011). Moreover, methylated forms of AsV common in terrestrial environments are also a concern as they can be reduced to the more cytotoxic methylated AsIII forms. Thus, methylated forms of As have the potential to more strongly disrupt plant metabolism at lower concentrations than the inorganic species.Like AsIII, the protonated, uncharged forms of the methylated As species MMAV and DMAV enter rice roots at least in part through the aquaporin channel OsLsi1 (Li *et al.*, 2009). However, the rate of uptake for MMAV and DMAV is much slower than that of AsIII or AsV (Abedin *et al.*, 2002; Raab *et al.*, 2007a; Abbas and Meharg, 2008). In contrast, the mobility within the plant of MMAV and DMAV appears to be substantially greater than that of AsIII or AsV (Marin *et al.*, 1992; Burló *et al.*, 1999; Raab *et al.*, 2007a; Li *et al.*, 2009; Carey *et al.*, 2010, 2011). While OsLsi1 has been implicated in the uptake of both MMAV and DMAV, OsLsi2 does not seem to be involved in their efflux (Li *et al.*, 2009). In animal systems, MMAIII is also transported through aquaporins (Liu *et al.*, 2006); however, it is not yet known whether OsLsi1, OsLsi2 or AsIII transporters are able to transport MMAIII. Arsenic can also be metabolized by various organisms to form arsenocholine, arsenobetaine, and arseno-sugars. These compounds have been detected in some terrestrial plants (reviewed by Dembitsky and Levitsky, 2004). However, it has not been demonstrated that these compounds can be produced by the plant, or whether they are simply taken up in those forms from the soil. The effects of these compounds on plant metabolism are largely unknown.

The results from a number of hydroponic experiments agree that As phytotoxicity depends on the chemical species supplied to the plant, but disagree on the identity of the most phytotoxic form of As (Marin *et al.*, 1992; Carbonell-Barrachina *et al.*, 1998a; Abbas and Meharg, 2008). These hydroponic experiments provide the clearest insights into the potency of externally supplied As on whole plant growth because they eliminate the complex and confounding phytoavailability issues that arise from differences in the mobility of various As species through the diverse growth substrates. The studies generally agree with the hydroponic survey of 46 different plant species (Raab *et al.*, 2007a) that the uptake of As by plants has the order AsIII > AsV > MMAV > DMAV, while translocation from the roots to the rest of the plant has the order DMAV > MMAV > AsV ≥ AsIII. However, no one As form appears to be consistently most phytotoxic. In two Spartina species, where the order of uptake was AsIII > AsV ≈ MMAV > DMAV, the order of phytotoxicity was DMAV ≈ MMAV > AsIII ≈ AsV (Carbonell-Barrachina et al., 1998a). This would suggest that DMAV, with lowest uptake and high phytotoxicity, exerted the most highly toxic effects within the plant. In contrast, the uptake order in rice was AsIII > MMAV > AsV > DMAV, an order that is similar to the order of phytotoxicity, which was MMAV > AsIII > AsV = DMAV (Marin *et al.*, 1992). Finally, the order for phytotoxicity in maize, a species with the typical order for uptake (Raab *et al.*, 2007a), was AsV > AsIII > DMAV (Abbas and Meharg, 2008) (figure 7.10).

Fig. 7.10: Arsenic contamination in rice and cooked rice

Source: Based on the review of literature

The inconsistent order of phytotoxicity of the various As species could be an indication that As has interacted differently with the available nutrients, or that the phytotoxic form of As is plant species dependent. Alternatively, the apparent inconsistency of the above results may be due to our incomplete understanding of the relative importance of the various.

As species to the mechanism of as toxicity. After all, the mechanism through which As causes phytotoxicity has not been definitively identified and the exact species of As that is the primary cause of toxicity is unknown. In this regard, the finding of MMAIII in plants (Li *et al.*, 2009; Ye *et al.*, 2010; Lomax *et al.*, 2012) is particularly intriguing. This As species is up to 18 times more cytotoxic to animal cells than AsIII (Styblo *et al.*, 2000; Naranmandura *et al.*, 2011). The phytotoxicity of MMAIII has not been tested.Another issue that needs to be included when considering the toxicology of As is that some forms of As may be under-represented or even missing from the evaluations of As speciation in plants. In a study on sunflower, 15-20% of the total tissue As was not recovered from the plant tissue, depending on the tissue and post-harvest storage time (Raab *et al.*, 2005). In beetroot, As was nearly quantitatively extractable from tissues with low As burden, but in tissues with higher As burdens, up to 75% of the As was not extracted (Száková *et al.*, 2010). Perhaps the speciation of this missing As, or indeed the molecules to which it may be bound, will give us important insights into the underlying mechanism of As toxicity. The above arguments indicate that we need a fuller understanding of the action of As at the cellular level. The structural similarities of AsV and Pi allow this form of the metalloid to substitute for Pi in biochemical reactions, potentially disrupting vital cellular processes. On the other hand, AsIII is highly reactive toward thiol groups, as are MMAIII and DMAIII. The binding of AsIII to the thiol groups of proteins or enzyme co-factors may alter or inhibit their activity, also exposing cellular processes to risk. Oxidative stress brought about by the inevitable production of reactive oxygen species (ROS) that occurs during As exposure has most recently gained favor as the main driver of As toxicity in plants. However, which cellular processes are most sensitive to As toxicity and which As species pose the greatest threats to plant cell health remain unclear.

ROLE OF ARSENIC IN NITROGEN METABOLISM IN PLANT

Biological nitrogen fixation, including the contribution made by symbioses in the root nodules of legumes, supplies a large proportion of the nitrogen in biological systems. The exposure of alfalfa root systems supporting well-established N_2-fixing symbioses with rhizobia to AsV demonstrated that symbiotic N_2fixation is sensitive to As toxicity (Porter and Sheridan, 1981). Moreover, alfalfa either grown in As-contaminated soil or exposed to AsIII had less than half of the total number of root nodules formed in the absence of added As (Carrasco *et al.*, 2005; Pajuelo *et al.*, 2008). Under controlled conditions, this reduction was due to a 90% decrease in the number of rhizobial infections (Pajuelo *et al.*, 2008). The use of an As-resistant strain of rhizobia in these experiments demonstrated that the decreased establishment of the symbiosis was not due to bacterial death. Rather, plant traits including root necrosis, root hair damage, and a shorter length of the root zone that was subject to infection were implicated (Pajuelo *et al.*, 2008). Transcript analysis indicated that AsIII exposure interferes with the expression of genes involved in early nodule development (Lafuente *et al.*, 2010). Together, these results suggest that As contamination of soil has the potential to strongly decrease N2 fixation in ecosystems involving legume-rhizobium symbioses. AsV also seems to disrupt N assimilation. Non-legumes obtain N from the soil predominantly as nitrate (NO''_3) or ammonium (NH_+^4) Inorganic N in the form of NH^+_4 is assimilated by the combined action of glutamine synthase (GS) and glutamate synthase (GOGAT) for entry into the organic molecule pool as glutamate (Foyer *et al.*, 2011). Roots of AsV-treated rice had decreased amounts of transcripts for a NO^-_3 transporter and for an NH+4 transporter (Norton *et al.*, 2008). Another experiment using whole rice seedlings also found a decrease in transcripts for a different NH^+_4 transporter (Chakrabarty *et al.*, 2009). The amount of nitrate reductase was repressed in whole seedlings of rice (Chakrabarty *et al.*, 2009), but induced in whole seedlings of Arabidopsis (Abercrombie *et al.*, 2008). Nitrate reductase, in combination with nitrite reductase, supplies NH^+_4 to GS for N assimilation. GS protein amount was lower in rice roots treated with AsV (Ahsan *et al.*, 2008). Although it is not clear if it was the cytosolic or plastid isoform that was reduced, the chloroplastic form was sensitive to oxidative fragmentation by hydroxyl radical (•OH; Ishida *et al.*, 2002), a ROS species produced during AsV exposure. While the details are far from clear, it appears that AsV interferes with both the supply of inorganic N to the assimilation pathway and the activity of the pathway itself.Arsenic exposure has been reported to cause dramatic changes in amino acid pools (Dwivedi *et al.*, 2010; Pavlík M. *et al.*, 2010). A key question is the extent to which the changes in the amounts of these amino acids is due to changes in amino acid biosynthesis or changes to protein metabolism. Exposure to As caused decreases in total plant protein abundance in P. ensiformis and P. vittata (Singh *et al.*, 2006), in total shoot protein abundance in red clover (Mascher *et al.*, 2002) and in soluble protein in maize (Stoeva *et al.*, 2003). Proteomic studies demonstrated that Rubisco, with its high capacity due to its great abundance to store N in the form of amino acids, can be targeted for destruction in AsV treated plants (Duquesnoy *et al.*, 2009; Ahsan *et al.*, 2010; Bona *et al.*, 2010). In Lemna minor, total protein increased at low AsV supply, but decreased at high As supply (Duman *et al.*, 2010), a relationship that may be linked to the stimulation of growth at low As supply that has been observed for numerous plants (Woolson *et al.*, 1971; Carbonell-Barrachina *et al.*, 1997, 1998b;Miteva, 2002; Chen *et al.*, 2010). Protein degradation has been recognized as an important source of respiratory carbon when carbohydrate levels are low (Araújo *et al.*, 2011). Thus, the lower protein abundance that generally accompanies As exposure, coupled with a likely As-induced decrease in carbohydrate metabolism that would hinder the biosynthesis of amino acids, suggests that any changes in the size of amino acid pools would be due to amino acids flowing from protein degradation.A number of genes involved in N transport appear to change expression in response to As. Amino acid transporters were down-regulated in response to AsV in roots and seedlings of rice (Norton *et al.*, 2008; Chakrabarty *et al.*, 2009). Interestingly, amino acid transporter gene transcript levels were not influenced by AsIII (Chakrabarty *et al.*, 2009), suggesting an area where the different modes of action of these compounds are manifested. Peptide and oligopeptide transporters have also been reported to be AsV responsive in rice, but reports disagree on the direction (Norton *et al.*, 2008; Chakrabarty *et al.*, 2009). Clearly, more work is needed in understanding the movements of N-containing compounds through the plant tissues during As exposure.

ROLE OF ARSENIC IN CARBON METABOLISM

A main effect of AsV on plant carbon metabolism is in stimulating the accumulation of ascorbate (Srivastava *et al.*, 2005; Singh *et al.*, 2006; Khan *et al.*, 2009), presumably to bolster protection against ROS. The effects of As on primary carbon metabolism in plants is largely unknown. However, the transcriptional profiles of genes encoding proteins involved in carbon metabolism are largely unaffected both in Arabidopsis and rice (Abercrombie *et al.*, 2008; Norton *et al.*, 2008; Chakrabarty *et al.*, 2009). Proteomic studies in the non-hyperaccumulating plants rice and maize (Requejo and Tena, 2005, 2006; Ahsan *et al.*, 2008, 2010) have shown that there are some changes in the abundance of proteins that participate in glycolysis and the citric acid cycle, but the changes are not consistent or systemic throughout either pathway. There are too few studies to fully understand the relevance of the changes that are observed. However, it appears that As does not have strong effects on gene expression related to carbon metabolism. This suggests that plant metabolism has sufficient plasticity to maintain adequate carbon flow without the need to adjust enzyme amounts in these central pathways. Robust assessment of the metabolite pools associated with primary metabolism is needed in plant tissues exposed to As to address this point directly.At the level of carbon input into metabolism, AsV, AsIII, and MMAIII application are all able to inhibit net photosynthesis (Porter and Sheridan, 1981; Marin *et al.*, 1993; Stoeva and Bineva, 2003). The light harvesting apparatus can be affected, with decreases seen in chlorophyll content (Porter and Sheridan, 1981; Stoeva and Bineva, 2003; Singh *et al.*, 2006; Rahman *et al.*, 2007; Duman *et al.*, 2010) and photosystem II activity (Stoeva and Bineva, 2003). These results are largely consistent across studies and suggest that As may reduce photosynthetic electron flow through the thylakoid membranes, decreasing the potential to produce ATP and NADPH, both of which are needed to fuel the carbon fixation reactions. Adding to this potential energy deficiency would be the likelihood of uncoupling thylakoid electron transport from ATP synthesis by the replacement of Pi by AsV in photophosphorylation (Avron and Jagendorf, 1959; Watling-Payne and Selwyn, 1974). On the other hand, chlorophyll can be used as a source of metabolic carbon when carbohydrate availability is low (Araújo *et al.*, 2011). This then raises the question of whether chlorophyll degradation limits photosynthesis or whether limitations on the supply of photosynthetic carbon trigger chlorophyll degradation (figure 7.11).

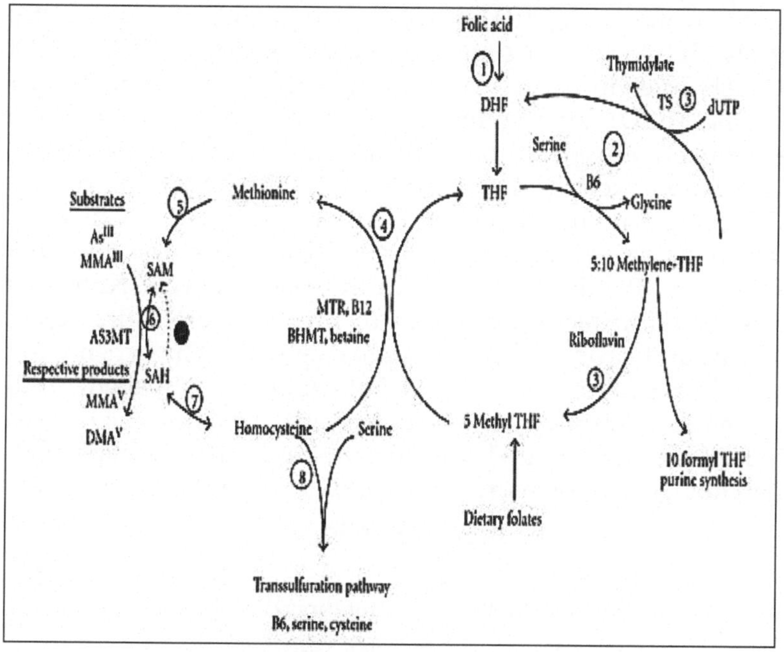

Fig. 7.11: Arsenic biochemistry in the plants

Source: Based on the review of literature

On the carbon fixation side of photosynthesis, the Rubisco large subunit content of rice leaves decreased with AsV treatment (Ahsan *et al.*, 2010). The Rubisco large subunit is encoded by the plastid DNA (Bock, 2007). Therefore, the decreased abundance of this protein not only indicates that As interferes with carbon fixation capacity, but raises the question of whether As also interferes with chloroplast DNA gene expression. However, in contrast to the decrease in Rubisco large subunit amount in rice, Rubisco small subunit transcripts increased in AsV-treated Arabidopsis (Abercrombie *et al.*, 2008). Whether the increased transcript abundance results in more Rubisco small subunit, or is a response to a decrease in active Rubisco is not yet known. AsIII inhibits the light activation of photosynthetic CO_2 fixation in isolated pea chloroplasts (Marques and Anderson, 1986). The inhibition is at the level of the light activation of enzyme activities associated with the reductive pentose phosphate pathway. While the extent of the effects of As on photosynthetic carbon metabolism are not fully understood, it appears likely that the toxicant decreases the amount of carbon available to the plant through decreased CO_2 fixation.

CONCLUSION

Photorespiration is a prominent path of carbon flow in most plants and includes the activity of the lipoamide-containing GDC. The dithiol group of dihydrolipoamide is a well known target for AsIII binding in animals (Dixon, 1996). Addition of this co-factor to animal cells is able to ameliorate AsIII toxicity (Wang *et al.*, 2011). In plants, lipoamide is found not only in GDC, but also in the four enzyme complexes mtPDC, ptPDC, OGDC, and BCOADC. All five lipoamide-containing complexes contain lipoamide dehydrogenase (LPD), an enzyme that catalyzes the transfer of electrons from the reduced dihydrolipoamide co-factor to NAD+ as part of the enzymatic reaction cycle of the complex. Like the lipoamide co-factor, the plant LPD enzymes are inactivated by AsIII, but not AsV (Chen *et al.*, 2010), presumably because of the binding of AsIII to the absolutely conserved dithiol present in LPD that takes part in the reaction cycle. Knock-out lines of Arabidopsis with decreased levels of mtLPD were more sensitive to AsV treatment and produced much higher levels of Gly when exposed to AsV than wild-type lines (Chen and Finnegan, unpublished), indicating that LPD is an important target for As toxicity in plants. LPD increased in amount in leaves of AsV-treated rice (Ahsan *et al.*, 2010), perhaps in response to the inhibition of one or more of the LPD containing complexes.

REFERENCES

Abou-Shanab RAI., Angle JS., Chaney RL (2006). Bacterial Inoculants Affecting Nickel uptake by *Alyssum murale* from Low, Moderate and High Ni Soils. Soil Biol. Biochem., 38: 2882-2889.

Agropedia.iitk.ac.in.node.

All India Coordinate Pulse Improvement Project.

Baum C, Hrynkiewicz K, Leinweber P, Meissner R (2006). Heavy-metal Mobilization and uptake by Mycorrhizal and Nonmycorrhizal Willows (*Salixdasyclados*). J Plant Nut. Soil Sci., 169: 516-522.

BB Bohlool,JK Ladha, DP Garrity, T George- for Sustainable Agriculture, 1992-Springer.

Bi YL, Li XL, Christie P (2003a). Influence of Early Stages of Arbuscular Mycorrhiza on uptake of Zinc and Phosphorus by Red Clover from a Low Phosphorus Soil Amended with Zinc and Phosphorus. Chemosphere, 50: 831-837.

Bijus.com.biology.rhizobium.

Bossier P, Hofte M, Verstraete W (1988). Ecological Significance of Siderophores in Soil. Adv. Microbiol. Ecol., 10: 385-414.

Braud A, Jezequel K, Vieille E, Tritter A, Lebeau T (2006b). Changes in Extractability of Cr and Pb in a Polycontaminated Soil after Bioaugmentation with Microbial Producers of Biosurfactants, Organic Acids and Siderophores. Water, Air and Soil Pollu., 6: 261-279.

Byjus.com.biology.rhizobium.

Cao A, Carucci A, Lai T, La Colla P, Tamburini E (2007). Effect of Biodegradable Chelating Agents on Heavy Metals Phytoextraction with *Mirabilis jalapa* and on its Associated Bacteria. Europ. J Soil Biol., 43: 200-206.

Carlot M, Giacomini A, Casella S (2002). Aspects of Plant Microbe Interactions in Heavy Metal Polluted Soil. Acta Biotechno., 22: 13-20.

Chen B, Shen H, Li X, Feng G, Christie P (2004a). Effects of EDTA Application and Arbuscular Mycorrhizal Colonization on Growth and Zinc uptake by Maize (*Zea mays* L.) in Soil Experimentally Contaminated with Zinc. Plant and Soil, 261: 219-229.

Chen B, Shen H, Li X, Feng G, Christie P (2004a). Effects of EDTA Application and Arbuscular Mycorrhizal Colonization on Growth and Zinc Uptake by Maize (*Zea mays* L.) in Soil Experimentally Contaminated with Zinc. Plant and Soil, 261: 219-229.

Chen BD, Li X., Tao HQ, Christie P, Wong MH (2003). The Role of Arbuscular Mycorrhiza in Zinc uptake by Red Clover Growing in a Calcareous Soil Spiked with Various Quantities of Zinc. Chemosphere, 50: 839-846.

Chen YX, Wang YP, Lin Q, Luo YM (2005). Effect of Copper-tolerant Rhizosphere Bacteria on Mobility of Copper in Soil and Copper Accumulation by *Elsholtzia splendens*. Environ. Intl., 31: 861-866.

Citesurx..ist..pus.edu/viewdoc/download.

Citterio S, Prato N, Fumagalli P, Aina R, Massa N, Santagostino A, Sgorbati S, Berta G (2005). The Arbuscular Mycorrhizal Fungus *Glomus mosseae* Induces Growth and Metal Accumulation Changes in *Cannabissativa* L. Chemosphere, 59: 21-29.

Di Gregorio S, Barbafieri M, Lampis S, Sanangelantoni AM, Tassi E, Vallini G (2006). Combined Application of Triton X-100 and Sinorhizobium sp. Pb002 Inoculum for the Improvement of Lead Phytoextraction by *Brassica juncea* in EDTA Amended Soil. Chemosphere, 63: 293-299.

Di Simine CD, Sayer JA, Gadd GM (1998). Solubilization of Zinc Phosphate by a Strain of *Pseudomonas fluorescens* Isolated from a Forest Soil. Biology and Fertility of Soils, 28: 87-94.

Dubbin WE, Louise Ander E (2003). Influence of Microbial Hydroxamate Siderophores on Pb(II) Desorption from a-FeOOH. Appl. Geochem., 18: 1751-1756.

Duijff BJ, Bakker PAHM, Schippers B (1991). Influence of Pseudobactin- 358 on the Iron Nutrition of Plants. In: Sixth International Fe Symposium.

Duss F, Mozafar A, Oertli JJ, Jaeggi W (1986). Effect of Bacteria on the Iron uptake by Axenically-cultured Roots of Fe-efficient and Fe-inefficient Tomatoes (*Lycopersiconesculentum* Mill.). J Plant Nut., 9: 587-598.

El-Kherbawy M, Angle JS, Heggo A, Chaney RL (1989). Soil pH, Rhizobia, and Vesicular-arbuscular Mycorrhizae Inoculation Effects on Growth and Heavy Metal uptake of Alfalfa (*Medicago sativa* L.). Biol. Fert. Soils, 8: 61-65.

Glick BR (2003). Phytoremediation: Synergistic use of Plants and Bacteria to Clean up the Environment. Biotechnol. Adv., 21: 383-393.

Guo Y, George E, Marschner H (1996). Contribution of an Arbuscular Mycorrhizal Fungus to the Uptake of Cadmium and Nickel in Bean and Maize Plants. Plant and Soil, 184: 195-205.

GWO'hara. RM Daniel- Soil Biology and Biochemistry, 1985-Elsevier.

Heggo A, Angle JS, Chaney RL (1990). Effects of Vesicular Arbuscular Mycorrhizal Fungi on Heavy Metal uptake by Soybean. Soil Biol. Biochem., 22: 856-869.

HH Zahra-Microbiology and Molecular Biology Reviews,1999-Am Soc Microbiol.

Hoflich G, Wiehe W, Kuhn G (1994). Plant Growth Stimulation by Inoculation with Symbiotic and Association Rhizosphere Microorganisms. Experientia 50.

Hofte M, Buysens S, Koedam N, Cornelis P (1993). Zinc Affects Siderophore-mediated High Affinity Iron uptake Systems in the Rhizosphere *Pseudomonas aeruginosa* 7NSK2. BioMetals 6: 85-91.

http://www.rsc.org/periodic-table/element/33/arsenic

https://brainly.in.Secondary school.Science.

https://en.wikipedia.org/wiki/Arsenic

https://www.hindawi.com.journals.ija.

https://www.ncbi.nlm.nih.gov.articles.

https://www.ncbi.nlm.nih.gov/pmc/articles/PMC3368394/

Joner EJ, Leyval C (1997). Uptake of 109Cd by Roots and Hyphae of a *Glomusmosseae/ Trifoliumsubterraneum* Mycorrhiza from Soil Amended with High and Low Concentrations. New Phytologist., 135: 353-360.

Jurkevitch E, Hadar Y, Chen Y (1988). Involvement of Bacterial Siderophores in the Remedy of Lime-induced Chlorosis in Peanut. Soil Sci. Soc. Amer. J., 52: 1032-1037.

Kayser G, Korckritz T, Markert B (2001). Bioleaching for the Decontamination of Heavy Metals. Wasser and Boden., 53: 54-58.

Leung HM, Ye ZH, Wong MH. (2006). Interactions of Mycorrhizal Fungi with *Pteris vittata* (As hyperaccumulator) in As-contaminated Soils. Environ. Poll., 139: 1-8.

Liao JP, Lin XG, Cao ZH, Shi YQ, Wong MH (2003). Interactions between Arbuscular Mycorrhizae and Heavy Metals under Sand Culture Experiment. Chemosphere, 50: 847-853.

Lopez ML, Peralta-Videa JR, Benitez T, Gardea-Torresdey JL (2005). Enhancement of Lead uptake by Alfalfa (*Medicagosativa*) using EDTA and a Plant Growth Promoter. Chemosphere, 61: 595-98.

Malcova R, Vosatka M, Gryndler M (2003). Effects of Inoculation with *Glomus intraradices* on Lead uptake by *Zea mays* L. and *Agrostiscapillaris* L. Appl. Soil Ecol., 23: 55-67.

Mmbr.asm.org.content.

Modern Techniques of Raising Field Crops.

Neubauer U, Nowack B, Furrer G, Schulin R (2000). Heavy Metal Sorption on Clay Minerals Affected by the Siderophore Desferrioxamine B. Environ. Sci. Technol., 34: 2749-2755.

Nfsm.gov.in.PulsesStatus2016.

O'Sullivan DJ, O'Gara F (1992). Traits of Fluorescent Pseudomonas spp. Involved in Suppression of Plant Root Pathogens. Microbiol. Rev., 56: 662-676.

Sc.org.pk/file.Download.aspk.archived papered.28.

Sharma A, Johri BN (2003a). Combat of Iron-deprivation through a Plant Growth Promoting Fluorescent Pseudomonas Strain GRP3A in Mung Bean (*Vigna radiata* L. Wilzeck). Microbiol. Res., 158.

Sharma A, Johri BN (2003b). Growth Promoting Influence of Siderophore-producing *Pseudomonas* Strains GRP3A and PRS9 in Maize (*Zea mays* L.) under Iron Limiting Conditions. Microbiol. Res., 158: 243-248.

Sheng XF, Xia JJ (2006). Improvement of Rape (*Brassica napus*) Plant Growth and Cadmium uptake by Cadmium-resistant Bacteria. Chemosphere, 64: 1036-1042.

Wang FY, Lin XG, Yin R (2007b). Role of Microbial Inoculation and Chitosan in Phytoextraction of Cu, Zn, Pb and Cd by *Elsholtzia splendense* a Field Case. Enviro. Pollu., 147: 248-255.

Web.inflibnet.ac.in/ojs/index. kJAS/articles.

Whiting SN, de Souza MP, Terry N (2001). Rhizosphere Bacteria Mobilize Zn for Hyperaccumulation by *Thlaspi caerulescens*. Enviro. Sci. Technol., 35: 3144-3150.

Wu QT, Deng JC, Long XX, Morel JL, Schwartz C (2006). Selection of Appropriate Organic Additives for Enhancing Zn and Cd Phytoextraction by Hyperaccumulators. J Environ. Sci., 18: 1113-1118.

Wu SC, Luo YM, Cheung KC, Wong MH (2006b). Influence of Bacteria on Pb and Zn Speciation, Mobility and Bioavailability in Soil: A Laboratory Study. Environ. Poll., 144.

www.csum.edu/hcbio27/biotechinology/lec10/lindemanhtml.

www.ncbi.nlm.nih.gov.articles.

www.ncbi.nlm.nih.gov.NCBI.Literature.Pub Med Central(PMC).

www.research gate.net/file.Post Loader.html?id....assetkey.

www.scholarresearchlibry.com.articles.

www.sciencedirect.com/science/articles/pii.

www.scoop.it.rhizobium-catabollism.

www.tandfonline.com/doi/abs.

www.usa.journals.com/wp-content.

Zaidi S, Usmani S, Singh BR, Musarrat J (2006). Significance of Bacillus Subtilis Strain SJ-101 as a Bioinoculant for Concurrent Plant Growth Promotion and Nickel Accumulation in *Brassicajuncea*. Chemosphere, 64: 991-997.

Pages: 126-147

Stress Tolerance and Plant Productivity

Edited by: Mr. Prasann Kumar and Dr. Pawan Kumar 'Bharti'

ISBN: 978-93-86841-56-8

Edition: 2018

Published by: Discovery Publishing House Pvt. Ltd., New Delhi (India)

8 Metals and Micronutrients-Food Safety Issue

Prasann Kumar

ABSTRACT

As awareness grows about food safety issues, the need for countries to provide greater assurance about the safety and quality of food also grows. The increase in world food trade and the advent of the Sanity and Phytosanitary (SPS) Agreement under the World Trade Organization (WTO) have also raised interest in food safety requirements. To ensure a strong presence in global markets, India realizes the need to meet these challenges and keep pace with international developments. Environmental pollution from hazardous metals and minerals can arise from natural as well as anthropogenic sources.

Key words: Anthropogenic,Basic, Crop, Disease,Environment, Phytosanity

INTRODUCTION

Natural sources are: seepage from rocks into water, volcanic activity, forest fires, etc. Pollution also arises from partitioning of polluting elements (which are concentrated in clay minerals with high absorption capacities), between sedimentary rocks and their precursor sediments and water(Gupta *et al.*, 2016, Latha *et al.*, 2013, ashwin *et al.*, 2016). With rapid industrialization and consumerist lifestyle, anthropogenic source of environmental pollution has increased. The pollution occurs both at the level of industrial production as well as the end use of the products and run-off. These toxic elements enter the human body mostly through food and water and to a lesser extent through inhalation of polluted air, use of cosmetics, drugs, poor quality herbal formulations. Of all the elements, the most important to consider in terms of food-chain contamination is arsenic (As), cadmium

Department of Agronomy, School of Agriculture, Lovely Professional University
Jalandhar - 144 411 (Punjab) (India)

(Cd), mercury (Hg), lead (Pb) and selenium (Se). Where soils are enriched in these elements, it is usually through the agricultural, industrial or urban activities of man, except for Se where high concentrations in soil are often derived from high-Se parent rock materials. The propensity for plants to accumulate and translocate these contaminants to edible and harvested parts depends largely on soil and climate factors, plant genotype and agronomic management(Benazir *et al.*, 2010, Beolchini *et al.*, 2011, Brar *et al.*, 2006, Calomiris *et al.*, 1984). Elevated As intake, especially of inorganic As, is most likely to arise from high-As drinking water than from ingestion of food. Cadmium and Se are of the greatest concern in terms of terrestrial food-chain contamination, with the former elements receiving most attention (Deb *et al.*, 2009). Worldwide, the probability of insufficient Se in the human diet exceeds that of toxicity, with deficiency usually associated with monotonous vegetarian diets in areas with Se-deficient soil (Table 8.1).

Table 8.1: Source of heavy metals

Metal	Industry
Chromium (Cr)	Mining, industrial coolants, chromium salts manufacturing, leather tanning
Lead (Pb)	Lead acid batteries, paints, E-waste, Smelting operations, Coal-based thermal power plants, ceramics, bangle industry
Mercury (Hg)	Chlor-alkali plants, thermal power plants, fluorescent lamps, hospital waste (damaged thermometers, barometers, sphygmomanometers), electrical appliances etc.
Arsenic (As)	Geogenic/natural processes, smelting operations, thermal power plants, fuel burning
Copper (Cu)	Mining, electroplating, smelting operations
Vanadium (Va)	Spent catalyst, sulphuric acid plant
Nickel (Ni)	Smelting operations, thermal power plants, battery industry
Cadmium (Cd)	Zinc smelting, waste batteries, e-waste, paint sludge, incinerations & fuel combustion
Molybdenum (Mo)	Spent catalyst
Zinc (Zn)	Smelting, electroplating

Source: Kumar *et al.*, 2012

Arsenic in Food

In most dietary As models, the food component is dominated by organo-As compounds, primarily in seafood, which are absorbed readily in the human gut, but are not metabolized and are rapidly excreted; inorganic As(III) and As(V) are considered the far greater health hazards (Chappel *et al.*, 1994). Food crops have highly variable and intermediate percentage of organo-As compounds. Adverse health effects of excess arsenic intake include the widely documented blackfoot disease in Taiwan, a peripheral vascular disease that can lead to gangrene of the extremities, as well as skin cancer and internal organ cancers. The cancers are believed to arise from long-term chronic exposures to relatively low levels of arsenic, but much uncertainty persists in the frequency of cancer at low doses and how the associated risk assessment should be computed (Chappel *et al.*, 1994). Arsenic may or may not be an essential nutrient for humans and, if it is, there are no estimates of daily requirement. The possibility has been raised, however, that the nutritional requirement could overlap with the chronic exposure doses associated with moderate cancer risk (Chappel *et al.*, 1994), a potential dilemma to rational regulation of As in foodstuffs and drinking water.

Interactions of As with other nutritive factors are largely unknown, except for a mutual antagonism with Se. There is some speculation that other nutritional factors may increase risk; low methionine intake is through to inhibit the normal detoxification of low-dose arsenic via biomethylation reactions (Chappel *et al.*, 1994).

Selenium in Food

Clearly demonstrated cases of Se toxicity in humans are rare, although a number of somewhat anecdotal reports are at least suggestive (National Research Council 1983). Widespread Se poisoning of livestock in seleniferous areas of western USA prompted human health studies in the 1930s that yielded equivocal results. A recent, more rigorous study by Longnecker *et al.*, 1991, yielded no conclusive evidence of Se-related health problem in farm families with daily Se intake as high as 720µg day $^{-1}$. Studies by Yang *et al.*, 1983, 1984 in the Hubei Province of China have provided the most unequivocal evidence of chronic Se toxicity in humans. Symptoms included hair brittleness and loss; streaking, brittleness and loss of nails; skin lesions; liver enlargement; and various gastrointestinal and neurological complaints; and even one family was recorded. At the time of study, daily intakes of Se ranged from 3200 to 6700 µg day $^{-1,}$ although a latter study reported incipient Se toxicosis at intakes >850 µg day $^{-1}$ (Yang *et al.*, 1989). The Chinese experience may be unique in that high soil and water Se was augmented by ashes from very high-Se coal that was burned locally and then applied as fertilizers material. Moreover, liming of local soils may have promoted oxidation of Se to the soluble, plant-available selenate ion (Yang *et al.*, 1983). Most importantly, Se toxicosis occurred in small, isolated farming communities with an almost 100% vegetarian diet comprising vegetables and grains produced locally. The worst outbreak of Se poisoning (1961-1964) coincides with a drought and a resulting failure of the local rice crop, and a consequent increase in consumption of high-Se maize and vegetables and a decrease in protein consumption; there is some evidence that Se toxicosis is associated with a low-protein diet (Yang *et al.*, 1983). The greater diversity and high quality of typical western diets greatly diminishes the probability of Se toxicosis elsewhere.

Worldwide, the probability of insufficient Se in the diet exceeds that of toxicity. Two relatively widespread syndromes have been documented in China for which Se deficiency is at least a primary factor. Kaschin-Beck disease has been documented in Siberia, North Korea and parts of China (Often in geographical association with Keshan disease), and is a type of osteoarthroathy (cartilage dysfunction and joint swelling) that also afflicts children. Daily Se intake associated with both disorders are estimated at just 7-11μg day^{-1} (Yang *et al.*, 1987), and blood Se levels are approximately one-half those found in New Zealand, where endemic selenium deficiencies in livestock (but not human) are common (Combs and Combs 1986). The occurrence of human Se deficiency in rural China is also, most likely, a result of the monotonous vegetarian diets comprising locally grown grains and produce (Combs and Combs 1986). There is currently considerable interest in the possible prophylactic use of dietary Se supplements to reduce incidence of cancer and heart disease, especially in countries where low-Se soils are prevalent.

Cadmium in Foods

Cadmium is a nonessential element in foods, and it accumulates principally in the kidney and liver. Cadmium concentration in foodstuff varies widely, with leafy vegetables and root crops generally having higher Cd concentrations than fruits crops or seeds (Table 8.2) although oilseeds may have high Cd concentration. With the impact of acute Cd toxicity through occupational exposure is well documented (IPCS 1992), the risk associated with life times low level exposure from food ingestion are not so well defined. Much of the information with regard to the latter pathways derives from studies in Japan (Ryan *et al.*, 1982; Friberg *et al.*, 1986; IPCS 1992) and China (Cal *et al.*, 1990) where the local population were exposed to contaminated food crops, principally rice, contaminated on accounts of adjacent industrial activities. The critical organ for long-term Cd exposure is the kidney, where Cd principally affects renal tubular function, irreversibly impairing re-absorption of protein, sugars and amino acids. Extreme case of cadmium toxicity leads to osteomalacia and bone fractures, as in the polluted areas in Japan (Itai-Itai disease). The affected population was mainly post-menopausal women and symptoms were closely linked to dietary deficiencies of Ca, Fe, Zn, protein, fat and vitamins D during the period of Cd exposure (Friberg *et al.*, 1986; Fox 1988; Nordberg 1996). The high level of Zn (1% Zn) in these soils may have acted as a protective Cd blocking agent, both for plant uptake and human absorption of Cd from foods (Chaney and Ryan 1994).

Table 8.2: Concentration of cadmium in the edible portion of food crops

Food Type	Total Number of Sample	Cd Concentrations (mg kg^{-1} dry wt)		
		Minimum	Maximum	Mean
Fruits	190	0.004	0.012	0.005
Vegetables				
Seed	394	0.016	0.130	0.028
Root/bulb	878	0.029	0.710	0.208
Fruit	322	0.021	0.540	0.237
Leaf	297	0.093	0.880	0.560
Field crops				
Grain	1302	0.014	0.210	0.047

Source: McLaughlin *et al.*, 1999

Mercury in Foods

Speciation of Hg is critical in determining toxicity, with methyl mercury being more toxic than other species (von Burg and Greenwood 1991). Mercury concentrations in food crops are generally low, with most of the dietary intake of Hg deriving from consumption of seafood (Hapke 1991). Mercuric poisoning on account of consumption of agricultural crops has been reported (In Iraq), but was due to consumption of seeds treated with mercuric fungicides (Bakir *et al.*, 1973). Levels of Hg in most field crops are sufficiently low to cause little concern from a human health viewpoint (Wiersma *et al.*, 1986).

Impact of Micronutrients on the Bioavailability of Contaminants in Foods

The interaction between micronutrient nutrition and the toxicity of heavy metals in foods has been reviewed recently (Goyer 1995), and more detailed reviews for Cd also available (Fox 1974, 1988; Andersen *et al.*, 1992b; Chaney *et al.*, 1996). Subsequent experiments examining retention of dietry Cd in animals at levels more relevant to Cd exposure through human food confirmed that Cu, Fe and Zn are ntagonists to Cd retention (Valberg *et al.*, 1976; Flanagan *etal.*, 1978; Shaikh and Smith 1980; Fox *et al.*, 1984; McKenna *et al.*, 1992). For instance, early work by Valberg *et al.*, 1976 investigates the intestinal uptake of ^{109}Cd in iron –deficient and iron-sufficient mice, and Cd retention (over a two-week period) increased from 2% in iron-sufficient animals to 3.8% in iron-deficient animals. While Zn deficiency has been shown to increase Cd retention in quail (Fox *et al.*, 1984), supplementation of Zn-sufficient (wheat/potato-based) diets with extra Zn had no effect on Cd retention in rats (Wing 1993). It is interesting to note that Lamphere *et al.* (1984) found supplemental Zn added to calf diets reduced Cd added in this experiment were high (50 mg/kg in feed) and outside the range relevant for most agricultural food crops. McKenna *et al.*, 1992 studied the effects on Cd retention by quail of level of intrinsic Zn (Zn with feed rather than added as a Zn salt to feed) in spinach. Their data, although not conclusive, also indicated that high dietary Zn is slightly protective in terms of Cd retention. With regard to evidence for micronutrient interaction with Cd retention in humans, data from controlled experimentation is, unfortunately, much more limited and appear restricted to the Fe/Cd interaction. Epidemiogical evidence for a Fe/Cd antagonism was given by Flanagan *et al.*, (1978), who studied Cd retention in a group of 22 men and women through tracer feeding experiments using ^{109}Cd. They found that Cd retention is more likely to be higher in females, who had lower body iron (serum Ferritin) levels than men (Figure 8.1).

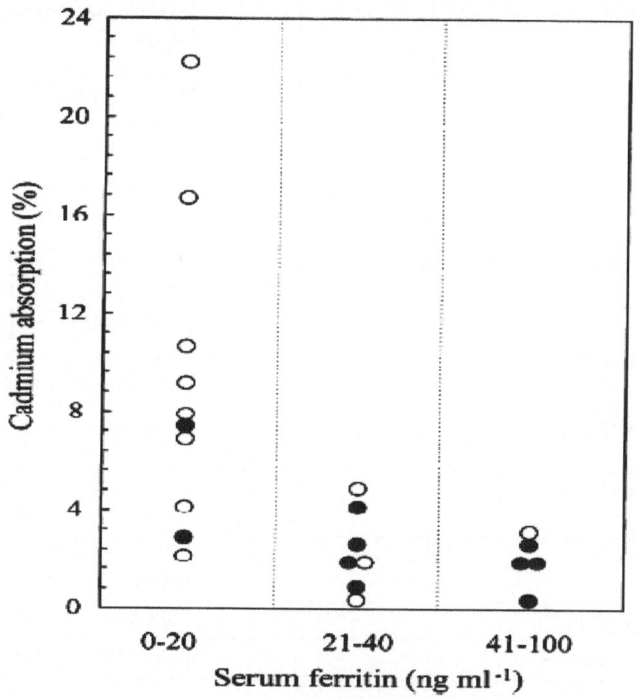

Fig. 8.1: Cadmium absorption in human volunteers in relation to body iron status

Source: McLaughlin *et al.*, 1999]

Where, (o) Females; (•) males

Management of Soil-Plant Transfer of Contaminants by Agronomic Means

Levels of most contaminants, except Cd, have rarely caused concern sufficient to require changes in agronomic practices to minimize food-chain contamination. With some countries introducing regulations to control Cd concentration in food staples (Walker 1988), some agricultural industries in many countries are introducing management practices to minimize the soil-plant transfer of Cd. Agronomic practices, that may be used to control Cd in crops, are given in table 8.3 along with an indication as to whether the effect has been demonstrated under realistic field conditions. A number of strategies are available to minimize Cd contamination of field crops, but mechanistic explanations for all the effects observed are incomplete.

Table 8.3: Agronomic management practices to control Cd accumulation in field crops. For each of the practices our summary of evidence is given by + if evidence is available and, - if there is no evidence and? If evidence is equivocal

Agronomic Management Practices	Laboratory Evidence	Field Evidence	References
Liming	+	?	Anderson and Nilsson 1974 Anderson and Siman 1991 Sparrow *et al.*, 1993a Oliver *et al.*, 1994a Li *et al.*,1996 Maiser *et al.*, 1997
Addition og Zn	+	+	Abdel-Sabour *et al.*, 1988 Choudhary *et al.*, 1995 Oliver *et al.*, 1994a
Addition of other micronutrients	+	-	Catalado *et al.*, 1983
Changes to low Cd fertilizer	+	?	Sparrow *et al.*, 1993b McLiaughlin *et al.*, 1995
P fertilizer type change	+	?	Reuss *et al.*, 1978 McLiaughlin *et al.*, 1995
N fertilizer type change	+	?	Willaert and Verloo 1992 Grant *et al.*, 1996
K fertilizer type change	+	+	Sparrow *et al.*,1994 Grant *et al.*, 1996
Fertlizer placement	+	+	Williams and David 1976 Sparrow *et al.*, 1992
Change crop rotation	-	+	Oliver *et al.*, 1993
Change tillage practices	?	-	Oliver *et al.*, 1993

Source: McLaughlin *et al.*, 1999

Liming is often suggested as primary management tool to minimize Cd accumulation by field crops. While beneficial effects of limining reducing plant Cd concentration have been clearly demonstrated in glasshouse experiments where Cd is added as the metal salt or in sewage sludge (John 1972; Andersson and Nilsson 1974; MacLean 1976; Williams and David 1976; Street *et al.*, 1978; Eriksson 1989), similar experiment with field crops on soils with low levels of Cd contamination have yielded conflicting or equivocal results (Anderson and Siman 1991; Sparrow *et al.*, 1993a; Oliver *et al.*, 1994a; Li *et al.*, 1996; Maier *et al.*, 1997). The reasons for this inconsistency are not known,but, at least in some cases, may be related to the relatively narrow pH range studied (Li *et al.*, 1996). In some studies where the minimum pH has been found around 5.5 further increase in pHhave not enhanced Cd uptake (Anderson and Siman 1991; Li *et al.*, 1996), perhaps due to minimal changes in Cd solubility over this pHrange. Changes in soil solution Ca may further complicate the liming response by causing increased completition with Cd for sorption sites (Anderssons 1976; Christensen 1984) and thus increasing plant uptake, or by competing for root binding sites such that Cd uptake is diminished. In atypical cases, where soils are naturally high in Cd, plant Cd levels may fail to show a response to liming because of extensive subsoil rooting and uptake of Cd; liming the plow layer would not affect Cd uptake from the subsoil (Li *et al.*, 1996). Nonetheless, in many field studies involving a range of soil types, plant uptake of Cd has been found to be a negative function of soil pH (Chumbley and Unwin1982; Alloway*et al.*, 1990; Eriksson 1990; Sillanpaa and Jansson 1992; Oliver *et al.*, 1994a). A number of authors have found increased Cd in crops as rates of fertilization were increased, in both pot and field experiments (Anderson 1976; Williams and David 1976; Anderson and Siman 1991; He and Singh 1994; Garnt *et al.*, 1996). This may be explained as follows:

[A] Increase in soil solution ionic strength that reduces soil surface negative charge, and thus Cd retention (Garcia-Miragaya and Page 1976);

[B] Fertilizars cations displacing Cd from exchange sites and leading to greater plant Cd uptake (Andersson 1976)

[C] pH reductions because of common formulations of both both N and P fertolizers (Reuss *et al.*, 1978; Willaert and Verloo 1992);

[D] Increased acquisition of Cd by roots on accounts of fertilization-induced root growth (Williams and David 1976; Grant *et al.*, 1996)

However, not all of these effects are manifested under field conditions where root exploration is more dispersed throughout the soil profile, and where rates of fertilization are often much lower than in pot experiments (McLaughlin *et al.*, 1995).

Potassium additions may also increase crop Cd concentrations (Sparrow *et al.*, 1994; Grant *et al.*, 1996) because the common use of KCl fertilizers increase soil solution Cl concentration which, in turn, increase total Cd in solution via formation of $CdCl_n^{2-n}$ ion pairs (McLaughlin *et al.*, 1997), enhancing uptake by plants (Smolders and McLaughlin 1996). Additions of KCl increase soil solution ionic strength and thus may decrease Cd retention, but this effect will tend to be small in comparison to chloro-complexation. Soil salinity has a marked effect in enhancing Cd uptake by field crops (Li *et al.*, 1994; McLaughlin *et al.*, 1994a), because of Cl-complexation enhancing the mobility and uptake of Cd by crops (Smolders and McLaughlin 1996). However, salinity cannot always be readily or economically manipulated, except by changing the site of production (especially fro dryland salinization) or by switching to higher quality irrigation water.The addition of Zn to the soil have been shown to reduce crop Cd concentrations significantly (Cataldo *et al.*, 1983; Abdel-Sabour *et al.*, 1988; McKenna *et al.*, 1993; Moragham 1993; Chaney *et al.*, 1994; Oliver *et al.*, 1994a; Choudhary *et al.*, 1995). This effect has been demonstrated in both common and durum wheat, and is particularly well-expressed under conditions of Zn deficiency (Oliver *et al.*, 1994a; Choudhary *et al.*, 1995). In a nutrient solution, the addition of Zn has been found to reduce short-term uptake of Cd (<24 h) using 109Cd-labelled solutions (Cataldo *et al.*, 1983). It has also been suggested that, under Zn deficiency, losses in membrane integrity may occur (Welch and Norvell 1993) leading to enhanced Cd uptake (Oliver *et al.*, 1994a), but for this to increase Cd uptake requires a (plant-available) Cd concentration gradient to exist from the soil to the root, which is unlikely (McLaughlin *et al.*, 1998). While interactions between plant Cd uptake and other micronutrients (Cu, Mn, Fe) have been demonstrated in solution culture, no glass-house or field evidence is available to confirm that micronutrient fertilization with elements other than Zn could be used as a Cd-management tool. Crop rotations, tillage andresidue handling practices affect a number of soil physical and chemical factors and have also been found to influence Cd uptake by field crops (Oliver *et al.*, 1993). The effects were smaller for tillage and residue handling (Oliver *et al.*, 1993), but crop rotation was found to markedly influence Cd concentrations. Wheat grown after legume crops, particularly lupins, had higher Cd concentrations in grain than wheat grown after fallow or other cereals. The reasons for these differences are still under investigation. Relatively large additions of organic soil amendements (manure, composts) may also decrease Cd uptake by crops, and are much likely to be effective in the case of sandy soils (Singh 1994)

Management of Soil-Plant Transfer of Contaminants by Palnt Breeding

Genetic variation in mineral uptake has been recognised from many years (Saric 1983) and there appears to be considerable potential for manipulation of uptake eof metal ions through plant breeding. There are now several examples of these genetic differences being exploited to develop crop cultivars with improved tolerance to particular ion deficiencies or excesses, or in the case of heavy metals, to improve food safety through reduced uptake (Wagner 1993; Clarke 1995; Li *et al.*, 1995a). Existing and propose maximum limits for Cd in foods has prompted searches for genetic differences in various crops. So far, manipulation of Cd concentration by breeding only seems to have been undertaken in sunflower (*Helianthusannus* L.) and durum wheat (*Triticumturgidum* cultivar group durum). These efforts were initiated to provide an economic, long-term means of reducing Cd concentration in these crops to ensure continued access to markets in countries with Cd limits. Cultivars with genetically low levels of Cd give farmers greater flexibility than restriction of crop production to soils with low available Cd, or to crop rotation that reduce Cd uptake. Of all the potentially toxic elements present in soil or added by man to soils, Cd and Se are of primary concern in terms of food-chain contamination. Problems due to Se-contamination of the food chain are predominantly arising from natural enrichment of soils and are limited to certain reginons with seleniferous soils. Cadmium concentrations in soil in many countries are increasing due to inadvertent additions in fertilizer, biosolids, soil amendments and additions from the atmosphere. Health problems due to Cd contamination of the food chain have been manifest only in situations of gross soil contamination, with a predominantly rice-based diet, where soil-plant and plant –human transfer of Cd would have been enhanced. Evidence for advance health effects arising from Cd contamination of foods is contentious, but human feeding studies have indicated that food Cd bioavailability is dependent on Fe nutition, and animal studies have indicated that Zn, Ca, P and other elements and food constituents affects Cd bioavailability. Plants breeding can minimize Cd accumulation in crops, and maximize concentrations of antagonists to Cd assimilations in humans. Agronomic management also offers options to minimize Cd transfer to crops. However, given the continuing accumulations of Cd in many fertilized agricultural soils and the difficulty of removing these elements from soil, it remains important that inputs of the metal to soil be minimized (Table 8.4).

Metals and Seeds: Biochemical and Molecular Implications and their Significance for Seed Germination

Seed have the embryo like new-fangled plant in tiny and encompass two major functions, reproductive and dispersal. Seed formation completes the process of plant reproduction and with seed germination, the next plant generation starts. Given the ever-increasing environmental pollution with metal, it is perhaps surprisingly that relatively few reports detail he impacts of metals on seed metabolism, viability, and germination in comparison to the numerous publications on the effects of metals in vegetative tissues, particularly roots and shoots.

Metal uptake and Transport to Seeds

The delivery of metals to seeds depends upon uptake by the mother plant, and subsequent transport to developing seeds. Due to the potential toxicity of excess levels of metals, their uptake and distribution and the intracellular concentration must be carefully regulated. Membrane transport systems and gene families involved in metal homeostasis include heavy metal ATPases, natural resistance-associated macrophage proteins (Nramps), cation diffusion facilitators (CDFs), the ZRT (zinc-regulated transporter)-, IRT (iron-regulated transporter)-like protein (ZIP) family and cation antiporter. Most of the genes families in plants are large compared to analogous families in other organisms, reflecting the need for plants to respond to fluctuating environmental conditions and metal availability with low and high affinity system, and the need to control metal transport at the cellular and organelle level (Hall and Williams 2003). The uptake of essential metals from the soil and subsequent transfer to the xylem for transport to other plant parts has been reviewed by Briat and Lobreaux (1997) and Colangelo and Guerinot (2006).

Table 8.4: Reports of genotypic differences in and breeding for Cd concentration in food crops

Crop	References
Wheat (*Triticum* spp.)	
Genotypic variation	Pettersson 1977
	Andersson and Pettersson 1981
	Oliver *et al.*, 1995
differences *T. aestivum* vs. *T. turgidum* L. c. group durum	Zook *et al.*, 1970
	Meyer *et al.*, 1982a
variation among *T. turgidum* L. var durum genotypes	Penner *et al.*, 1995
genetics of differences in *T. turgidumL. vardurum*	Clarke, 1995
Barley (*Hordeum vulgare* L.)	
genotypic variation	Chang *et al.*, 1982
Rice (*Oryza* spp.)	
variation among *O. japonica, O. indica, O. javanica* and hybrids	Morishita *et al.*, 1987
Sunflowe (*Helianthus annus* L.)	Li *et al.*, 1995a
genotypic variation	Li *et al.*, 1995b
breeding and genetics	
Lettuce (*Lactuca sativa* L.)	Crews and Davies 1985
	Harrison 1986
	Thomas and Harrison 1989
	Xue and Harrison 1991
	Florijin *et al.*, 1991
Maize (*Zea mays* L.)	
genotypic variation	Hinesly *et al.*, 1978
Potato (*Solanum tuberosum* L.)	Harris *et al.*, 1981
genotypic variation	Isermann *et al.*, 1983

Source: McLaughlin *et al.*, 1999

Metal Delivery to Seeds

Metals are normally found at the highest concentrations in the roots, and at the lowest concentrations in the reproductive tissues (Malan and Farrant 1998; Shanker *et al.*, 2005). This is because metals are sequestrated into the vacuoles of root and shoot tissue and the subsequent availability of free metals in the symplast can be low. For example, concentrations of Cd and Ni in soyabean were 30 and 20 times, respectively, and higher in roots than in the leaves. Cadmium concentration was lower in the seeds, whereas the concentration of Ni was the same in both leaves and seeds (Malan and Farrant 1998).

Essential metals, e.g. Fe, need to be transported to the developing seeds (Figure 8.2). Mineral transport of seeds is believed to occur via the phloem, because movement of the xylem sap is driven by transpiration, which is limited by impermeability of the seed coat as demonstrated in soyabean (Laszlo 1994; Stacey *et al.*, 2008). Radiotracer experiments of the phloem loading of Fe in Pisum sativum showed that Fe delivery f the seed occurred throughout the period of seed development. Predominate source of Fe is through continuous uptake via the roots rather than mobilization of stored reserves from other tissues, which supplied about 20-30% of seed Fe (Grusak 1994). Similarly, remobilization of reserve from senescing leaves has been estimated to supply at most 40% of the metal content of *Arabidopsis* seeds (Curie *et al.*, 2009). Non-essential metals are also transported to seeds, and this represents a problem in crop species, where the levels of metals present in seeds can exceed safe limits for human consumption. For example, Cd is transported to developing seeds of Indian mustard via the phloem as a result of shift in the source-sink relationship as seeds fill and draw increasing levels of photosynthates during the process of seed set. Cadmium has been proposed to enter the phloem through two possible mechanisms: direct transfer from the xylem in stems or rapid export from the leaves before the Cd is compartmentalized into the vacuole (Shankaran and Ebbs 2008).

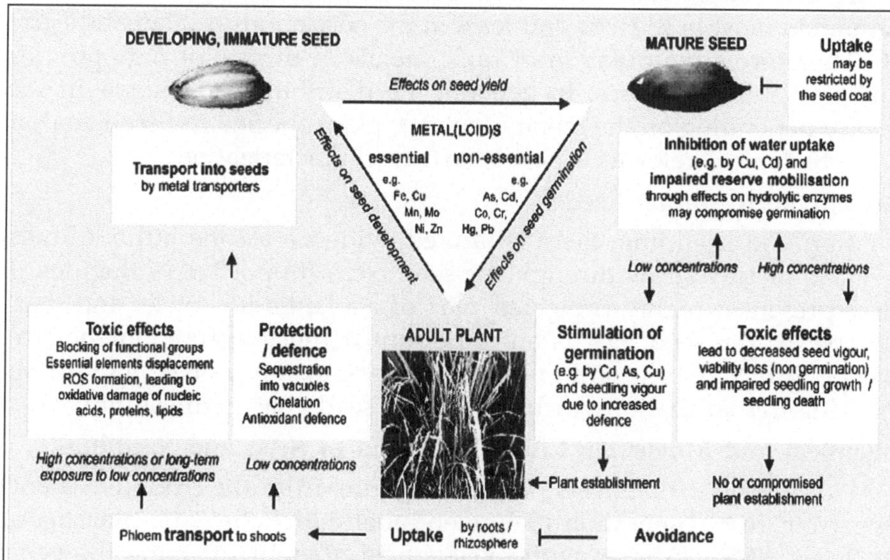

Fig. 8.2: Simplified scheme summarizing our current knowledge of the effects of metal on seeds

Source: Kraner and Colville 2011

Metal Distribution within Seeds

Iron in developing seeds was found mainly in the vacuole of perivascular cells in the embryo and cotyledons of non-endospermic seeds, e.g. those of most Leguminous and Brassicaceae species, and in embryo and aleurone layer of endospermic seeds, e.g. those of species belonging to the Poaceae and Solanaceae families. Transport of Fe into the vacuole is mediated by VIT1, and expression of VIT1 is high in developing seeds. The distribution of Cd, Zn and Pb in the seeds of the metal hyperaccumulator Thlaspi praecox was investigated using micro-proton-induced X-ray emission (micro-PIXE). Cadmium was found in the greatest abundance in cotyledons> radicle > seed coat. In comparison, Zn, Fe and Cu were greater in radicle > cotyledons > seed coat. Lead was not; detected, suggesting that it was excluded from seeds. Within the cotyledon, both Cd and Zn were present at higher levels in the epidermis compared to the Mesophyll, but the reverse was observed was observed for Cu and Fe. Cadmium and Zn were located in the aleurone layer and, whereas Cu and Fe accumulated more in the testa. The mechanisms for Cd delivery of seeds may be different to those of the other metals, which are likely to be transported via the phloem as complexes with NA, because Cd readily forms complexes with thiol groups and Cl. Cadmium hyperaccumulation in seeds was thought to be responsible for reduced seed biomass and germination, and the increased dormancy of *Thlaspi* seeds collected from the most polluted sites (Vogel-Mikus *et al.*, 2007). In soyabean seeds Cd was present at the highest concentrations in the testa and cotyledons and at low levels in the embryonic axis, while Ni accumulated most in the axis and least in the cotyledons (Malan and Farrant 1998). Therefore, accumulation of toxic metals at this point may provide a means of chemical defence. In general, the distribution of metals in seeds may vary depending on the metal involved, plant species and seed anatomy, and the biological relevance needs further characterization.

Metal uptake by Intact Seeds

After seed shedding, there is limited evidence for the influx of metals into intact, mature seeds through the seed coat, supportive of the idea that seeds represent a highly protected part of a plant's life cycle, and that in many species the seed coat is an important defence against abiotic stress. However, great inter-specific variation exists in the morphology of seed coats (Moise *et al.*, 2005), which will affect seed coat permeability.

Biochemical and Molecular Effects of Metal in Seed and Seedlings

Many of the toxic effects of metals results from the oxidative damage arising from ROS generation (Schutzendubel and Polle 2002; Sharma and Dietz 2009). ROS can react with nucleic acid, thereby affecting the genetic code in the embryo, and can react with seed storage compounds such as proteins and lipids. Hence, ROS can compromise germination and seedling establishment with potentially mutagenic effects on the next plant generation.

Table 8.5: Summary of the metal on seed germination and seedling growth in different plant species

Plants	Metal Treatment	Concentration(μM)	TC	Seedling Growth	References
Apium graveolens	$CrCl_3$	0	100%	Lr reduced at all coc, Ls reduced by 1000μM	Scoccianti *et al.*, 2006
		10-1000	98-65%		
		10000	0%		
Arabidopsis thaliana	$CdSO_4$	0	82.6%	Lr and Msl reduced by ≥ 10μM	Sharma and Kumar 2002
		50	No effect		
		100	72%		
		200	54%		
Brassica pekinensis	$Cu(NO_3)_2$	0	100%	Lr reduced by ≥ 31μM, Ls reduced by ≥ 500μM	Xiong and Wang 2005
		8-125	No effect		
		500	43.3%		
		2000	0%		
Bowiea volubilis	Control		93%		
	$CuSO_4$. $5H_2O$	4-40	No effect	Lr reduced at all concentration	Street *et al.*, 2007
	$ZnSO_4.7H_2O$	3.5-35	No effect	Lr reduced at all concentration	
	$CdCl_2.H_2O$	3-11	No effect	Lr reduced by ≥ 3μM	
	$HgCl_2$	2-7.5	78%	Lr reduced by 7.5 μM	
	$(CH_3COO)_2Pb.3H_2O$	1-5	No effect	No effect	

(Table Contd…)

Plants	Metal Treatment	Concentration(μM)	TC	Seedling Growth	References
Calamagrostis epigeios	Control	0	77%		Madzhugina *et al.*, 2008
	$CuSO_4$	1000-5000	50-25%	Not reported	
	$ZnSO_4$	1000	No effect	Not reported	
		2000-5000	50-20%	Not reported	
	$Pb(NO_3)_2$	1000-5000	60-12%		
Dorycnium pentaphyllum	Control		79.3%		Lefevre *et al.*, 2009
	$ZnSO_4$	100-1000	No effect		
	$CdCl_2$	10	55%	Lr, Ls, Mr and Ms reduced	
		100	88%		
		1000	Delayed		
			40%	Lr, Ls, Mr and Ms reduced	
Eruca sativa	Control		85%		Ozdener and Kutbay 2009
	$Cd(NO_3)_2 \cdot 4H_2O$	81-810	No effect	Lr reduced at all concentration Ls reduced by ≥ 240 μM. No growth at ≥ 650 μM	
		1620-3240	59-44%		
	$CuSO_4.5H_2O$	20-100	No effect		
		200-800	73%		
		1000	47.8%		
		2000-4000	<10%		
	$ZnSO_4.7H_2O$	87-2610	No effect		

(Table Contd…)

Plants	Metal Treatment	Concentration(μM)	TC	Seedling Growth	References
	$NiSO_4.6H_2O$	95-950	No effect	Lr reduced by ≥ 230 μM. Ls reduced by ≥ 300μM. No growth at ≥ 760 μM	
Eucomis auumnalis	Control		90%		Street *et al.*, 2007
	$CuSO_4.5H_2O$	4-200	60%	Lr reduced at all concentration and Ls reduced by ≥ 8 μM	
	$ZnSO_4.\ 7H_2O$	3.5-170	60%	Lr reduced at all concentration and Ls reduced by ≥ 35 μM	
	$CdCl_2.\ H_2O$	3-11	61%	No effect	
	$HgCl_2$	4-7.5	83%	No effect	
	$(CH_3CO)_2Pb.3H_2O$	1-5	No effect	No effect	
Helianthus annuus	Control	0	70%	Lr increased by ≤32 μM, reduced by ≥ 65 μM.Ls increased at all concentration	Jadia and Fulekar 2008
	$Cd(NO_3)_2.4H_2O$	16-160	65-40%		
	$CuSO_4.\ 5H_2O$	20-200	75-50%	Lr increased by ≤ 80μM, reduced by ≥ 160 μMLs increased at all concentration	
	$Ni(NO_3)_2$	27-270	66-43%	Lr increased ≤ 110μM, reduced by ≥ 220μM. Ls increased at all concentration	

(Table Contd…)

Plants	Metal Treatment	Concentration(µM)	TC	Seedling Growth	References
	$Pb(NO_3)_2$	15-150	70-46%	Lr increased by ≤ 60µM reduced by ≥ 120 µM.	
	$Zn(NO_3)_2.6H_2O$	17-170	74-94%		
Lupinus luteus	$PbCl_2$	1500	No effect	Lr reduced by ≥ 300µM	Kopyra and Gwozdz 2003
				Lr reduced by ≥ 500µM	
Merwillia natalensis	Control		96%		Street *et al.*, 2007
	$CuSO_4.5H_2O$	4-200	No effect	Lr reduced at all conc. Ls reduced by ≥ 8 µM	
	$ZnSO_4.\ 7H_2O$	3.5-170	No effect	Lr and Ls reduced by ≥ 35 µM	
	$CdCl_2$	3-11	No effect	Ls reduced at all concentration Lr reduced by ≥ 5 µM	
	$HgCl_2$	4-7.5	No effect	Ls reduced by all concentration	
Oryza sativa	$CdCl_2$	0	100%	Ls reduced by all concentration. No growth at 1000 µM. No root formation at all concentration	Ahsan *et al.*, 2007b
		200-800	Reduced		
		1000	0%		

Source: Kranner and Colville 2011

Metal Effects on Proteins

Like other tissue, seeds contain enzymes and membrane bound proteins, but many seed types also accumulate proteins as major storage reserves. Proteins can undergo oxidative modification through direct reaction with ROS, and also through interaction with the aldehyde products of lipid peroxidation. Aldehyde produced through lipid peroxidation can initiate browning reactions, through non-enzymatic condensation with free amino groups of proteins or nucleic acids. The resulting glycosylamine is rearranged to form the 1-amino-α-deoxyketose, which is subsequently degraded into amino acids or carbonyl intermediates. These react with other amino groups to form advanced glycosylation end –products (AGE). Proteomic studies of the effects of metals on protein expression during seed germination revealed differential expression of various proteins. In maize seeds treated with potassium dichromate, 22 proteins were up-regulated, some of which are antioxidants. Other up-regulated proteins are involved in stress response and sugar metabolism. In addition,metallothionein levels increased with Cr concentration (Labra *et al.*, 2006). In germinating rice seeds treated with Cu, 50 proteins were differentially expressed. Expression of 18 proteins was increased to including globulin-like proteins, suggesting that Cu exposure inhibited glycoprotein pathways enzymes, a transducin and rice receptor-like protein kinase, which are likely to have roles in stress signaling, and a binding immunoglobulin protein (BiP; a Dna K-type molecular chaperone) that prevents protein unfolding under stress conditions. Two metabolic proteins were up-regulated: dehydroquinate dehydratase, an enzyme of the shikimate pathway for synthesis of phenyalanine, tyrosine and tryptophan; and aldose reductase, which is involved in polyol synthesis. The seven proteins that declined following Cu treatment including α-amylase, which degrades starch to provide metabolites for respiration, providing further evidence for the down-regulation of glycolysis in response to Cu. Enolase of the PEP cycle also decreased as did a protein disulphide isomerase and glutathione- S-transferase (GST) (Ahsan *et al.*, 2007).

Metals Effects on Lipids

Membrane and seed storage lipids are another target for ROS arising from exposure to excess concentrations of metals and various changes in lipid content and composition result from growth in metal-contaminated soil. Plant genes activated by metal stress include gene encoding enzymes with fatty acid peroxidase activity such as α-dioxygenase, peroxidase (POX) and lipoxygenases. Another other functions, these enzymes catalyse peroxidation of polyunsaturated membrane lipids leading to loss of membrane integrity. Compositional changes were observed in peeper seedlings cultured in Cd solutions. Lipid peroxidation is indicative of oxidative stress and has been reported in many plant species following exposure to metals including Cu (Ahsan *et al.*, 2007a), Hg (Cargnelutti *et al.*, 2006; Cho and Park 2000), Pb (Wang *et al.*, 2008; Cavusoglu *et al.*, 2009), Cr (Sinha *et al.*, 2005; Pandey *et al.*, 2009).

Genotoxic Effects of Metal Exposure

The phytotoxicity of excess concentrations of metals is in part due to the damage of nucleic acids, which is clearly unwanted in developing or germinating seeds. Hydroxyl radicals are highly damaging and are responsible for an estimated 10,000 and 100, 000 DNA base modifications in a single cell per day. In addition to base modifications, metal binding to the cell nucleus causes other pro-mutagenic damage including inter- and intra –molecular crosslinking of DNA and proteins, DNA strand breaks, rearrangements and depurination (Briat and Lebrun 1999). Mercury, Pb and As all exert clastogenic and mutagenic effects. The clastogenicity arises affinity of metallic salts for thiol groups, which leads to mitotic spindle disturbances. In terms of disruption to cell division, Hg is more potent than As and Pb (Patra *et al.*, 2004). Laboratory tests of various mercurial compounds have shown a number of Genotoxic effects, which were dependent on the concentration, the type of compounds and the target species and target organ. Chromosomal damage was reported during germination of seeds of several wheat species, rye and pea. All forms of Pb appear to have similar effects on mitosis, and tend to cause spindle disturbance resulting in c-mitosis, in which normal anaphase separation of the chromosomes is prevented, so that resulting nuclei has double the number of chromosomes (Fankhauser and Humphrey 1952). The most common Genotoxic effects reported for As exposure involves mitotic spindle disturbance. In *Hordenum vulgare* seeds the frequency of chromosomal abnormalities was proportional to the concentration of As (Bandyopadhyay and Maity 1995). Cadmium has also been reported to cause chromosomal aberrations, with cytogenetic analysis of Pisum sativum root tips from seeds germinated on different concentrations of Cd revealing the increased frequency of abnormalities such as fragments, precocious separation, laggards, single and double bridges and stickiness. Again, the total number of aberrations increased in a concentration dependent manner (Siddiqui *et al.*, 2009).

CONCLUSION

Seeds contain enzymes and membrane bound proteins, but many seed types also accumulate proteins as major storage reserves. Proteins can undergo oxidative modification through direct reaction with ROS, and also through interaction with the aldehyde products of lipid peroxidation. Aldehyde produced through lipid peroxidation can initiate browning reactions, through non-enzymatic condensation with free amino groups of proteins or nucleic acids. The resulting glycosylamine is rearranged to form the 1-amino-α-deoxyketose, which is subsequently degraded into amino acids or carbonyl intermediates. These react with other amino groups to form advanced glycosylation end –products (AGE). Proteomic studies of the effects of metals on protein expression during seed germination revealed differential expression of various proteins. In maize seeds treated with potassium dichromate, 22 proteins were up-regulated, some of which are antioxidants. Other up-regulated proteins are involved in stress response and sugar metabolism.

REFERENCES

Abhijit Gupta, JyotiJoia, AdityaSood, RidhiSood, Candy Sidhu and GaganjotKaur. (2016) Microbes as Potential Tool for Remediation of Heavy Metals: A Review, Journal of Microbial & Biochemical Technology, 8:4.

AshaLatha, P., and S. Sandeep Reddy. (2013) Review on Bioremediation-Potential Tool for Removing Environmental Pollution International Journal of Basic and Applied Chemical Sciences: 2277-2073.

Ashwini M, Veena Gayathri Krishnaswamy and Nabila Fathima., (2016) Removal of Chromium by a Bacterial Consortium Isolated from Kolar Gold Fields and Chromium Contaminated sites, Environment Conservation Journal 17(1&2): 109-118.

Benazir, J. Fathima, Suganthi R., Rajvel D., Padmini Pooja M and Mathithumilan B, (2010) Bioremediation of Chromium in Tannery Effluent by Microbial Consortia. African Journal of Biotechnology 9.21: 3140-3143.

Beolchini, Francesca, Fonti V, Dell Anno A, Vegilo F, (2011) Bio-mobilization of Heavy Metals from Contaminated Sediments by Acidophilic Microbial Consortia. Chemical Engineering Transactions 4: 833-888.

Bestawy, Ebtesam El, (2013) Bioremediation of Heavy Metal-contaminated Effluent using Optimized Activated Sludge Bacteria. Applied Water Science 3(1): 181-192.

Brar, Satinder K., M. Verma; R.Y. Surampalli; K. Misra, R.D. Tyagi; N. Meunier; and J.F. Blais (2006) - Bioremediation of Hazardous Wastes—A Review. Practice Periodical of Hazardous, Toxic, and Radioactive Waste Management 10(2): 59-72.

Calomiris, Jon J., John L. Armstrong, and Ramon J. Seidler, (1984) Association of Metal Tolerance with Multiple Antibiotic Resistance of Bacteria Isolated from Drinking Water. Applied and Environmental Microbiology 47(6): 1238-1242.

Deeb, Bahig El, and Abdullah D. Altalhi, (2009) Degradative Plasmid and Heavy Metal Resistance Plasmid Naturally Coexist in Phenol and Cyanide Assimilating Bacteria. American J BiochemBiotechnol 5 (2): 84-93.

Dixit, Ruchita, *et al.* (2015) Bioremediation of Heavy Metals from Soil and Aquatic Environment: An Overview of Principles and Criteria of Fundamental Processes. *Sustainability* 7(2): 2189-2212.

Focardi, Silvia, MilvaPepi, and Silvano E. Focardi. (2013) Microbial Reduction of Hexavalent Chromium as a Mechanism of Detoxification and Possible Bioremediation Applications. Agricultural and Biological Sciences, Biodegradation-life of Science 12: 321-347.

Garbisu, C., and I. Alkorta. (2003) Basic Concepts on Heavy Metal Soil Bioremediation. European Journal of Mineral Processing and Environmental Protection. 3(1): 58-66.

GawaliAshruta, A.V.D. Nanoty, and U.K. Bhalekar (2014) Biosorption of Heavy Metals from Aqueous Solution using Bacterial EPS. EPS 2 (4): 373-377.

Girma, Gosa, (2015) Microbial Bioremediation of some Heavy Metals in Soils: An Update Review. Indian Journal of Scientific Research 6(1): 147.

Greaney, Karen Marie, (2005) An Assessment of Heavy Metal Contamination in the Marine Sediments of Las Perlas Archipelago, Gulf of Panama. School of Life Sciences Heriot-Watt University, Edinburgh.

Jahani, Samaneh, FatemiFaezeh, Ali Firoz-e-zare Mohammad, Reza Zolfaghar and Mohammad (2015), Isolation and Characterization of *Acidithiobacillus ferrooxidans* Strain FJS from Ramsar, Iran. Electronic Journal of Biology 11:4.

Jain, Akshata, T.H. Udayashankara, and Lokesh, K.S. (2014) Bioremediation of Heavy Metals using Mixed Bacterial Culture from Contaminated Soil of Abandoned Kolar Gold Mine Residue. International Journal of Engineering Research and Technology. 3(8)

Jankaite, Audrone, and SauliusVasarevièius. (2005) Remediation Technologies for Soils Contaminated with Heavy Metals. Journal of Environmental Engineering and Landscape Management 13 (2): 109-113.

Kiran, K. (2012) Spectrophotometric Determination of Iron in Water Samples using 3-hydroxy benzyl Amino Benzoic Acid. International Journal of Environmental Sciences 3(1): 20.

Arpita Kulshreshtha, Ranu Agrawal, Manika Barar, Shilpi Saxena, (2014) A Review on Bioremediation of Heavy Metals in Contaminated Water. IOSR–J Environ SciToxicol Food Tech 8: 44-50.

Kumar, A., Bisht. B.S., Joshi.V.D., Dhewa. T. (2011) Review on Bioremediation of Polluted Environment: A Management Tool. International Journal of Environmental Sciences 1(6): 1079.

Lambert, M., B.A. Leven, and R.M. Green, (2000) New methods of Cleaning up Heavy Metal in Soils and Water. Environmental Science and Technology Briefs for Citizens. Kansas State University, Manhattan, KS.

Marques, Ana PGC, António OSS Rangel, and Paula ML Castro (2009) Remediation of Heavy Metal Contaminated Soils: Phytoremediation as a Potentially Promising Clean-up Technology. Critical Reviews in Environmental Science and Technology 39 (8): 622-654.

Merina Paul Das and Neha Kumari., (2016) A Microbial Bioremediation Approach: Removal of Heavy Metal Using Isolated Bacterial Strains from Industrial Effluent Disposal Site. Int. J. Pharm. Sci. Rev. Res., 38(1), 19: 111-114.

Mishra, Debaraj, and Young Ha Rhee (2014) Microbial Leaching of Metals from Solid Industrial Wastes. Journal of Microbiology 52 (1): 1-7.

Oliveira, Helena. Chromium as an Environmental Pollutant: Insights on Induced Plant Toxicity. Journal of Botany 2012: (2012).

Paranthaman, S.R. and Karthikeyan, B. Bioremediation of Paper Mill Effluent on Growth and Development of Seed Germination (*Vignamungo*). CIBTech Journal of Biotechnology 2015 Vol. 4 (1): 22-26.

QiuZhuo Zhang; Achal, V.; Xiang WeiNing; Wang DuanChao (2014) Identification of Heavy Metal Resistant Bacteria Isolated from Yangtze River, China. International Journal of Agriculture and Biology 16 (3): 619-623.

Rampelotto, Pabulo Henrique. Extremophiles and Extreme Environments. (2013): 482-485.

Su, Chao (2014) A Review on Heavy Metal Contamination in the Soil Worldwide: Situation, Impact and Remediation Techniques. Environmental Skeptics and Critics 3(2): 24.

Subramanian, Sangeetha, Silviya Sam, and Gurunathan Jayaraman (2012) Hexavalent Chromium Reduction by Metal Resistant and Halotolerant *Planococcusmaritimus* VITP21. African Journal of Microbiology Research 47: 7339-7349.

Tripathi, M., and S.K. Garg (2010) Studies on Selection of Efficient Bacterial Strain Simultaneously Tolerant to Hexavalent Chromium and Pentachlorophenol Isolated from Treated Tannery Effluent. Research Journal of Microbiology 5 (8): 707-716.

Vieira, Regine HSF, and Boya Volesky Biosorption (2010): A Solution to Pollution? International Microbiology 3 (1): 17-24.

Wuana, Raymond A., and Felix E. Okieimen (2011) Heavy Metals in Contaminated Soils: A Review of Sources, Chemistry, Risks and best Available Strategies for Remediation." Isrn Ecology 2011, Article ID 402647.

Yang, Tao, ZhengXu, Jiankang Wen and Limei Yang (2009) Factors Influencing Bioleaching Copper from Waste Printed Circuit Boards by *Acidithiobacillus ferrooxidans. Hydrometallurgy* 97 (1): 29-32.

Zhitong Yaoa, Jinhui Lib, HenghuaXiec and CongHaiYuc, (2012) Review on Remediation Technologies of Soil Contaminated by Heavy Metals." *Procedia Environmental Sciences* 16: 722-729.

Pages: 148-158

Stress Tolerance and Plant Productivity
***Edited by:* Mr. Prasann Kumar and Dr. Pawan Kumar 'Bharti'**
ISBN: 978-93-86841-56-8
***Edition:* 2018**
***Published by:* Discovery Publishing House Pvt. Ltd., New Delhi (India)**

9 Role of Farming Practices on Environment

Prasann Kumar

ABSTARCT

As environmental conditions effect to agricultural practices, agricultural practices also have effects on the environment. Namely; agriculture affects of global flowing of greenhouse gases. The main reason for the destruction of forest land is to obtain agricultural land. As a result of agricultural land, obtaining, greenhouse gases are created at the same time. These greenhouse gases show the second major negative impact after the negative effects of greenhouse gases, which created by the using of the fossil fuels.

Key words: Agriculture, Biotic, Crop, Cadmium, Drop, Effect, Forage, Grass, Husbandry

INTRODUCTION

Forests collect carbon 20 or 40 times more than agricultural lands and most of the carbon is released into the atmosphere when forests has been destroyed to open agricultural land (Kamer, and Gürlek, 2003). The environmental impact of agriculture is the effect that different farming practices have on the ecosystems around them, and how those effects can be traced back to those practices. The environmental impact of agriculture varies based on the wide variety of agricultural practices employed around the world. Ultimately, the environmental impact depends on the production practices of the system used by farmers. The connection between emissions into the environment and the farming system is indirect, as it also depends on other climate variables such as rainfall and temperature.Globally agriculture sector feeds over 7 billion people, but is also a major cause of several environmental degradation. Agricultural activities emit 25%-33%

Department of Agronomy, School of Agriculture, Lovely Professional University
Jalandhar - 144 411 (Punjab) (India)

of greenhouse gases (Edenhofer *et al.* 2014, Tubiello *et al.* 2014); Around 50% of the world's habitable land has already been converted to farming land so overall, farmland covers 38% of the world's land area (FAO 2016a); account for >70% of freshwater withdrawals (Molden, 2007), drive deforestation and habitat fragmentation (Ramankutty and Foley 1999) and resultant biodiversity loss (IUCN 2016); and eutrophy and acidify natural aquatic and terrestrial ecosystems with agrochemicals (Vitousek *et al.* 1997). There are two types of indicators of environmental impact: "means-based", which is based on the farmer's production methods, and "effect-based", which is the impact that farming methods have on the farming system or on emissions to the environment. An example of a means-based indicator would be the quality of groundwater, which is affected by the amount of nitrogen applied to the soil. An indicator reflecting the loss of nitrate to groundwater would be affect-based (van der Warf and Petit, 2002). The means-based evaluation looks at farmers' practices of agriculture, and the effect-based evaluation considers the actual effects of the agricultural system. For example, means-based analysis might look at pesticides and fertilization methods that farmers are using, and affect-based analysis would consider how much CO_2 is being emitted or what the Nitrogen content of the soil is (van der Warf and Petit, 2002)?

The environmental impact of agriculture involves a variety of factors from the soil, to water, the air, animal and soil variety, people, plants, and the food itself. Some of the environmental issues that are related to agriculture are climate change, deforestation, genetic engineering, irrigation problems, pollutants, soil degradation, and waste.

Sustainable Agriculture is farming in sustainable ways based on an understanding of ecosystem services, the study of relationships between organisms and their environment. It has been defined as "an integrated system of plant and animal production practices having a site-specific application that will last over the long term", for example:

- Satisfy human food and fiber needs
- Enhance environmental quality and the natural resource base upon which the agricultural economy depends
- Make the most efficient use of non-renewable resources and on-farm resources and integrate, where appropriate, natural biological cycles and controls
- Sustain the economic viability of farm operations
- Enhance the quality of life for farmers and society as a wholecauses of Agricultural Pollution (Gold, 2009).

Fig. 9.1: Concept of sustainable agriculture
Source: Based on review of literature

Chemical Fertilizers

Unlike pesticides, fertilizers are not directly toxic. However, their presence in freshwater and marine areas alters the nutrient system, and in consequence the species composition of specific ecosystems. Their most dramatic effect is eutrophication – resulting in an explosive growth of algae due to excess nutrients. This depletes water of dissolved oxygen, which in turn can kill fish and other aquatic life. These are mostly nitrogen and phosphorus based chemicals like ammonia and nitrates that in correct amounts boost the fertility of the soil. But in most cases these are used in more quantity than required and hence tend to be retained in the soil not adding to its goodness (Figure 9.2).

Fig. 9.2: Chemical fertizers as the concentrated source of nutrition
Source: Based on Review of Literature

Chemical Pesticides

The use of pesticides, fertilizers and other agrochemicals has increased hugely since the 1950s. For example, the amount of pesticide sprayed on fields has increased 26-fold over the past 50 years. These chemicals don't just stay on the fields they are applied to. Some application methods – such as pesticide spraying by aeroplane – lead to pollution of adjacent land, rivers or wetlands (Schwarzenbach *et al.* 2010).Due to inappropriate water management and irrigation technology, fertilizers and pesticides also commonly run-off from fields to adjacent rivers and lakes and contaminate groundwater sources. These chemicals eventually end up in the marine environment too. When pests and insects cause losses on a large scale, this leads to economic fallout for the farmers. Pesticides and insecticides like organochlorines, organophosphates and carbonates are toxic to the pests. They also tend to bio accumulate, *i.e.* they collect in the body of the organism and lead to chronic poisoning. This can be passed up the food chain. Some pesticides also are absorbed naturally by the plants themselves and stored their different parts. Pesticides are not discriminatory in nature as they also cause harm to beneficial insects such as bees and pollinators. Synthetic pesticides such as 'Malathion', 'Rogor', 'Kelthane' and 'confidor' are the most widespread method of controlling pests in agriculture. Pesticides can leach through the soil and enter the groundwater, as well as linger in food products and result in death in humans. Pesticides can also kill non-target plants, birds, fish and other wildlife (EPA, 2016). A wide range of agricultural chemicals are used and some become pollutants through use, misuse, or ignorance. Pollutants from agriculture have a huge effect on water quality. Agricultural nonpoint source (NPS) solution impacts lakes, rivers, wetlands, estuaries, and groundwater. Agricultural NPS can be caused by poorly managed animal feeding operations, overgrazing, plowing, fertilizer, and improper, excessive, or badly timed use of Pesticides. Pollutants from farming include sediments, nutrients, pathogens, pesticides, metals, and salts (USEPA, 2015).

Heavy Metals

Cadmium, fluoride, radioactive elements like uranium are regularly found in the parent minerals from which the fertilizers are obtained. Dangerous metals such as Mercury, Lead, Arsenic, Chromium, and Nickel are seen in traces in Zinc rich wastes from the steel industries which are used as fertilizers. These are often not removed from the because of the high cost involved (Figure 9.3).

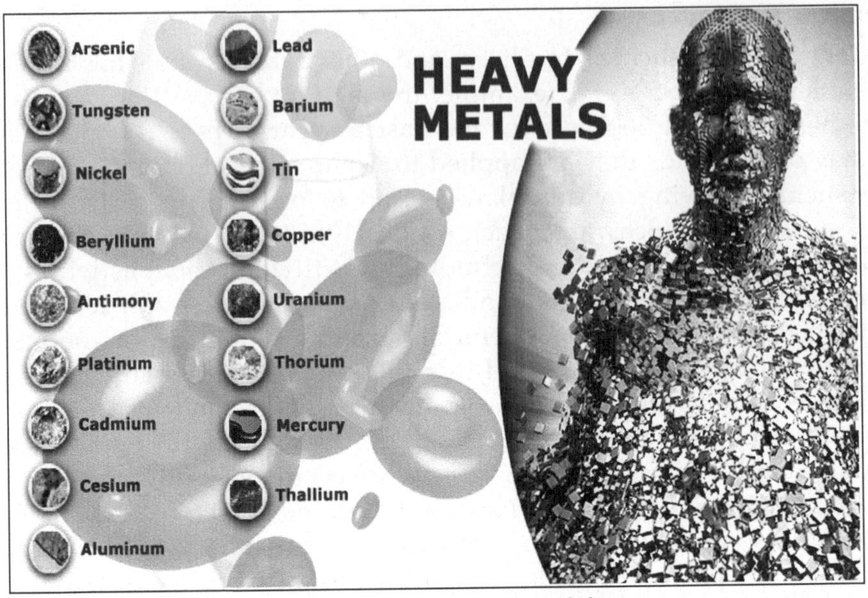

Fig. 9.3: Heavy metal toxicity

Source: Based on review of literature

Excessive Tillage of the Land

Overturning, digging or stirring leads to release of greenhouse gases produced in the ground such as nitrous oxide. Wrong soil tillage with regards of without any concern field location, soil structure and climate conditions cause to soil moving with rain in other words cause erosion. This situation not only cause to inefficient soils, it also pollutes streams and fills up dams with soil etc. serious environmental problems. Cultivation of natural ecosystems has led to a marked decline in soil C storage, such that conservation, agricultural practices are widely recommended as options to increase soil C storage, thereby mitigating climate change (Luo *et al.* 2010). Conservation tillage is an alternative tillage method of farming which is more sustainable for the soil and the surrounding ecosystem. This is done by allowing the residue of the previous harvest crops to remain in the soil before tilling for the next crop. Conservation tillage has shown to improve many things such as soil moisture retention, and reduce erosion. Some disadvantages are the fact that more expensive equipment is needed for this process, more pesticides will need to be used, and the positive effects take a long time to be visible (Holland, 2004) (Figure 9.4).

Soil Erosion

Land degradation stretches to about 30% of the total global land area. The problem persists, with a reported loss rate of about 10 million hectares per year (Nkonya *et al.* 2016). Loss of soil material due to poor management causes soil to become infertile. When natural vegetation is cleared and when farmland is ploughed, the exposed topsoil is often blown away by wind or washed away by rain.Erosion due to soy production, lose 55 million tons of topsoil every year (WWF, 2006). This leads to reduced soil fertility and degraded land. Other major crops that cause soil erosion include coffee, cassava, cotton, corn, palm oil, rice, sorghum, tea, tobacco, and wheat (Carey and Oettli, 2006).

Fig. 9.4: Tillage practice in the soil
Source: Based on the Review of Literature

Soil Sedimentation

The soil or sediments carried off into water bodies cause a lot of harm. Sedimentation reduces the transportation capability of navigation channels. It reduces the amount of sunlight reaching the water beds affecting the plants and animals living in it. The turbidity it causes interferes with the feeding patterns of the fishes and affects their population. Sedimentation also affects the transport and accumulation of water pollutants.

Soil carried off in rain or irrigation water can lead to sedimentation of rivers, lakes and coastal areas. The problem is exacerbated if there is no vegetation left along the banks of rivers and other watercourses to hold the soil (Centre for Science in the Public Interest, 2005). Sedimentation causes serious damage to freshwater and marine habitats, as well as the local communities that depend on these habitats.It's not just the eroded soil that is damaging: pesticides and fertilizers carried in rainwater and irrigation runoff can pollute waterways and harm wildlife (Figure 9.5).

Fig. 9.5: Soil sedimentation

Source: Based on review of literature

Introduction of Foreign Species

Many instances of foreign species of plants, animals and insects were introduced to control pests and weeds. But after a while these have taken over and become nuisances themselves. They cause harm to indigenous flora and fauna competing for the natural resources, and also cause changes in the biodiversity. There has been loss of many indigenous beneficial creatures due to this kind of biological pest control.

Genetic Modification to Increase Resistance to Pest and Diseases

A raging topic of debate today, it is a cause of concern for many that these crops will lead to the loss of many original species and may become weeds themselves. If these will be toxic to consumers ranging from insects to humans is to be studied in depth.

Animal Management

Farms specializing in rearing cattle, sheep, goats, pigs, and poultry must have strict regulations concerning the disposal of manure and other associated waste material. These must not be indiscriminately disposed in the surrounding areas. They cause pollution of the air as well as the water. 18 percent of Greenhouse gases are said to be generated by farm animals. The large amounts of manure created, carry pathogens that are harmful to humans too. Proper animal waste management can reduce the huge bulk of it, making it easier to use.

Mechanisms (Types) of Agricultural Pollution

Leaching and Ground Water Poisoning

When chemicals accumulate in the soil, depending on its water solubility and soil structure, it percolates through reaching the ground water, causing its contamination. This also depends on the rainfall. For example, after applying pesticides on crops in sandy areas, if excessive irrigation is done, the pesticide chemicals leach into the ground. Leaching occurs not only in the fields, but also at the manufacturing, mixing and disposal sites.

Water Runoff

Globally, the agricultural sector consumes about 70% of the planet's accessible freshwater – more than twice that of the industry (23%), and dwarfing municipal use (8%). Unsustainable water use harms the environment by changing the water table and/or depleting ground water supplies (Clay, 2004).

Excessive irrigation can also increase soil salinity and wash pollutants and sediment into rivers – causing damage to freshwater ecosystems and species as well as those further downstream, including coral reefs and coastal fish breeding grounds. Only a fraction of fertilizers and other chemical additives are utilized in the fields. The major bulk mixes in the runoff water and flows into the nearby watercourses. This is mainly in the form of nitrates and phosphates.The main causes of wasteful and unsustainable water use are:

- Leaky irrigation systems
- Wasteful field application methods
- Cultivation of thirsty crops not suited to the environment.

The problem is made worse by misdirected subsidies, low public and political awareness of the crisis, and weak environmental legislation.

Eutrophication

Eutrophication is also called water nutrient enrichment. When chemicals rich in nitrogen and phosphorus are flushed into the water from farms, this increases the nutrient levels in the water. This encourages the growth of the plants.

Algae benefit greatly from this. When they flourish and bloom, they use up most of the oxygen levels in the water body leaving very little for the other life forms in it. This leads to the death of the fish and other animals in the water that cannot swim away to safety.

Algae blooms restrict the penetration of sunlight into the water. This affects the photosynthesis in plants and does not allow the restoration of oxygen levels by this process. Ultimately the water becomes unfit to support any form of life.Certain toxins are also released by the algae themselves,which travel up the food chain and affect the higher life forms adversely.

Prevention of Agricultural Pollution

The priority is to keep the nitrogen and phosphorus rich nutrients from running off into the water sources near fields and animal farms.

- Prevention can never be a solo effort. The state governments, farmers' organisations, collectives and cooperatives, educational institutions and conservation groups need to work together for regulating and reducing farming related water pollution.
- Planning the application of fertilizer at the right time, in the right quantity with the correct methods can reduce the run off
- Planting certain grasses and clovers that can absorb and recycle the additional nutrients and prevent soil erosion. Planting rows of trees and shrubs around fields and along the borders of the stream or lake also help in the same way.
- Over tilling of the soil must be avoided to prevent soil erosion and soil compaction.
- Managing the correct disposal of animal wastes and keeping farm animals away from water will reduce the nitrogen pollution of the water.
- Composting, solid, liquid separation, anaerobic digestion and lagoons are different ways of managing animal manure. Of these anaerobic digestion is the most effective. It involves the use of anaerobic bacteria and heat. The products of this process are nutrient rich liquid used as fertilizer and methane gas that can be burned to produce electricity and heat. Anaerobic digestion is a best method for controlling odour associated with manure management.

Effects of Agricultural Pollution

Since agricultural pollution is not alone standing entity, its effects are carried over as water pollution and air pollution. It affects every aspect of the environment and every organism from the earthworm to humans. Some of the adverse effects are as follows:

- Drinking or swimming in water with dangerous levels of algal bloom causes rashes, stomach and liver problems, respiratory illnesses and neurological effects.
- Infants drinking water with high levels of nitrates get affected by the blue baby syndrome which is often fatal. Symptoms are shortness of breath and blue tinted skin.
- Formation of dead zones or hypoxic areas, where no aquatic life exists; Examples Chesapeake Bay and Gulf of Mexico.
- Entry of toxins from algal blooms into the food chain hurts larger animals like dolphin's seals and turtles etc.

- Air pollution with nitrogen oxides leads to occurrences of smog because of the formation of ozone. Ozone pollution damages trees and forests.

These impacts are likely to increase globally over the next several decades because of increases in population growth and income-dependent dietary shifts towards more meat-based diets (Tilman *et al.* 2011; Bajzelj *et al.* 2014; Tilman and Clark, 2014; Springmann *et al.* 2016).

Increasing agricultural input efficiency, reduces a food's environmental impact because of the environmental impacts of producing agricultural inputs such as fertilizer, pesticides, and livestock feeds. However, the environmental benefits of increasing agricultural input efficiency would not be equal across all systems, with improvements in agricultural input efficiency having the largest environmental benefit in the least efficient systems. Further, improving efficiency in more efficient systems, may only be possible at an economic cost. Emphasis should therefore be placed on improving efficiency in less efficient systems, although efficiency improvements in more efficient systems would still have environmental benefits (Clark and Tilman, 2017).

CONCLUSION

Agricultural pollution also causes heavy economic losses. Cleaning up contaminated waters is costly. Tourism is affected by decrease in fishing and boating activities. Visibility at tourist locations and scenic spots are reduced by air pollution. Marble and limestone buildings are damaged by ozone pollution. Fishing and shellfish industries are also losing money to contamination. Real estate value that always arises when ground water and nearby water sources are in good condition suffer when the opposite happens. Safe drinking water and clean water habitats are the rights of every living being. Let's become more responsible in our agricultural practices in order to preserve this and make this available to all.

REFERENCES

Bajzelj, B., Richards, K.S., Allwood, J.M., Smith, P., Dennis, J.S., Curmi, E. and Gilligan, C.A. (2014). Importance of Food-demand Management for Climate Mitigation. *Nat. Clim. Change*, 4: 924-9.

Carey, C. and Oettli, D. (2006). Determining Links between Agricultural Crop Expansion and Deforestation. A Report Prepared for the WWF Forest Conversion Initiative.

Centre for Science in the Public Interest (2005). Cruel Oil: How Palm Oil Harms Health, Rainforests and Wildlife.

Clark, M. and Tilman, D. (2017). Comparative Analysis of Environmental Impacts of Agricultural Production Systems, Agricultural Input Efficiency, and Food Choice. *Environ. Res. Lett.* 12: 064016.

Clay, J. (2004). World Agriculture and the Environment: A Commodity-by-Commodity Guide to Impacts and Practices Island Press.

Edenhofer O *et al.* 2014 Climate Change 2014: Mitigation of Climate Change (Cambridge: Cambridge University Press)

EPA (2015). "Agricultural Nonpoint Source Fact Sheet". United States Environmental Protection Agency. EPA. Retrieved 22 April 2015.

EPA (2016). "Risks of Pesticide Use". EPA. EPA. Retrieved 23 April 2016.

Gold, M. (2009). What is Sustainable Agriculture?. United States Department of Agriculture, Alternative Farming Systems Information Center.

Holland, J.M. (2004). The Environmental Consequences of Adopting Conservation Tillage in Europe: Reviewing the Evidence. *Agriculture, Ecosystems & Environment*, 103(1): 1-25.

Kamer, F. and Gürlek, S. (2003). GeliÞmekte Olan Ülkelerde Tarým-Çevre-Ekonomi EtkileÞimi. *Doðuþ Üniv. Dergisi.*, 4(2): 197-206.

Luo, Z., Wang, E. and Sun, O.J. (2010). Soil Carbon Change and its Responses to Agricultural Practices in Australian Agro-ecosystems: A Review and Synthesis. *Geoderma*, 155: 211-223.

Molden, D. (2007). Comprehensive Assessment of Water Management in Agriculture Water for Food, Water for Life: A Comprehensive Assessment of Water Management in Agriculture (London: Earthscan International Water Management Institute)

Nkonya, E. *et al.* (eds.) (2016). Economics of Land Degradation and Improvement – A Global Assessment for Sustainable Development, DOI 10.1007/978-3-319-19168-3_1

Ramankutty, N. and Foley, J.A. (1999). Estimating Historical Changes in Global Land Cover: Croplands from 1700 to 1992. *Glob. Biogeochem. Cycles*, 13: 997-1027.

Schwarzenbach, R.P., Egli, T., Hofstetter, T.B., von Gunten, U. and Wehrli, B. (2010). Global Water Pollution and Human Health. *Annu. Rev. Environ. Resour.*, 35: 109-136.

Springmann, M., Godfray, H.C.J., Rayner, M. and Scarborough, P. (2016). Analysis and Valuation of the Health and Climate Change Cobenefits of Dietary Change. *Proc. Natl Acad. Sci. USA*, 113: 4146-51.

Tilman, D. and Clark, M. (2014). Global Diets Link Environmental Sustainability and Human Health. *Nature*, 515: 518-22.

Tilman, D., Balzer, C., Hill, J. and Befort, B.L. (2011). Global Food Demand and the Sustainable Intensification of Agriculture. *Proc. Natl Acad. Sci.USA*, 108: 20260-4.

Tubiello, F.N., Salvatore, M., Cóndor Golec, R.D., Ferrara, A., Rossi, S., Biancalani, R., Federici, S., Jacobs, H. and Flammini, A. (2014). Agriculture, Forestry and Other Land Use Emissions by Sources and Removals by Sinks vol 2 (Rome: Food and Agriculture Organization of the United Nations) pp. 4-89.

van der Warf, H. and Petit, J. (2002). "Evaluation of the Environmental Impact of Agriculture at the Farm Level: A Comparison and Analysis of 12 Indicator-based methods". *Agriculture, Ecosystems and Environment*. 93 (1-3): 131-145. doi:10.1016/S0167-8809(01)00354-1. Retrieved 21 April 2015.

Vitousek, P.M., Aber, J.D., Howarth, R.W., Likens, G.E.A.P., Schindler, D.W., Schlesinger, W.H. and Tilman, D. (1997). Human Alteration of the Global Nitrogen Cycle: Sources and Consequences. *Ecol. Appl.*, 7: 737.

WWF (2006). Facts about Soy Production and the Basel Criteria.

Pages: 159-177

Stress Tolerance and Plant Productivity

Edited by: Mr. Prasann Kumar and Dr. Pawan Kumar 'Bharti'

ISBN: 978-93-86841-56-8

Edition: 2018

Published by: Discovery Publishing House Pvt. Ltd., New Delhi (India)

10 Irrigation with Special Reference to Crop Production

Prasann Kumar

ABSTRACT

Irrigation helps grow agricultural crops, maintain landscapes, and revegetate disturbed soils in dry areas and during periods of inadequate rainfall. Irrigationalso has other uses in crop production, including frost protection, suppressing weed growth in grain fields and preventing soil consolidation.The water requirement has been increasing more and more especially in agriculture.

Key words: Agriculture, Biotic, Crop, Density, Energy, Forage

INTRODUCTION

The agricultural sector makes use of 75% of the water withdrawn from river, lakes and aquifers (Wallace, 2000). In recent years irrigated land has developed rapidly. Water increasingly often becomes a limiting factor in food production, especially in dry climates. In dry climates, water sources are very limited since the amount of rainfall is very low. For example, in southern Libya the amount of rainfall is about 19 mm year. As the total size of the hot dry areas in the world is about 45-50 million square kilometers (Dregne, 1976) which means one third of the total land area of the world.In dry climates the availability of water for irrigation of crops is limited, which restricts the possibility for cultivation of crops. For that reason a lot of research has been done to develop methods to protect water and using less amount of fresh water as far as possible without effects on crop yield, and to increase water use efficiency in irrigation without any negative effects on crop yields.Thus, irrigation scheduling is one of the best methods which can help us to realize these aims. The

Department of Agronomy, School of Agriculture, Lovely Professional University
Jalandhar - 144 411 (Punjab) (India)

irrigation schedule consists of two parts; the first part is to determine the water requirement (the right amount of water). This can be done by different methods, like determine the amount of evapotranspiration of the crop. The second part is to estimate the right time to supply the water to plants. There are several methods that can be used to decide when to irrigate crops. Irrigation scheduling involves determining both the timing of irrigation and the quantity of water to apply. It is an essential daily management practice for a farm manager growing irrigated crops. Proper timing of irrigation can be done by monitoring the soil water content or monitoring the crop in the field. Plant stress responses provide the most direct measure of identifying the plant demand for water. However, it should be noted that while plant stress indicators provide a direct measure of when water is required, they do not provide a direct volumetric measure of the volume of water required to be applied. The crop water requirement is defined as the amount of water required to compensate the evapotranspiration loss from the cropped field (Allen *et al.*, 1998). Many researchers describe it as the total water needed for evapotranspiration. Therefore, the water requirement can be decided by determining the actual evapotranspiration (Figure 10.1).

Fig. 10.1: Irrigation schedule of the crops
Source: Based on review of literature

The crop water requirement can be related to the amount of water used by a reference crop. The reference crop typically is grass or alfalfa that is well irrigated and covers 100% of the ground. The reference evapotranspiration ET_0 includes the water evaporated from the soil surface and the water transpired by the plants.The daily reference evapotranspiration ET_0 can also be calculated from daily climate data like temperature, wind speed, sunshine and relative humidity. There are several methods used to calculate or measure ET_0. The most common methods are Penman method, Pan Evaporation and Blaney-Criddle method. The climate data can be obtained from a weather station. The actual evapotranspiration can be calculated by multiplying the calculated reference evapotranspiration by a crop coefficient factor, K_c. The crop coefficient factor values represent the crop type and its characteristics and the development of the crop.The successful irrigation scheduling requires good understanding of the knowledge of soil, water holding capacity, crop water use, and crop sensitivity to moisture stress at different growth stages. This requires consideration about the effective rainfall, and availability of irrigation water (Waskom, 1994) (Figure 10.1). The irrigation scheduling tips:

- Know the controller and how to change watering times.
- Adjust the watering times (number of minutes)and the frequency of watering (daily, twice a week, etc.) based on weather conditions.
- Change settings to adjust for seasonal differences and reset the timer when needed.
- Utilities should consider offering regular scheduling updates and tips throughout the irrigation season.

Table 10.1: Sample watering schedule

Zone and Plant Type	Sprinkler Type	# of Starts	Minutes Per Start	Total Minutes
1. Lawn 2. Lawn	Spray Spray	3 3	6 6	18 18
3. Groundcover	Spray	3	4	12
4. Shrubs	Drip	1	16	16
5. Garden	Spray	2	10	20
6. Trees	Drip	1	20	20

Source: Based on review of literature

FACTORS AFFECTING THE IRRIGATION INTERVAL

The interval between irrigations and the amount of water to apply at each irrigation depend on how much water is held in the root zone and how fast it is used by the crop. This is determined by:

- Soil texture
- Soil structure/water penetration
- Depth of effective root zone of the soil

- The crop grown
- The stage of development of the crop

SOIL TEXTURE

Soil texture refers to the feel of the soil. There are three types of particles that make up the soil; these are classified as sand, silt or clay depending on their size. The proportion of these particles in the soil determines the feel or texture of the soil and the size of the micropores between the particles, as well as the amount of water that can be stored in them. Soils are classified into texture classes such as clay loams, heavy clays, loams and sandy loams, as determined by the proportion of sand, silt and clay in the soil (Table 10.2).

Table 10.2: Available moisture according to texture (mm of plantavailable water per meter)

Soil Texture	Range	Average
Sand	Up to 65	49
Loam	155 to 172	164
Clay loam	155 to 172	164
Clay	137 to 147	137

Source: Based on review of literature
Note: that this is not a complete list of soil texture classes.

SOIL STRUCTURE

Soil structure refers to the natural aggregation of soil particles that are stable when wetted. The size and shape of these aggregates affect the way they stack together and the size of the pore spaces between them. A well structured soil contains many pores that will hold water and air and air infiltration of water into the soil. A poorly structured soil has fewer large pores; it will have a reduced water-holding capacity and poor water infiltration, and will probably restrict root growth. It is clear that a well structured soil will give plant roots an environment favourable to healthy growth and the extraction of water and nutrients. The structures of many soils have been damaged by years of cultivation and compaction by traffic; others have been damaged by sodicity. This has led to the development of soil crusting and hardpans,which reduce water penetration and retention and restrict root growth. This results in a reduction in plant growth. Some natural features of a soil may affect its structure independent of the soil management. For example, a sodic soil is likely to be poorly structured and will restrict air and water movement through the soil (Figures 10.2 & 10.3).

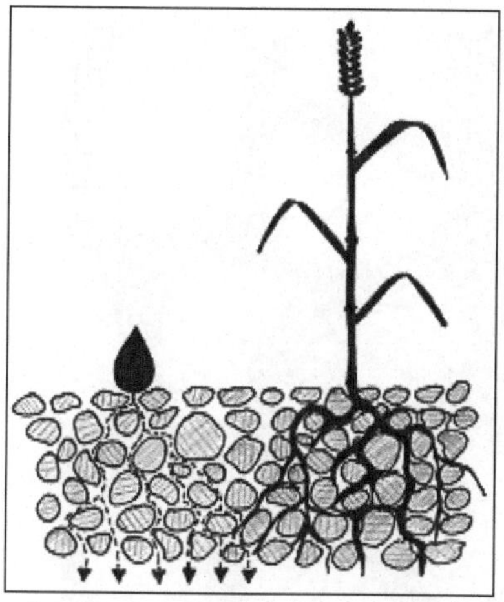

Fig. 10.2: A well structured soil

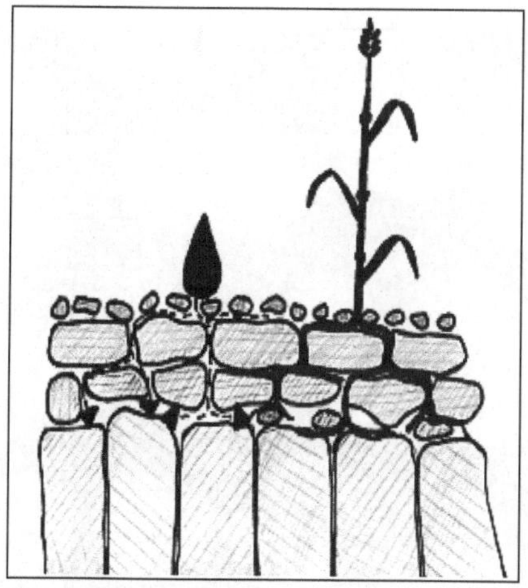

Fig. 10.3: A poorly structured Soil

Source: Based on review of literature

SOIL WATER CONSIDERATIONS

Before you consider your soil moisture status you need to understand a few terms. These include:

1. Field capacity
2. Wilting point
3. Saturation
4. Refill point.

SATURATION

Immediately after a soil has been irrigated it is at saturation. Almost all of the soil pore spaces are filled with water and verylittle air remains. If the drainage is adequate, water will drain awayfrom the larger pore spaces and allow some air to enter the soil. Thistakes about 48 hours, depending on the soil type. If the internaldrainage of the soil is restricted the soil becomes waterlogged. With noair in the soil, the roots begin to die from lack of oxygen.

FIELD CAPACITY

Once the soil has drained by gravity for about 48 hours, water isheld in the pore spaces by surface tension around the soil particle, andlittle further drainage will take place.This condition is called fieldcapacity, and at this time the soil is holding as much water as it can (Figure 10.4). In soil that is well structured, there is also enough air inthe soil to supply plant roots with the oxygen needed for them to liveand grow (Figure 10.4).

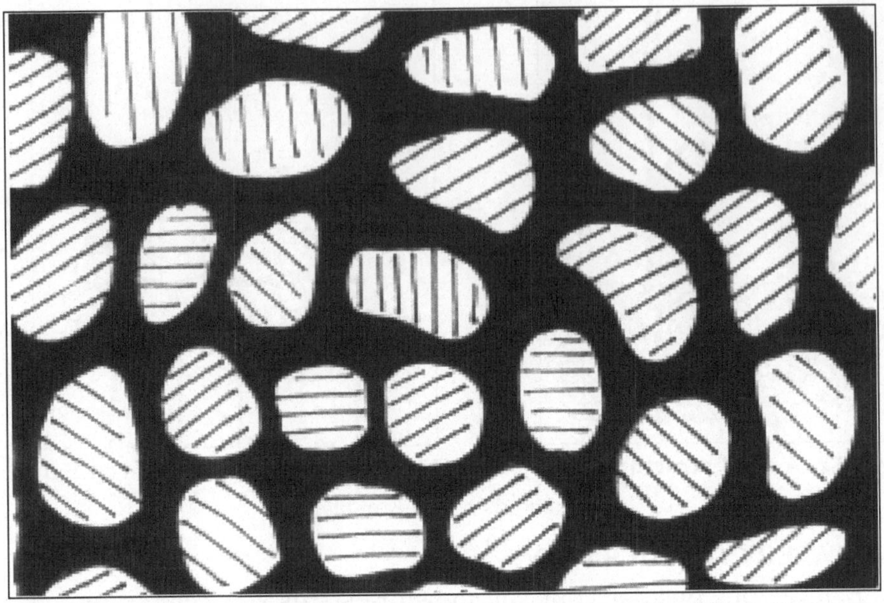

Fig. 10.4: Saturation (soil contains no air, water totally fills soil pores)
Source: Based on review of literature

To fine-tune your allowable depletion figures for your soil, dig a hole and assess the soil moisture immediately before irrigating to see if your allowable depletion figure is correct. If the soil is still too wet for irrigation, increase the figure you use of 10 mm. If the soil is too dry just before irrigation, reduce your figure by 10 mm. Continue thisprocess until you arrive at a suitable figure. The water storage in a soil must be balanced against the plant water use. Plant water use is affected by two main influences: the leaf area of thecrop or pasture and the daily evaporation. Plant water use is proportional to evaporation. The higher the evaporation, the higher the plant's water use. Evaporation is affected by humidity and temperature, so plant water use in summer is much higher than in winter. Plants draw water from the soil via the roots and release this water as vapour into the air via the leaves. If the plant (or crop) has a large amount of fresh, green leaves, then water use will be higher. High water use is a desirable characteristic, since yields are well correlated with water use. Soon after emergence a crop has only a small amount of leaf material, so water use is relatively low, while water use will be higher when the crop reaches the maximum leaf area. The crop factoris a number used to calculate the water use. It accounts for the crop leaf area. Crop factors vary between times of the year and stage of crop growth. Check with your local horticultural adviser for crop factor information.

The Daily Crop Water Use

To calculate the crop water use, multiply the crop factor by the dayor weekly evaporation totals.Daily crop water use (mm) = crop factor × daily evaporation (mm) Example: In December sweet corn has a crop factor of 1.0. On a particular daythe evaporation is 14 mm. Therefore, crop water use (mm) = 1.0 × 14 mm = 14 mm (on that particular day) Evaporation data Evaporation data can be obtained by:

- Calling your local post office, which keeps weather data
- Waterwatch no longer available. Evaporation data can be obtainedthrough the website www.clw.csiro.au/services/weather or check with your local horticultural advisor.The service provides evaporation figures for the last 10 days andforward estimates for the next six weeks. The data are measured inGriffith, but are reasonably accurate for the Murray Valley and MIA (Figures 10.5 & 10.6, Table 10.3).

Fig. 10.5: Cracking clay soil showing the large cracks that occur when these soils dry

Source: Based on a review of the literature

Fig. 10.6: Irrigation tool

Source: Based on review of literature

Table 10.3: A summary of the main classes of irrigation scheduling approaches, indicating their main advantages and disadvantages

	Advantages	Disadvantages
I. Soil water measurement		
(a) Soil water potential (tensiometers, psychrometers, etc.) (b) Soil water content (gravimetric; capacitance/TDR; neutron probe)	Easy to apply in practice; can be quite precise; at least water content, measures indicates 'how much' water to apply; many commercial systems available; some sensors (especially capacitance and time domain sensors) readily automated	Soil heterogeneity requires many sensors (often expensive) or extensive monitoring programme (e.g. neutron probe); selecting a position that is representative of the root-zone is difficult; sensors do not generally measure the water status at root surface (which depends on evaporative demand)
II. Soil water balance calculations		
(Require estimate of evaporation and rainfall)	Easy to apply in principle; indicate 'how much' water to apply	Not as accurate as direct measurement; need accurate local estimates of precipitation/runoff; evapotranspiration estimates require good estimates of crop coefficients (which depend on crop development, rooting depth, etc.); errors are cumulative, so regular recalibration needed
III. Plant 'stress' sensing		
(Includes both water status measurement and plant response measurement)	Measures the plant stress response directly; integrates environmental effects; potentially very sensitive	In general, does not indicate 'how much' water to apply; calibration required to determine 'control thresholds'; still largely at research/development stage and little used yet for routine agronomy (except for thermal sensing in some situations)
(a) Tissue water status	It has often been argued that leaf water status is the most appropriate measure for many physiological processes (e.g. photosynthesis), but this argument is generally erroneous (as it ignores root–shoot signalling)	All measures are subject to homeostatic regulation (especially leaf water status), therefore, not sensitive (isohydric plants); sensitive to environmental conditions which can lead to short-term fluctuations greater than treatment differences

(Table Contd...)

	Advantages	Disadvantages
(i) Visible wilting	Easy to detect	Not precise; yield reduction often occurs before visible symptoms; hard to automate
(ii) Pressure chamber (Ψ)	Widely accepted reference technique; most useful if estimating stem water potential (SWP), using either bagged leaves or suckers	Slow and labour intensive (therefore expensive, especially for predawn measurements); unsuitable for automation
(iii) Psychrometer (Ψ)	Valuable, thermodynamically based measure of water status; can be automated	Requires sophisticated equipment, and high level of technical skill, yet still unreliable in the long term
(iv) Tissue water content (RWC, leaf thickness [γ- or β-ray thickness sensors], fruit or stem diameter)	Changes in tissue water content are easier to measure and automate than water potential measurements; RWC more directly related to physiological function than is total water potential in many cases; commercial micromorphometric sensors available	Instrumentation generally complex or expensive, so difficult to get adequate replication; water content, measures (and diameter changes) subject to same problems as other water status measures; leaf thickness sensitivity limited by lateral shrinkage
(v) Pressure probe	Can measure the pressure component of water potential which is the driving force of xylem flow and much cell function (e.g. growth)	Only suitable for experimental or laboratory systems

Source: Based on review of literature

Direct, Irrigation Method

In this project water is directly diverted from the river into the canal by constructing a diversion structure like weir or barrage across the river with some pondage to take care of diurnal variations. It also effects of raising the river water level, which is then able to flow into the offtaking channel by gravity. The flow in the channel is usually controlled by a gated structure and this, in combination with the diversion structure is also sometimes called the headworks. If the water from such headworks is available throughout the period of growth of crops irrigated by it, it is called a perennial irrigation scheme. In this type of projects, the water in the offtaking channels ofthe river carries water throughout the year. It may not be necessary, however, to provide irrigation water to the fields during monsoon. In some places local rainfall would be sufficient to meet the plant water needs. In case of a non-perennial river the offtaking channel would be carrying water only for certain periods in a year depending upon the availability of supply of the source. Another form of direct irrigation is the inundation irrigation which may be called a river-canal irrigation. In this type of irrigation there is no irrigation work across the river to control the level of water in the river. Inundation canal off-taking from a river is a seasonal canal which conveys water as and when available in the river. This type of direct irrigation is usually practiced in deltaic tract that is, in areas having even and plane topography. It is feasible when the normal flow of te river or stream throughout the period of growth of crop irrigated, is never less than the requirements of the irrigated crops at any time of the base period. A direct irrigation scheme of irrigation using river water diversion head works typically be laid out as in figure 10.7. Though the diversion structure raises the river water level and is just sufficient to force some water into the channel, the stored water in the pond created behind doesn't have sufficient storage volume it may however be able to take care of any diurnal variation in the river water. An example of this scheme is the DVC irrigation project on the Damodar river with the barrage located in Durgapur (Figure 10.7).

Storage Irrigation Method

For this type of irrigation schemes part of the excess water of a river during monsoon, which otherwise would have passed down the river as a flood is stored in a reservoir or tank found at the upstream of a dam constructed across a river or stream. This stored water is then used for irrigation is adopted when the flow of the river or stream is in excess of the requirements of irrigated crops during a certain part of the year but falls below requirements or is not available at all in the Version 2 CE IIT, Kharagpur river during the remaining part of the year. Since the construction site of a storage reservoir is possible in regions of undulating topography, it is usually practiced in non deltaic areas.

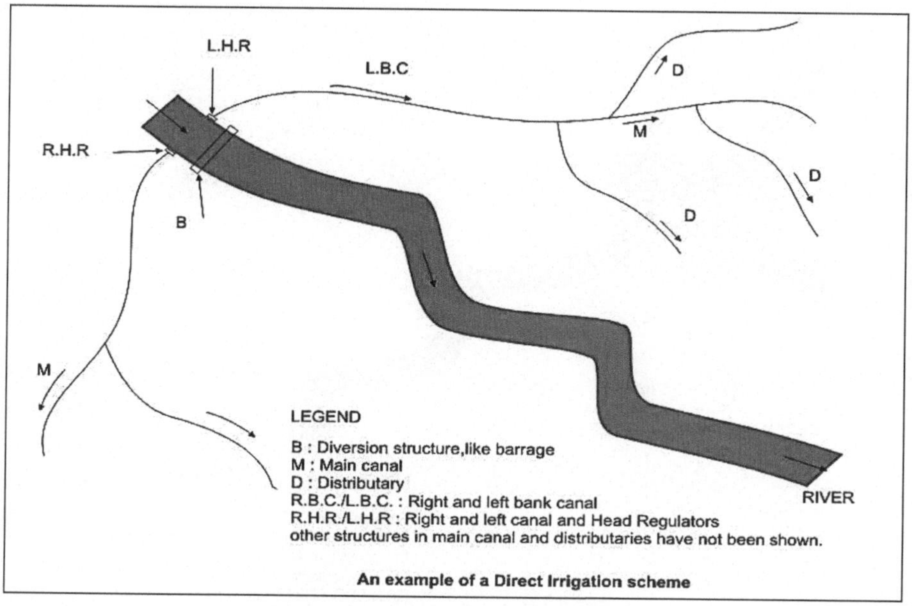

Fig. 10.7: DVC irrigation project

Source: Based on review of literature

A general layout of this irrigation scheme may typically be laid out as shown in figure 10.8. In the third type of scheme the storage head works or the dams has to be equipped with ancillary structure like outlet, sluice, spillway, log chutes, etc. The storage created by the dam behind the reservoir is substantial compared to that behind a barrage and may inundate a large tract of land, depending on the topography. The capacity of the reservoir is generally determined systematically by knowing possible withdrawal demands (in this case for irrigation) over the weeks and months of a year and corresponding expected inflows. An example for this type of scheme is the Indira Sagar project on the Narmada River. Of course, apart from serving irrigation demand the project also generates electricity. Hence it is actually a multipurpose project. Another type of storage, irrigation method envisages the storage of water at some place in the hilly terrain of the river where the construction of the dam is possible. A barrage is constructed at any downstream location, where the terrain is flatter Version 2 CE IIT, Kharagpur and canals take off as in a usual direct irrigation method (Figures 10.8 & 10.9).

Surface Irrigation Methods

In this system of field water application the water is applied directly to the soil from a channel located at the upper reach of the field. It is essential in these methods to construct designed water distribution systems to provide adequate control of water to the fields and proper land preparation to permit uniform distribution of water over the field.

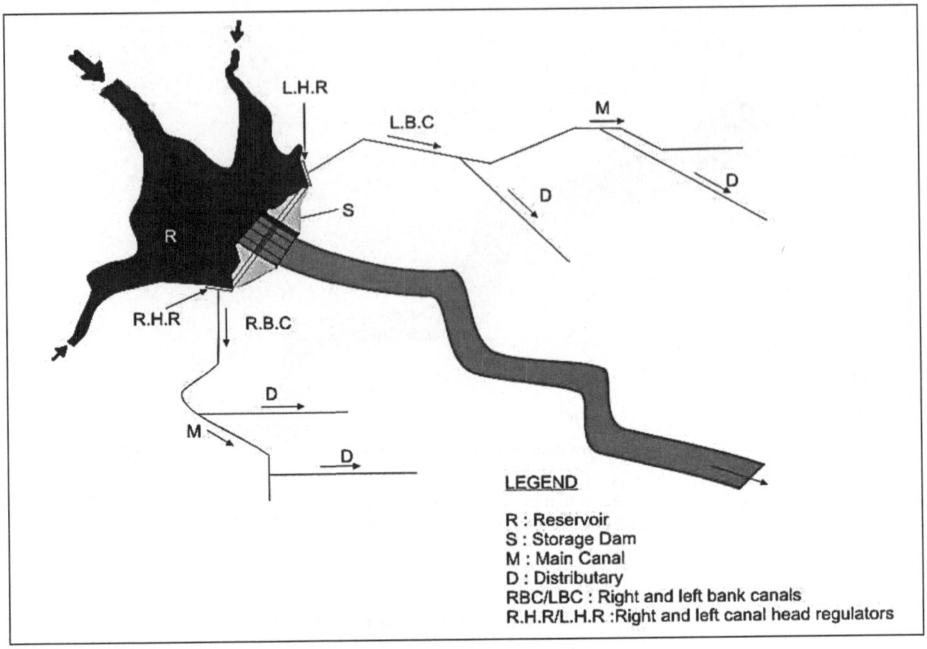

Fig. 10.8: A typical layout of the storage, irrigation scheme incorporating dam
Source: Based on review of literature

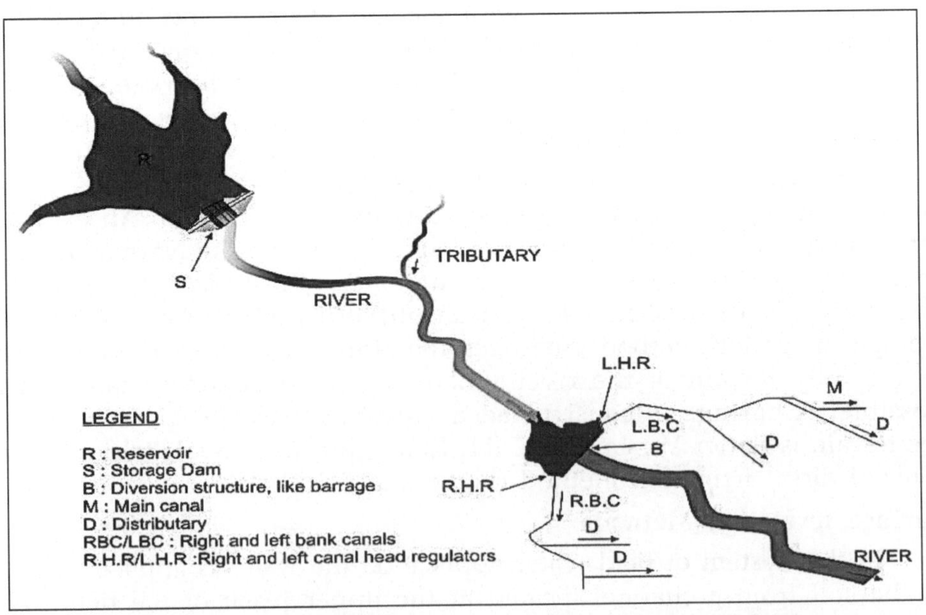

Fig. 10.9: A typical layout of a storage, irrigation scheme incorporating a dam with a barrage on its downstream
Source: Based on review of literature

One of the surface irrigation method is flooding method where the water is allowed to cover the surface of land in a continuous sheet of water with the depth of applied water just sufficient to allow the field to absorb the right amount of water needed to raise the soil moisture up to field capacity,. A properly designed size of the irrigation stream aims for proper balance against the intake rate of the soil, the total depth of water to be stored in the root zone and the area to be covered giving a reasonably uniform saturation of soil over the entire field. Flooding method has been used in India for generations without any control what soever and is called uncontrolled flooding. The water is made to enter the fields bordering rivers during folds. When the flood water inundates the flood plane areas, the water distribution is quite uneven, hence not very efficient, as a lot of water is likely to be wasted as well as soils of excessive slopes are prone to erosion. However the adaptation of this method doesn't cost much. The flooding method applied in a controlled way is used in two types of irrigation methods as under: (1) Border irrigation method; (2) Basin irrigation method: As the names suggest the water applied to the fields by this inundates or floods the land, even if temporarily. On the other hand, there are many crops which would try better if water is applied only near their root zone instead of inundating.Such an irrigation method is called the Furrow irrigation method. All these methods are discussed in the subsequent sections (Figure 10.10).

Fig. 10.10: Furrow irrigation methods

Source: Based on review of literature

Basin Irrigation

Basins are flat areas of land surrounded by low bunds. The bunds prevent the water from flowing to the adjacent fields. The basins are filled to desired depth and the water is retained until it infiltrates into the soil. Water may be maintained for considerable periods of time. Basin method of irrigation can be formally divided into two, viz; the check basin method and the ring basin method. The check basin method is the most common method of irrigation used in India. In this method, the land to be irrigated is divided into small plots or basins surrounded by checks, levees (low bunds). Each plot or basin has a nearly level surface. The irrigation water is applied by filling the plots with water up to the desired depth without overtopping the leves and the water retained there is allowed to infiltrate into the soil. The leves may be constructed for temporary use or may be semi permanent for repeated use as for paddy cultivation. The size of the levees depends on the depths of water to be impounded as on the stability of the soil when wet. Water is conveyed to the cluster of check basins by a system of supply channels and lateral field channels or ditches. The supply channel is aligned on the upper side (at a higher elevation) of the field for every two rows of plot as shown in the figure. The size of basins depends not only on the slope but also on the soil type and the available water flow to the basins. Generally, it is found that the following holds good for basin sizes. Basin size should be small if the

1. Slope of the land is steep
2. Soil is sandy
3. Stream size to basin is small
4. Required depth of irrigation application is small
5. Field preparation

   is done by hand or animal traction Basin size can be large if the:

   1. Slope of the land is flat
   2. Soil is clay
   3. Stream size to the basin is large
   4. Required depth of the irrigation is large
   5. Field preparation is mechanized

Basin irrigation is suitable for many field crops. Paddy rice grows best when its roots are submerged in water and so basin irrigation is the best method for use with the crop. The other form of basin irrigation is the ring basin method which is used for growing trees in orchards. In this method, generally for each tree, a separate basin is made which is usually circular in shape. Sometimes, basin sizes are made larger to include two more trees in one basin. Water to the basins is supplied from a supply channel through small field channels conveyed the basins with the supply channel. Trees which can be irrigated successfully using the ring basin method include citrus and banana. Basins can also be constructed on hillside. Here, the ridges of the basins are constructed as in contour border method thus making the only difference between the two is in the application of water. In the border method, the water is applied once during an irrigation cycle and is allowed to flow along the field and as the water infiltrates, till the supply is cutoff. In the basin method, as in a rice field the water is higher at a desired level of the basin. Basin irrigation is suitable for many field crops. Paddy rice grows best when its roots are submerged in water and so basin irrigation is the best method for use with this crop.

Furrow Irrigation

Furrows are small channels, which carry water down the land slope between the crop rows. Water infiltrates into the soil as it moves along the slope. The crop is usually grown on ridges between the furrows. This method is suitable for all row crops and for crops that cannot stand water for long periods, like 12 to 24 hours, as is generally encountered in the border or basin methods of irrigation. Water is applied to the furrows by letting in water from the supply channel, either by pipe siphons or by making temporary breaches in the supply channel embankment. The length of time the water is to flow in the furrows depends on the amount of water required to replenish the root zone and the infiltration rate of the soil and the rate of lateral spread of water in the soil. Furrow irrigation is suitable to most soils except sandy soils that have very high infiltration water and provide poor lateral distribution water between furrows. As compared to the other methods of surface irrigation, the furrow method is advantageous as: (1) Water in the furrows contacts only one half to one-fifth of the land surface, thus reducing puddling and clustering of soils and excessive evaporation of water. (2) Earlier cultivation is possible Furrows may be straight laid along the land slope, if the slope of the land is small (about 5 percent) for lands with larger slopes, the furrows can be laid along the contours.

Sprinkler Irrigation System

Sprinkler Irrigation is a method of applying irrigation water which is similar to rainfall. Water is distributed through a system of pipes usually by pumping. It is then sprayed into the air and irrigated entire soil surface through spray heads so that it breaks up into small water drops which fall to the ground. This is achieved by distributing water through a system of pipes usually by pumping which is then sprayed into the air through sprinklers so that it breaks up into small water drops which fall to the ground. The system of irrigation is suitable for undulating land, with poor water availability, sandy or shallow soils, or where a uniform application of water is desired. No land leveling is required as with the surface irrigation methods. Sprinklers are, however, not suitable for soils which easily form a crust. The water that is pumped through the pump, pipe, sprinkler system must be free of suspended sediments. As otherwise there would be chances of blockage of the sprinkler nozzles. A typical sprinkler irrigation system consists of the following components:

- Pump unit
- Mainline and sometimes sub mainlines
- Laterals
- Sprinklers

Fig. 10.11: Furrow water methods
Source: Based on review of literature

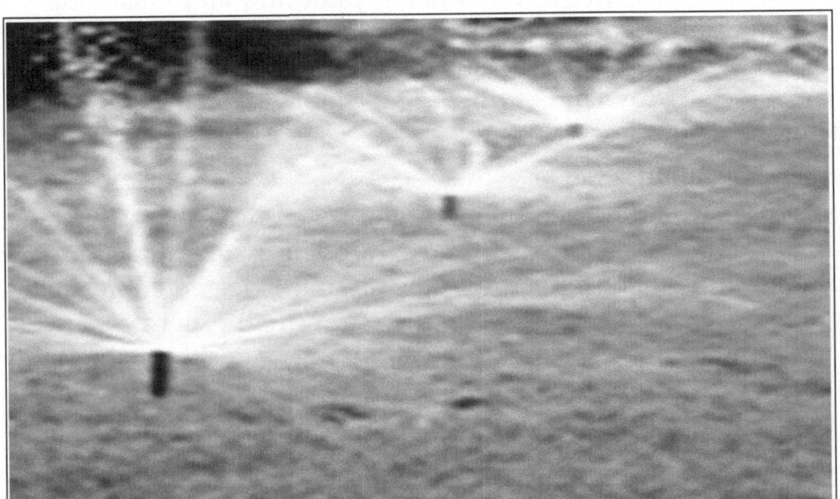

Fig. 10.12: Sprinkler irrigation system
Source: Based on the review of literature

Drip Irrigation System

Drip Irrigation system is sometimes called trickle irrigation and involves dripping water onto the soil at very low rates (2-20 litres per hour) from a system of small diameter plastic pipes filled with outlets called emitters or drippers. Water is applied close to the plants so that only part of the soil in which the roots grow is wetted, unlike surface and sprinkler irrigation, which involves wetting the whole soil profile. With drip irrigation water, applications are more frequent than with other methods and this provides a very favourable high moisture level in the soil in which plants can flourish. Figure 10.13 shows a typical layout of the drip irrigation system. A typical drip irrigation system consists of the following components:

- Pump unit
- Control Head
- Main and sub main lines
- Laterals
- Emitters and drippers

The drip irrigation system is particularly suited to areas where water quality is marginal, land is steeply sloping or undulating and of poor quality, where water or labour are expensive, or where high value crops require frequent water applications. It is more economical for orchard crops than for other crops and vegetables since the orchards plants as well as rows are widely spaced. Drip irrigation limits the water supplied for consumptive use of plants. By maintaining a minimum soil moisture in the root zone, thereby maximizing the water saving. A unique feature of drip irrigation is its excellent adaptability to saline water. Since the frequency of irrigation is quite high, the plant base always remains wet which keeps the salt concentration in the plant zone below the critical. Irrigation efficiency of a drip irrigation system is more than 90 percent. Drip irrigation usage in India is expanding rapidly. There is even some Government subsidy to encourage its use. From about 1000 hectare in 1985, the area under drip irrigation increased to 70860 hectare in 1991, with the maximum developments taking place in the following states:

- Maharashtra (32924 hectare)
- Andhra Pradesh (11585 hectare)
- Karnataka (11412 hectare). The drip irrigated crops is mainly used to irrigate orchards of which the following crops are important ones (according to a 1991 survey):
    - Grapes (12000 hectare)
    - Bananas (6500 hectare)
    - Pomegranates (5440 hectare)
    - Mangoes

Fig. 10.13: Drip irrigation system
Source: Based on review of literature

CONCLUSION

- Most collective irrigation systems cannot adopt crop-based and water saving irrigation scheduling methods in view of the lack of reliability and flexibility in the water supply.
- Reliable water supply demands a technically good design, which is adjusted to local conditions, good quality construction and proper operation and maintenance.
- Equity in the water supply is seldom achieved due to the inadequacy of adjustable outlets in functioning properly over a wide range of flow, the wide deviation of scheduling practices, loose management.
- Simple operational procedures may provide short-term solutions to improve reliability of supply, but long-term solutions need to be found in the modernization and automation of the irrigation system.
- The lack of adequate flow control and measurement devices are the main constraints in introducing effective water supply.
- Several good concepts, methods and equipment are available, but not yet widely introduced due to lack of knowledge and understanding of available techniques.
- Integral computer models are useful for project planning, design and evaluation, but have proved too cumbersome for day-to-day operation.
- The cost of irrigation modernization cannot be borne by farmers alone.

REFERENCES

Anonymous 1998. Comprehensive Report on "Sprinkler Irrigation in India". Indian National.

Committee on Irrigation and Drainage, Ministry of Water Resources, Government of India: 31-36.

Criddle, W.D., Davis, S., Pair, C.H., Shockley, D.G., 1956. Methods for Evaluating Irrigation Systems. Agricultural Handbook No. 82, SCS, USDA, Washington, D.C.

Deshmukh, M.T. 1970. Hydraulics of Flow in Irrigation Furrows. M.Sc. Thesis, Division of Agricultural Engineering, P.G. School, I.A.R.I., New Delhi, 156 p.

Hurd, C.J. 1969. Sprinkler Irrigation Guidebook. U.S. Agency for International; Development, Washington. D.C.

Karmeli, D. and J. Keller. 1975. Trickle Irrigation Design. Rain Bird Sprinkler Mfr. Corporation, Glendora, CA, USA.

Michael, A.M. 1978. Irrigation – Theory and Practice, Vikas Publishing House, New Delhi: 585-685.

Mine Hart, J.1976. A Guide to Application of Irrigation Water. U.S. Agency for International Development, New Delhi.

Molenaar, A. 1960, Irrigation by Sprinkler. FAO, Rome 91p.

Murty, V.V.N. 1998. Land and Water Management Engineering. Second Edition, Kalyani Publishers, Ludhiana: 291-352.

Schwab, G.O., D.D. Fang Meier, W.J. Elliot and R.K.Frevert.1993. Soil and Water Conservation Engineering, Fourth Edition. John Wiley & Sons, Inc., New York.

Sharma, R.K., K.K. Nathan, Ashok Kumar, H.R.Singh and Khushi Ram. 2006. Performance Evaluation of Sprinkler Irrigation in a Rural Watershed. Journal of Soil and Water Conservation, 5 (3): 61-69.

Visalakshi, K.P. and Rajput, T.B.S. 1998. Surge Flow – An Innovative Technology for Water Conserving Irrigation. Proc. National Seminar on "Water Management for Sustainable Agriculture - Problems and Perspectives for the 21st Century," Water Technology CentreIARI, New Delhi: 179-182.

Index

◆◆◆◆◆◆